THE GAMES OF '36

A PICTORIAL HISTORY OF THE 1936 OLYMPICS IN GERMANY

by **Stan Cohen**

Pictorial Histories Publishing Company, Inc.
Missoula, Montana

LIBRARY OF CONGRESS
CATALOG CARD NO. 96-67534

ISBN 1-57510-009-6

First Printing April 1996

Typography Arrow Graphics
Cover Graphics Mike Egeler

The cover painting by Robert Gunn was featured in the January/February 1976 issued of *The Saturday Evening Post*, one of his seven paintings in the Great Moments in U.S. Olympic History collection. It shows the three winners of the long jump: Jesse Owens of the United States, Luz Long of Germany and Naoto Tajima of Japan, plus German officials. The painting is in the U.S. Olympic Committee's art collection and is used by permission of the committee.

PICTORIAL HISTORIES PUBLISHING CO., INC.
713 South Third Street West, Missoula, Montana 59801

Introduction

THIS IS A STORY about people and events that took place 60 years ago in Nazi Germany. It has all the elements of a great novel—power struggles, political intrigue, anti-Semitism, treachery, personal triumph and patriotism.

It is the story of the 1936 summer Olympic games held in Berlin and the 1936 winter Olympic games held in Garmisch-Partenkirchen. It could be called the most political Olympics of all time, or at least until the 1980 Moscow games.

The cast of characters includes Adolf Hitler, Hermann Göring, Joseph Goebbels, Leni Riefenstahl, Avery Brundage, Baron Pierre de Coubertin, the founder of the modern Olympics, and some of the greatest athletes of the 20th century.

The games took place amid controversy over an attempted boycott, the first proposed for political purposes in Olympic history. Many firsts also took place at both the winter and summer games. The first use of television in Olympic history. The introduction of both basketball in the summer games and alpine skiing in the winter games. The largest audience to view a baseball game, the largest and most complex sports facilities ever constructed for a summer Olympics or, for that matter, for any sports competition.

The games were a tremendous propaganda boost for the Nazi government that was trying to portray an image of peace and prosperity while stifling all political opposition and imprisoning religious, ethnic and other people at odds with the government.

Germany in 1936 was completely dominated by Adolf Hitler and his Nazi thugs. The suppression of the Jews was on-going but had not yet seen the massive deportations to concentration camps. German troops had occupied the Rhineland in early March without any counter moves by the French or British. Hitler's rearmament plan was progressing and later in the year he would forge a pact with Fascist Italy and Japan and intervene in the Spanish Civil War. Europe would be in turmoil for the next three years until the German invasion of Poland on Sept. 1, 1939, that started World War II.

I have spent considerable time and effort contacting as many living participants as possible. Some were very cooperative, some did not respond. After 60 years it is remarkable how many are still alive and active. The focus of this book is on the American team, its triumphs and its tribulations. It is fitting that this book be published 60 years after the events and in the year of the centennial games in Atlanta, Georgia.

For those who want a comprehensive history of the 1936 games, I suggest they check out some of the books in the bibliography. With the number of photos and information available I could only touch on some of the sports and personalities.

A great many people helped with this project. I must give special thanks to Alice Hodge, Annette Kelly, Marty Glickman, John Macionis, Marshall Wayne, Dick Durrance, Betty Woolsey, Mary Young, Clarita Bright and Herman Goldberg who provided information, photos and artifacts.

Preston Levi, librarian at the International Swimming Hall of Fame and Michael Salmon of the Amateur Athletic Foundation were very helpful, along with the staffs of the U.S. Olympic Committee, National Baseball Hall of Fame, Wrestling Hall of Fame, New England Ski Museum, Ketchum-Sun Valley Historical Society, The Bundesarchiv in Koblenz, Germany, William Woods College, National Archives, Library of Congress, Lake Placid Historical Society, Garmisch-Partenkirchen Chamber of Commerce, Ohio State Archives, University of Illinois Archives, *The Saturday Evening Post*, and the U.S. Naval Academy Athletic Department.

The following also provided help: John Reynolds, Larry Sypolt, Dave Gilbert, Karen Huff, Peter Lunn, Blaine Taylor, Morton Lund, Jim Osborne, John Griffin, Helga Hosford, Kevin Fitzsimons, Dave Shlansky, Sam Balter, and Derek Symer of the U.S. Holocaust Memorial Museum. Robert Gunn of Olathe, Kansas, and the U.S.O.C. provided the cover art, Mike Egeler provided the cover graphics, Kitty Herrin of Arrow Graphics typeset the book and Carol Van Valkenburg edited the manuscript.

—Stan Cohen, 1996

1936
OLYMPICS
Olympic History

The Founder's View

"The main issue in life is not the victory but the fight: the essential is not to have won but to have fought well. To spread these precepts is to pave the way for a more valiant humanity, stronger, and consequently more scrupulous and more generous. These words extend across whole domains and form the basis of a healthy and happy philosophy.

"The Olympic movement gives the world an ideal which reckons with the reality of life, and includes a possibility to guide this reality toward the great Olympic Idea: 'Joie des muscles, culte de la beauté; travail pour le service de la famille et de la société; ces trois éléments unis en un faisceau indissoluble.'

"May joy and good fellowship reign, and in this manner, may the Olympic Torch pursue its way through the ages, increasing friendly understanding among nations, for the good of a humanity always more enthusiastic, more courageous and more pure."

—BARON PIERRE DE COUBERTIN

The founder of the modern Olympics, Baron Pierre de Coubertin was born in Paris, France, on Jan. 1, 1863. He was the son of a painter of historical and religious subjects, Charles Louis Fredi Baron de Coubertin.

At age 20 de Coubertin began work to introduce sports in French schools. The first interscholastic meets in France were organized in 1889, and in 1891 the first Franco-British football match was played. This interest in sports sparked his desire to direct a revival of the current Olympic games.

In 1894 as a young writer and educator, de Coubertin first presented his plan for the Olympic revival to an international meeting on amateur sports convinced that athletics should play a large part in the educational development of young people.

Even then he warned against what later became known as "commercialization" of sport.

De Coubertin's idea won approval and the International Olympic Committee was born. The first games were held in 1896 with Athens, the ancient site, appropriately selected. A special marble stadium was built though it lacked a really suitable running track. The games were set up in four-year intervals, although in 1904 the games were mainly an American affair at the St. Louis World's Fair. It was not until the 1908 games in London that they became a true international event.

Baron Pierre de Coubertin

De Coubertin frequently was at odds with the French sports bodies and felt that his work had not met the appreciation it should. In bitterness he left his native land and spent the latter part of his life in Switzerland.

For 31 years he worked actively as president of the International Olympic Committee. He was succeeded in 1925 by Count de Baillet-Latour and became honorary president for life.

Baron Pierre de Coubertin died of a stroke in Geneva, Switzerland, on Sept. 2, 1937, a year after the XI Olympiad in Germany. His heart was removed, as directed by his will, placed on white satin in a wooden box, and shipped to Olympia, Greece, for entombment. Crown Prince Paul of Greece put de Coubertin's heart in the base of a commemorative marble stele, the kind of honor that had eluded de Coubertin in his lifetime.

Sites for the Olympic Games

Summer
Ist Olympiad, 1896, Athens, Greece
IInd Olympiad, 1900, Paris, France
IIIrd Olympiad, 1904, St. Louis, Missouri, USA
1906, Athens, Greece *(not official)*
IVth Olympiad, 1908, London, England
Vth Olympiad, 1912, Stockholm, Sweden
VIth Olympiad, 1916, Berlin, Germany *(not held)*
VIIth Olympiad, 1920, Antwerp, Belgium
VIIIth Olympiad, 1924, Paris, France
IXth Olympiad, 1928, Amsterdam, Holland
Xth Olympiad, 1932, Los Angeles, California, USA
XIth Olympiad, 1936, Berlin, Germany

Winter
Ist Olympiad, 1924, Chamoix, France
IInd Olympiad, 1928, St. Moritz, Switzerland
IIIrd Olympiad, 1932, Lake Placid, New York, USA
IVth Olympiad, 1936, Garmisch-Partenkirchen, Germany

Count Henri de Baillet-Latour was a Belgian aristocrat who became IOC president in 1925 and presided over the 1936 Olympic games. He was IOC president until 1942.

In 1913 Baron Pierre de Coubertin designed the five Olympic rings symbol and flag. The six colors (including the white background) represented the fraternity of all nations with no exceptions. The 1936 games were the beginning of the pageantry traditions. Banners and flags with the white swastika against a red background were displayed side by side with the Olympic flags.

Members of the International Olympic Committee listen to the preparations for the German games at a working conference in Oslo in 1935.

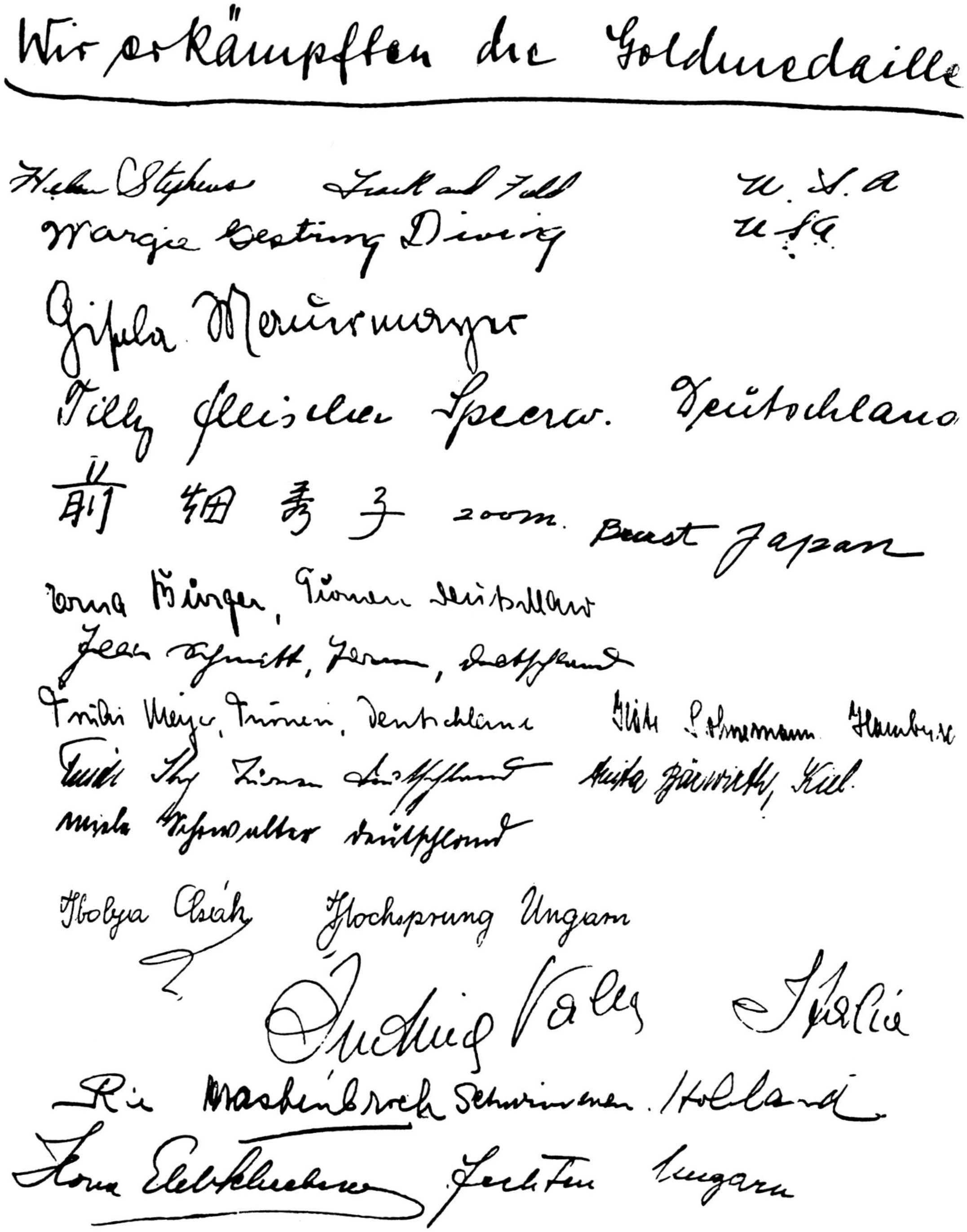

Wir erkämpften die Goldmedaille
Helen Stephens Track and Field U.S.A
Margie Gestring Diving U.S.A.
Gisela Mauermayer
Tilly Fleischer Speerw. Deutschland
200m. Breast Japan
Ibolya Csák Hochsprung Ungarn
Schwimmen. Holland
Fechten Ungarn

These autographs of gold medal winners are in a book once owned by an unnamed German gold medal winner. The book is now owned by John Reynolds, Walnut, California. Not all the names can be identified. **United States**—Helen Stephens, 100-meter run; Marjorie Gestring, diving. **Germany**—Gisela Mauermayer, discus; Tilly Fleischer, javelin; Gymnastics: Women's Combined Team—Erna Bürger, Julie Schmitt, Trudi Meyer, Friedel Iby, Käthe Sohnemann, Anita Bärwirth. **Japan**—Detsuo Hamuro, 200-meter breast stroke. **Hungary**—Ibolya Csak, high jump; Ilona Schacmerer, foil (fencing).

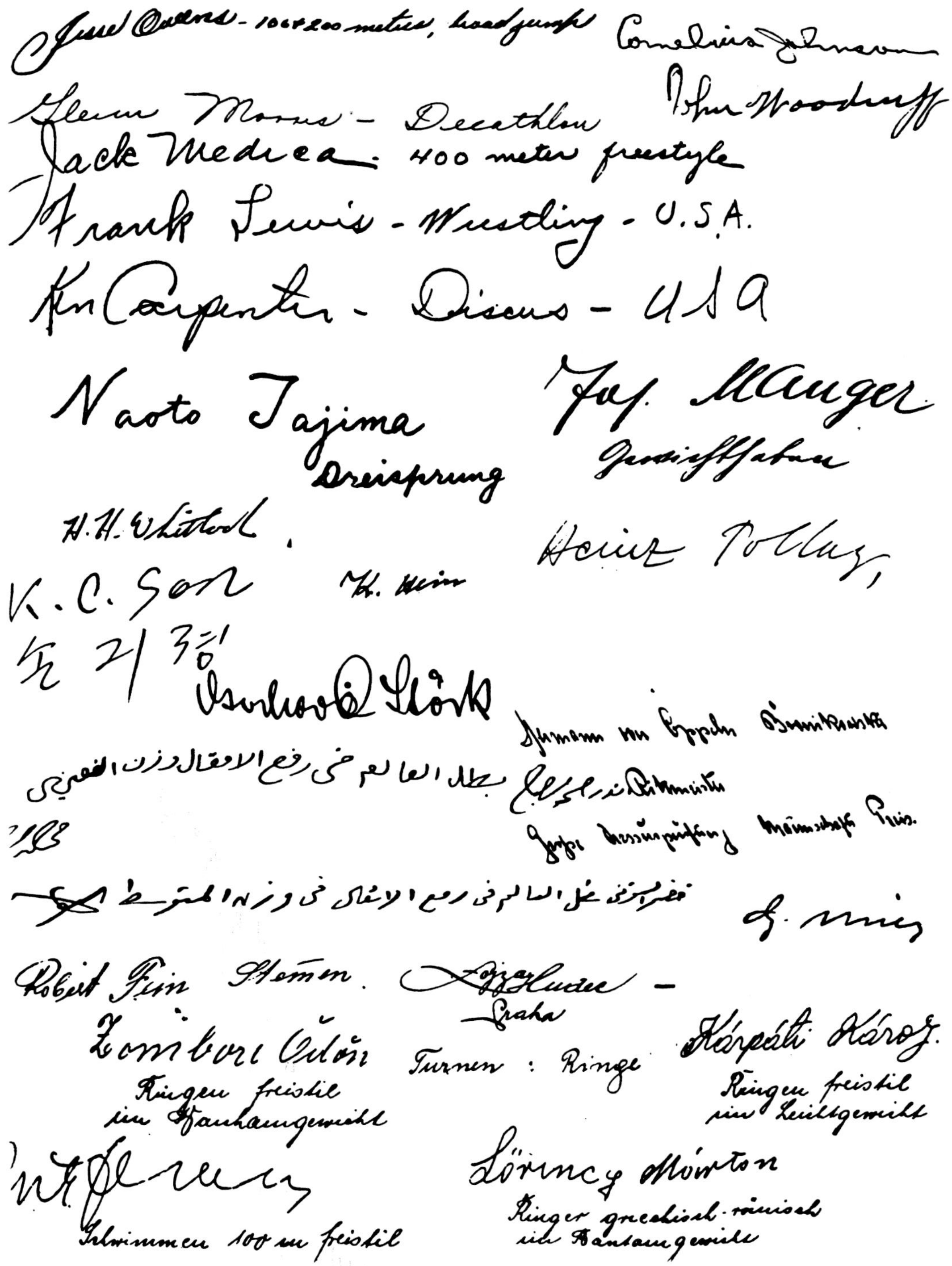

United States—Jesse Owens, 100-meter run, 200-meter run, broad jump, 400-meter relay; Cornelius Johnson, running high jump; Glenn Morris, decathlon; John Woodruff, 800-meter run; Frank Lewis, welterweight wrestling; Ken Carpenter, discus. **Germany**—Joseph Menger, super heavyweight, weight lifter; Karl Hein, 161-pound hammer throw; Heinz Pollan, dressage—individual and team; Herman von Oppelin-Broniskowski, dressage—team. **Japan**—Kitei Son, marathon; Naoto Tajima, hop, step and jump. **Hungary**—Ödön Zombori, bantam weightlifting; Ferenc Csík, 100-meter freestyle swimming; Károly Kárpáti, lightweight weightlifting; Márton Lörincz, Greco-Roman bantamweight wrestling. **United Kingdom of Great Britain**—Harold Whitlock, 50,000-meter walk. **Egypt**—Khadr E. Touni, middleweight weightlifting; Ibrahim Hassan Shams, lightweight weightlifting. **The Netherlands**—"Rie" Hendrika Mastenbroek, 100-meter and 400-meter freestyle swimming. **Austria**—Robert Fein, lightweight weightlifting

WINNERS IN THE ELEVENTH OLYMPIC GAMES

TRACK AND FIELD

Men

	GOLD MEDAL	SILVER MEDAL	BRONZE MEDAL
100 METER DASH	Jesse Owens (*USA*)	R. H. Metcalfe (*USA*)	M. B. Osendarp (*Netherlands*)
200 METER DASH	Jesse Owens (*USA*)	M. M. Robinson (*USA*)	M. B. Osendarp (*Netherlands*)
400 METER RUN	Archie Williams (*USA*)	A.G.K. Brown (*Great Britain*)	J. E. LuValle (*USA*)
800 METER RUN	John Woodruff (*USA*)	M. Lanzi (*Italy*)	P. A. Edwards (*Canada*)
1500 METER RUN	Jack Lovelock (*New Zealand*)	G. Cunningham (*USA*)	L. Beccali (*Italy*)
5,000 METER RUN	Gunnar Hoeckert (*Finland*)	Lehtinen (*Finland*)	J. Jonsson (*Sweden*)
10,000 METER RUN	Ilmari Salminen (*Finland*)	A. Askola (*Finland*)	V. Iso-Hollo (*Finland*)
MARATHON	Kitei Son (*Japan*)	E. Harper (*Great Britain*)	Shoryu Nan (*Japan*)
400 METER RELAY	United States*	Italy	Germany
1600 METER RELAY	Great Britain	United States	Germany
110 METER HURDLES	Forrest Towns (*USA*)	D. O. Finlay (*Great Britain*)	F. D. Pollard (*USA*)
400 METER HURDLES	Glenn Hardin (*USA*)	J. W. Loaring (*Canada*)	M. S. White (*Philippines*)
3,000 METER STEEPLECHASE	Volmari Iso-Hollo* (*Finland*)	K. Tuominen (*Finland*)	A. Dompert (*Germany*)
50,000 METER WALK	Harold Whitlock (*Great Britain*)	A. T. Schwab (*Switzerland*)	A. Bubenko (*Latvia*)
SHOT-PUT	Hans Woellke (*Germany*)	S. Bärlund (*Finland*)	B. Stöck (*Germany*)
DISCUS THROW	Kenneth Carpenter (*USA*)	G. G. Dunn (*USA*)	G. Oberweger (*Italy*)
JAVELIN THROW	Gerhard Stoeck (*Germany*)	Y. Nikkanen (*Finland*)	K. Toivonen (*Finland*)
HAMMER THROW	Karl Hein (*Germany*)	E. Blask (*Germany*)	O. A. Warngard (*Sweden*)
BROAD JUMP	Jesse Owens (*USA*)	L. Long (*Germany*)	N. Tajima (*Japan*)
HIGH JUMP	Cornelius Johnson (*USA*)	D. Albritton (*USA*)	D. Thurber (*USA*)
POLE VAULT	Earle Meadows (*USA*)	J. Nishida (*Japan*)	S. Oe (*Japan*)
HOP, STEP AND JUMP	Naoto Tajima (*Japan*)	M. Harada (*Japan*)	J. P. Metcalfe (*Australia*)
DECATHLON	Glenn Morris (*USA*)	R. Clark (*USA*)	J. Parker (*USA*)

Women

100 METER DASH	Helen Stephens (*USA*)	St. Walasiewicz (*Poland*)	K. Krauss (*Germany*)
80 METER HURDLES	Tresbisonda Valla (*Italy*)	A. Steuer (*Germany*)	E. G. Taylor (*Canada*)
400 METER RELAY	United States*	Great Britain	Canada
HIGH JUMP	Ibolya Csak (*Hungary*)	D. Odam (*Great Britain*)	E. Kaun (*Germany*)
JAVELIN THROW	Tilly Fleischer (*Germany*)	L. Krüger (*Germany*)	M. Kwasiewska (*Poland*)
DISCUS THROW	Gisela Mauermayer (*Germany*)	J. Weiss (*Poland*)	P. Mollenhauer (*Germany*)

SHOOTING

RAPID-FIRE PISTOL	C. van Oyen (*Germany*)	H. Hax (*Germany*)	T. Ullmann (*Sweden*)
PRECISION PISTOL	T. Ullmann (*Sweden*)	E. Krempel (*Germany*)	C. des Jammonnières (*France*)
SMALL-BORE RIFLE	W. Rogeberg (*Norway*)	R. Berzseny (*Hungary*)	W. Karas (*Poland*)

EQUESTRIAN

Team Events

GRAND DRESSAGE	Germany	France	Sweden
THREE-DAY	Germany	Poland	Great Britain
PRIX DES NATIONS	Germany	Netherlands	Portugal

Individual Events

GRAND DRESSAGE	Heinz Pollay (*Germany*)	F. Gerhard (*Germany*)	Podhajsky (*Austria*)
THREE-DAY	Ludwig Stubbendorf (*Germany*)	E. Thomson (*USA*)	H. Lundung (*Denmark*)
PRIX DES NATIONS	Kurt Hasse (*Germany*)	H. Rang (*Rumania*)	J. v. Platthy (*Hungary*)

WEIGHT-LIFTING

FEATHERWEIGHT CLASS	Anthony Terlazzo (*USA*)	S. H. Soliman (*Egypt*)	J. Shams (*Egypt*)
LIGHTWEIGHT CLASS	Mohammed Ahmed Mesbah (*Egypt*)		K. Jansen (*Germany*)
MIDDLEWEIGHT CLASS	Khadr El Touni (*Egypt*)	R. Ismayr (*Germany*)	A. Wagner (*Germany*)
LIGHT-HEAVYWEIGHT CLASS	Louis Hostin* (*France*)	E. Deutsch (*Germany*)	W. Ibrahim (*Egypt*)
HEAVYWEIGHT CLASS	Joseph Menger (*Germany*)	V. Psenicka (*Czechoslovakia*)	A. Luhäar (*Estonia*)

* Retained title.

	GOLD MEDAL	SILVER MEDAL	BRONZE MEDAL

SWIMMING

Men

100 METER FREE STYLE	Ferenc Csik (*Hungary*)	M. Yusa (*Japan*)	Sh. Arai (*Japan*)
100 METER BACK-STROKE	Adolph Kiefer (*USA*)	A. van de Weghe (*USA*)	M. Kiyokawa (*Japan*)
200 METER BREAST-STROKE	Detsuo Hamuro (*Japan*)	E. Sietas (*Germany*)	R. Koike (*Japan*)
400 METER FREE STYLE	Jack Medica (*USA*)	S. Uto (*Japan*)	S. Makino (*Japan*)
1500 METER FREE STYLE	Noboru Terada (*Japan*)	J. Medica (*USA*)	S. Uto (*Japan*)
800 METER RELAY	Japan*	United States	Hungary
SPRINGBOARD DIVING	Dick Degener (*USA*)	M. Wayne (*USA*)	A. Greene (*USA*)
PLATFORM DIVING	Marshall Wayne (*USA*)	E. Root (*USA*)	H. Stork (*Germany*)

Women

100 METER FREE STYLE	Rita Mastenbroek (*Netherlands*)	J. M. Campbell (*Argentina*)	G. Arendt (*Germany*)
100 METER BACK-STROKE	Dina Senff (*Netherlands*)	R. Mastenbroek (*Netherlands*)	A. Bridges (*USA*)
200 METER BREAST-STROKE	Hideko Machata (*Japan*)	M. Genenger (*Germany*)	J. Sörensen (*Denmark*)
400 METER FREE STYLE	Rita Mastenbroek (*Netherlands*)	R. Hveger (*Denmark*)	L. K. Wingard (*USA*)
400 METER RELAY	Netherlands	Germany	United States
SPRINGBOARD DIVING	Marjorie Gestring (*USA*)	K. Rawls (*USA*)	D. Poynton Hill (*USA*)
PLATFORM DIVING	Dorothy Poynton Hill* (*USA*)	V. Dunn (*USA*)	K. Köhler (*Germany*)

WRESTLING

Catch-as-Catch-Can

BANTAMWEIGHT CLASS	Oedon Zombori (*Hungary*)	R. Flood (*USA*)	J. Herbert (*Germany*)
FEATHERWEIGHT CLASS	Kustaa Pihlajamäki (*Finland*)	F. E. Millard (*USA*)	G. Jönssen (*Sweden*)
LIGHTWEIGHT CLASS	Karoly Karpati (*Hungary*)	W. Ehrl (*Germany*)	K. Pihlajamäki (*Finland*)
WELTERWEIGHT CLASS	Frank Lewis (*USA*)	T. Andersson (*Sweden*)	J. Schleimer (*Canada*)
MIDDLEWEIGHT CLASS	Emile Poilvé (*France*)	R. L. Voliva (*USA*)	A. Kirecci (*Turkey*)
LIGHT-HEAVYWEIGHT CLASS	Knut Fridell (*Sweden*)	A. Neo (*Estonia*)	E. Siebert (*Germany*)
HEAVYWEIGHT CLASS	Kristjan Palusalu (*Estonia*)	J. Klapuch (*Czechoslovakia*)	H. E. Nyström (*Finland*)

Graeco-Roman

BANTAMWEIGHT CLASS	Martin Lörincz (*Hungary*)	E. Svensson (*Sweden*)	J. Brendel (*Germany*)
FEATHERWEIGHT CLASS	Yasar Erkan (*Turkey*)	A. Reini (*Finland*)	E. Karlsson (*Sweden*)
LIGHTWEIGHT CLASS	Lauri Koskela (*Finland*)	J. Herda (*Czechoslovakia*)	V. Väli (*Estonia*)
WELTERWEIGHT CLASS	Rodolf Svedberg (*Sweden*)	F. Schäfer (*Germany*)	E. Virtanen (*Finland*)
MIDDLEWEIGHT CLASS	Ivar Johansson (*Sweden*)	L. Schweikert (*Germany*)	J. Palotás (*Hungary*)
LIGHT-HEAVYWEIGHT CLASS	Axel Cadier (*Sweden*)	E. Bietags (*Latvia*)	A. Neo (*Estonia*)
HEAVYWEIGHT CLASS	Kristjan Palusalu (*Estonia*)	J. Nyman (*Sweden*)	K. Hornfischer (*Germany*)

GYMNASTICS

Men

ALL-AROUND TEAM	Germany	Switzerland	Finland
ALL-AROUND INDIVIDUAL	Alfred Schwarzmann (*Germany*)	E. Mack (*Switzerland*)	K. Frey (*Germany*)
LONG HORSE	Alfred Schwarzmann (*Germany*)	E. Mack (*Switzerland*)	M. Volz (*Germany*)
SIDE HORSE	Konrad Frey (*Germany*)	E. Mack (*Switzerland*)	Bachmann (*Switzerland*)
FLYING RINGS	Alois Hudec (*Czechoslovakia*)	L. Stukelj (*Yugoslavia*)	M. Volz (*Germany*)
PARALLEL BARS	Konrad Frey (*Germany*)	M. Reusch (*Switzerland*)	K. Schwarzmann (*Germany*)
HORIZONTAL BAR	Aleksanteri Saarvala (*Finland*)	K. Frey (*Germany*)	K. Schwarzmann (*Germany*)
FREE HAND	George Miez (*Switzerland*)	E. Walter (*Switzerland*)	Frey (*Germany*) & Mack (*Switzerland*)

Women

ALL-AROUND TEAM	Germany	Czechoslovakia	Hungary

* Retained title.

	GOLD MEDAL	SILVER MEDAL	BRONZE MEDAL
		CYCLING	
1,000 METER SCRATCH	Toni Merkens (*Germany*)	A. G. Van Vliet (*Netherlands*)	L. Chaillot (*France*)
4,000 METER PURSUIT	France	Italy	Great Britain
1,000 METER STANDING START	A. G. Van Vliet (*Netherlands*)	P. Georget (*France*)	R. Karsch (*Germany*)
2,000 METER TANDEM	Germany	Netherlands	France
100 KILOMETER ROAD	R. Charpentier (*France*)	G. Lapebie (*France*)	E. Nievergelt (*Switzerland*)
		YACHTING	
MONOTYPE CLASS	Kaghelland (*Netherlands*)	Krogman (*Germany*)	Scott (*Great Britain*)
STAR CLASS	Germany	Sweden	Netherlands
SIX METER CLASS	Great Britain	Norway	Sweden
EIGHT METER CLASS	Italy	Norway	Germany
		ROWING	
SINGLE SCULLS	Gustav Schaefer (*Germany*)	J. Hasenöhrl (*Austria*)	D. H. Barrow (*USA*)
DOUBLE SCULLS	Great Britain	Germany	Poland
PAIRS WITHOUT COXSWAIN	Germany	Denmark	Argentina
PAIRS WITH COXSWAIN	Germany	Italy	France
FOURS WITHOUT COXSWAIN	Germany	Great Britain	Switzerland
FOURS WITH COXSWAIN	Germany	Switzerland	France
EIGHT-OARED SHELLS	United States*	Italy	Germany
		CANOEING	
		Short Course	
CANADIAN SINGLES	F. Amyot (*Canada*)	B. Karlik (*Czechoslovakia*)	E. Koschik (*Germany*)
CANADIAN DOUBLES	Czechoslovakia	Canada	Austria
KAYAK SINGLES	Gregor Hradetsky (*Austria*)	H. Cämmerer (*Germany*)	J. Kraaier (*Netherlands*)
KAYAK DOUBLES	Austria	Germany	Netherlands
		Long Course	
KAYAK SINGLES	Ernest Krebs (*Germany*)	F. Landertinger (*Austria*)	E. Riedel (*USA*)
KAYAK DOUBLES	Germany	Austria	Sweden
COLLAPSIBLE SINGLES	Gregor Hradetsky (*Austria*)	N. Eberhard (*France*)	X. Hörmann (*Germany*)
CANADIAN DOUBLES	Czechoslovakia	Canada	Austria
COLLAPSIBLE DOUBLES	Sweden	Germany	Netherlands
		BOXING	
FLYWEIGHT CLASS	Kaiser (*Germany*)	Matta (*Italy*)	Laurie (*USA*)
BANTAMWEIGHT CLASS	Sergo (*Italy*)	Wilson (*USA*)	Ortiz (*Mexico*)
FEATHERWEIGHT CLASS	Casanova (*Argentina*)	Catterall (*South Africa*)	Miner (*Germany*)
LIGHTWEIGHT CLASS	Harangi (*Hungary*)	Stepulow (*Estonia*)	Agren (*Sweden*)
WELTERWEIGHT CLASS	Suvio (*Finland*)	Murasch (*Germany*)	Petersen (*Denmark*)
MIDDLEWEIGHT CLASS	Despeaux (*France*)	Tiller (*Norway*)	Villareal (*Argentina*)
LIGHT-HEAVYWEIGHT CLASS	Michalot (*France*)	Vogt (*Germany*)	Risiglione (*Argentina*)
HEAVYWEIGHT CLASS	Runge (*Germany*)	Lovell (*Argentina*)	Nilsen (*Norway*)
		FENCING	
		Foils	
TEAM	Italy	France	Germany
INDIVIDUAL	G. Gaudini (*Italy*)	E. Gardère (*France*)	G. Bocchino (*Italy*)
WOMEN'S INDIVIDUAL	Elek Schacherer (*Hungary*)	H. Mayer (*Germany*)	E. Preis (*Austria*)
		Epée	
TEAM	Italy	Sweden	France
INDIVIDUAL	F. Riccardi (*Italy*)	S. Ragno (*Italy*	G. Cornaggia (*Italy*)
		Saber	
INDIVIDUAL	Endre Kabos (*Hungary*)	G. Marzi (*Italy*)	A. Geray (*Hungary*)
TEAM	Hungary	Italy	Germany

* Retained title.

Contents

The Flags of the Participating Nations

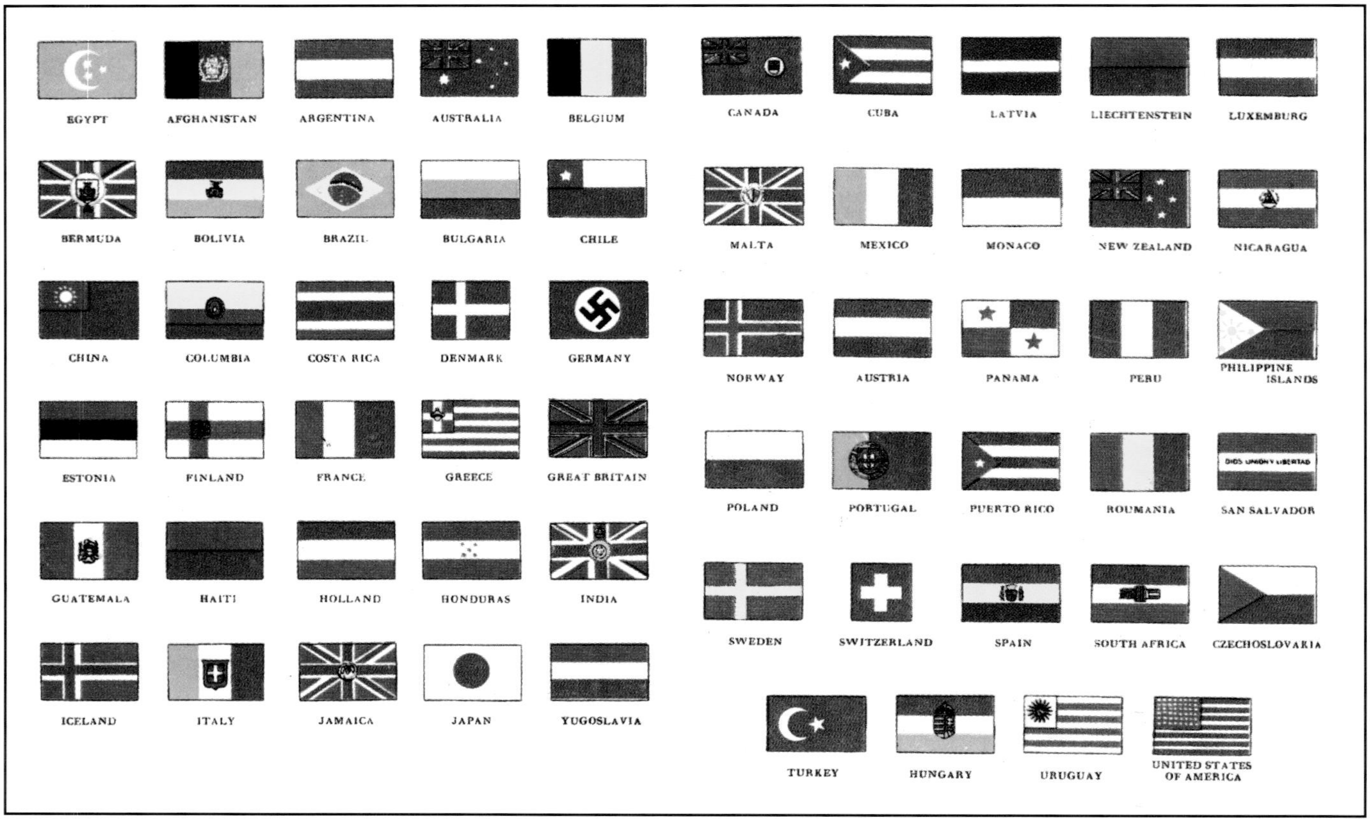

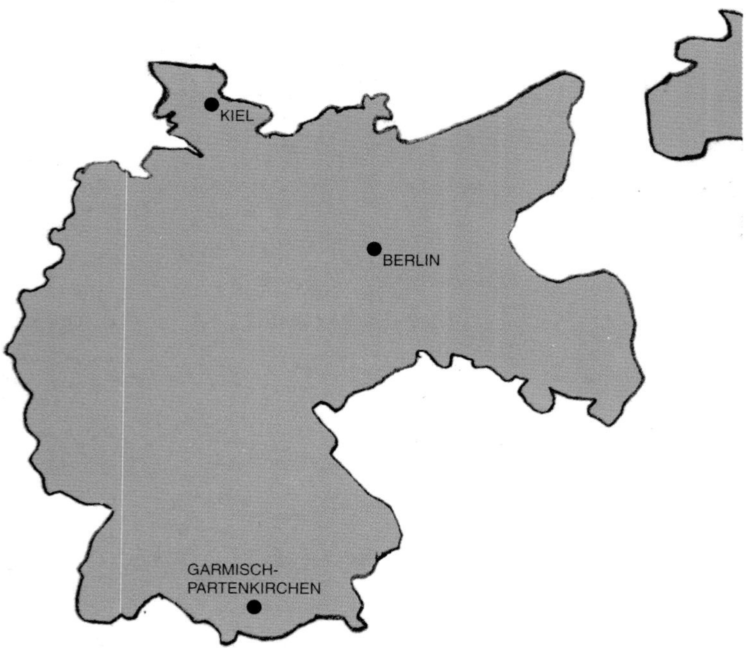

Photo Identification

AP—Associated Press
BA—Bundesarchiv, Koblenz, Germany
ISHF—International Swimming Hall of Fame
KSVHS—Ketchum-Sun Valley Historical Society, Don and Gretchen Fraser memorabilia collection
LC—Library of Congress
NA, GRIO—National Archives, German Railroad Information Office Collection
NA, HH—National Archives, Heinrich Hoffman Collection
NBHF—National Baseball Hall of Fame
NESM—New England Ski Museum Collection
OSU—Ohio State University Archives
UIA—University of Illinois Archives, Avery Brundage Collection
WASM—Western American SkiSport Museum

Photos not credited are from the collection of the author.

Dedicated to all the 1936 Olympians who represented the United States in an historic event.

1936
O L Y M P I C S

Controversy over U.S. Participation

AT THE 29TH session of the International Olympic Committee in Barcelona, Spain, in May 1931, committee members awarded the 1936 Olympic games to Germany. The vote was 43 for Berlin and 16 for Barcelona. The vote symbolized the reintegration of Germany into the international sports community after World War I, although the country had reentered the Olympic games in 1928.

The summer games were awarded to Berlin and the winter games to the twin villages of Garmisch-Partenkirchen in Bavaria.

In 1931 the Weimer Republic was in power but in constant turmoil. Two years later the Nazi party under the leadership of Adolph Hitler had taken power. The new government was not initially enthusiastic about the games, but finally realized their tremendous propaganda value.

The Nazi government rose to power based on a dogma of anti-Semitism, coupled with a belief in the superiority of the Aryan race and a concentrated suppression of its own people. By 1935 the world had awakened to the Nazi's actions and many countries, the United States among them, threatened a boycott or removal of the games to another site. Religious, labor, athletic, and fraternal groups were among those advocating a boycott and brought pressure to bear on the USOC.

Avery Brundage made a trip to Berlin to see for himself if Germany was abiding by international law and not suppressing her people, especially her Jewish population. On his return he expressed the opinion that the games should go on, that it was not the place of the IOC to interfere in the internal policies of the host country. The American Olympic Committee eventually voted to participate in the games.

Germany had cleaned up her act, at least outwardly, before the games, and had even placed a Jewish athlete on the winter and summer teams.

Many Americans and Europeans had arranged to hold a "People's Olympics" or "Workers' Games" in Barcelona in 1936, but the Spanish Civil War broke out in July, just before the games were to begin.

After the games were over it was agreed that Germany had put on the best-organized Olympic games ever. It didn't take long, however, for her to sink back into the abyss of suppression and aggression, which eventually led to the war and the downfall of the "Thousand Year Reich" in only 12 years.

UNDER CONSTRUCTION—PASSABLE BUT DANGEROUS -:- By BURRIS JEN

The Case Against Participation

The following is from a booklet entitled *Preserve the Olympic Ideal: A statement of the Case Against American Participation in the Olympic Games at Berlin*, published by the Committee on Fair Play in Sports, New York City.

"The question whether America should participate in the Eleventh Olympiad, if it is held in Nazi Germany, is now being debated throughout the length and breadth of the country. In the last analysis this question will have to be and will be decided by American athletes themselves. If we know them correctly, they will not permit it to be decided for them either by the International Olympic Committee or by the American Olympic Committee which, in order to obtain the high prerogative of making up the American athlete's mind for him, represent him as the forgotten man, themselves as his only friend, and everyone else as his betrayer.

"In all the history of American sport American athletes have never had to decide a more momentous question. It is not too much to say that upon their decision rest the future and the integrity of amateur athletics throughout the world. For as America goes on this question the world will go, the American Olympic Committee to the contrary, notwithstanding. In view of the importance of the question, it is highly desirable that it should be debated thoroughly and dispassionately and that all the relevant facts should be made known. Only in this way will it be possible to answer the question wisely and in the best interests of athletics and athletes. The American Olympic Committee has issued a pamphlet presenting the case for American participation. The purpose of this booklet is to present the case against American participation.

"Anyone who wants both sides of the question ought to read both of these discussions; and, of course, American athletes will not be content to hear only one side.

"In discussing the question we shall depart from the technique of the American Olympic Committee in one respect. The American Olympic Committee has appealed to every passion and prejudice which in their low opinion of the American athlete he might conceivably possess. By attempting to make the opposition to American participation appear as an attempt by Jews to use the Olympic Games to serve their own selfish purposes to the detriment of athletics and athletes, they seek to appeal to and to arouse prejudice against the Jew. Indeed, to their everlasting shame, some members of the American Olympic Committee have gone so far as to threaten the Jews of America with retaliatory anti-Semitic measures if the opposition should be successful. By trying to make the opposition appear as an attempt by Communists to destroy the Olympic Games themselves, they seek to appeal to prejudice against Communism and Communists, although they know, of course, that such American leaders as Hugh S. Johnson, Alfred E. Smith and William Green, such sports writers as Westbrook Pegler, Paul Gallico and John Kieran, and such athletes as James Bausch, Jack Shea, Carmen Barth, Evelyn Furtsch, who are opposed to American Olympic participation, are no more communistic than the members of the American Olympic Committee themselves. By trying to make the opposition appear as a movement composed exclusively of elements who know nothing about and have no interest in athletics, they seek to arouse the prejudice of the athlete against the non-athlete. And so on, almost without limit and apparently without conscience.

"We have sufficient faith in the justice and correctness of our position to wish to have the matter of American participation considered on its merits, and sufficient confidence in the intelligence of American athletes to believe, as the American Olympic Committee apparently does not believe, that they are capable of considering and deciding the matter in that way. Therefore, on our part, we shall appeal to the reason of American athletes rather than to their imaginary passions and prejudices. We do not believe that appeals to passion and prejudice have any place in the discussion of a question fraught with so much significance for the future of sport and athletics.

"Let us now see precisely what this issue is which American athletes must and will decide for themselves in spite of the desire of Messrs. Sherrill, Brundage and others, to decide it for them."

Following are some of the testimonials the committee published in the booklet to support its view.

"It is obvious that our participation in the Berlin Olympics is not a Jewish question, not a Catholic question, but an American question. The principles of democracy, of opportunity, of fair play which Nazi practice discards are vital to every American."

—*New York Evening Post*, October 22, 1935

"It was Sunday afternoon, the closing moments of the 1932 Olympiad in Los Angeles. Over the western parapets of the big Coliseum 104,000 persons were standing bareheaded. Flags of all nations stirred in the breeze. Then they extinguished the Olympic torch, to be re-lighted four years later in Berlin—or so they said.

"Damon Runyan was next to me.

"'Even God is with you folks,' he said, pointing to the glorious sunset, and there was a choke in his voice, as there was in that of anyone else who tried to speak. It was no time for speaking.

"So how can a nation that seeks to supplant this God of ours hope to catch that spirit, that 'lost chord'? Germany's pagan putsch makes its acceptance of the real Olympic oath either an impossibility or a hypocrisy. Let Germany read well that Olympic oath and then dare ask the privilege to be world hosts."

—Mark Kelly, *Los Angeles Examiner*

"Now that it is admitted that the German Olympics are to be a political undertaking intended to glorify the Nazi program, the American Olympic Committee has no right to commit American support to participation."

—Westbrook Pegler, *New York World Telegram*

"I read in the papers yesterday that Germany now proposes to wipe from the war records the names of Jewish war veterans who were killed or maimed in her defense. If a nation is so lacking in sportsmanship to its own war dead what reason is there for irate General Sherrill to insist on participation in games that are founded on sportsmanship in a country that ignores it?"

—Ed Sullivan, *New York Daily News*

"I hope that the United States will withdraw from Olympic participation or have the Games removed to another country. The sport world never had a better opportunity to give an example of good sportsmanship in international sport relations."

—Dr. A.D. Browne, former vice president,
National Collegiate Conference

"Nobody can compete in an atmosphere such as exists in Nazi Germany."

—Stella Walsh, sprinting champion

The pamphlet concludes with the following statement:

"All that has been set down here is a matter of public record. There is no hearsay between these pages. The case against Nazi Germany has been proven by the words and deeds of Nazis from Adolf Hitler to the lowest ranking storm trooper. The Olympic code has been violated by the nation which expects other nations, who hold it sacred, to gather round her in honorable and friendly contest for supremacy in the world of sport. And by such violation Nazi Germany has proven herself unworthy to be an Olympics contestant—let alone a host to the other Olympic entrants throughout the world."

A Nazi Leader's View

"According to the teachings of the so-called Liberals sport is supposed to be a uniting link between nations. International sports meets are sponsored in the spirit of reconciliation. Frenchmen kiss the cheeks of German girls, roses and flags are exchanged, national anthems are played and 'clever' words of 'peace' are spoken—but all the sport in the world cannot cancel those shameful paragraphs in the Versailles Treaty regarding the war guilt.

"Frenchmen, Belgians, Polaks and Jew-Niggers run on German tracks and swim in German pools. Good money is thrown away and nobody can truthfully say that international relationships between Germany and its enemies have been bettered. Only a few treasonable persons and anti-German pacifists claim such accomplishments when speaking in Geneva and Prague.

"As a matter of fact we consider them (the Olympic games) ... propaganda. The ... private clubs or a ... the name of Ger... The state will n...

from a booklet ... Ideology," a...

COMMITTEE *on* FAIR PLAY *in* SPORTS

NO AMERICAN PARTICIPATION *in the* OLYMPIC GAMES *under* NAZI AUSPICES

20 Vesey Street, New York City

Tel BARCLAY 7-0875-0879

Temporary Committee

GEORGE GORDON BATTLE
DR. HENRY SMITH LEIPER
Chairmen

FRANCIS A. HENSON
Treasurer

WILLIAM B. CHAMBERLAIN
Executive Secretary

LEE BRICK
Assistant Secretary

BERDA S. HORN
Associate Secretary

WILLIAM G. SCHRAM
Comptroller

JOSEPH A. BABOR
HON. RICHARD J. BEAMISH
FRANCIS BIDDLE
DR. FRANZ BOAS
HEYWOOD BROUN
DR. HUGH ELMER BROWN
REV. EDMUND B. CHAFFEE
DEAN E. W. CHUBB
GOV. JAMES M. CURLEY
DR. HARRY EMERSON FOSDICK
DR. JOHN C. FUTRALL
IRVING [illegible]
HON. JAMES W. GERARD
DR. FRANK P. GRAHAM
MARTHA GRUENING
REV. HERMAN J. HAHN
ARTHUR GARFIELD HAYS
DR. JOHN HAYNES HOLMES
DR. PAUL HUTCHINSON
DR. RAYMOND A. KENT
DR. FRANK KINGDON
FREDA KIRCHWEY
SENATOR JESSE H. METCALF
LUCILLE B. MILNER
RICHARD NEUBERGER
DR. REINHOLD NIEBUHR
DR. ELLEN F. PENDLETON
REV. A. CLAYTON POWELL, JR.
FRANK RITCHIE
REV. MILLARD L. ROBINSON
MERRILL E. ROOT
JOHN A. RYDER
C. W. SAVAGE
WILLIAM JAY SCHIEFFELIN
JACK SHEA
GEORGE N. SHUSTER
LAWRENCE E. SPIVAK
REV. E. V. STANFORD, O.S.A.
NORMAN THOMAS
OSWALD GARRISON VILLARD
DR. E. GRAHAM WILSON
DR. MARY E. WOOLLEY

November 15, 1935

Dr. Godfrey Dewey
Lake Placid Club
New York

Dear Dr. Dewey:

Knowing your interest in preserving the high standards of sportsmanship and the Olympic ideals, we take the liberty of bringing to your attention the enclosed pamphlet entitled "Preserve the Olympic Ideal".

The pamphlet presents a description of the situation in Germany and the violation by the present regime of the Olympic regulations and of the pledges given to the International Olympic Committee, to the American Olympic Committee, and to the Amateur Athletic Union of the United States. The facts contained therein are well authenticated.

We should be interested in having your comment on this pamphlet.

Very sincerely yours,

George Gordon Battle

Henry Smith Leiper
Co - Chairmen

Former judge Jeremiah T. Mahoney, a Catholic and president of the AAU, formed the Committee on Fair Play in Sports to channel and make more effective the growing alarm over the news about Nazi atrocities and to counter Avery Brundage's contention that the games should not be boycotted.

ANK By Jerry Doyle.

Germany—The Ideal Place For The Olympics

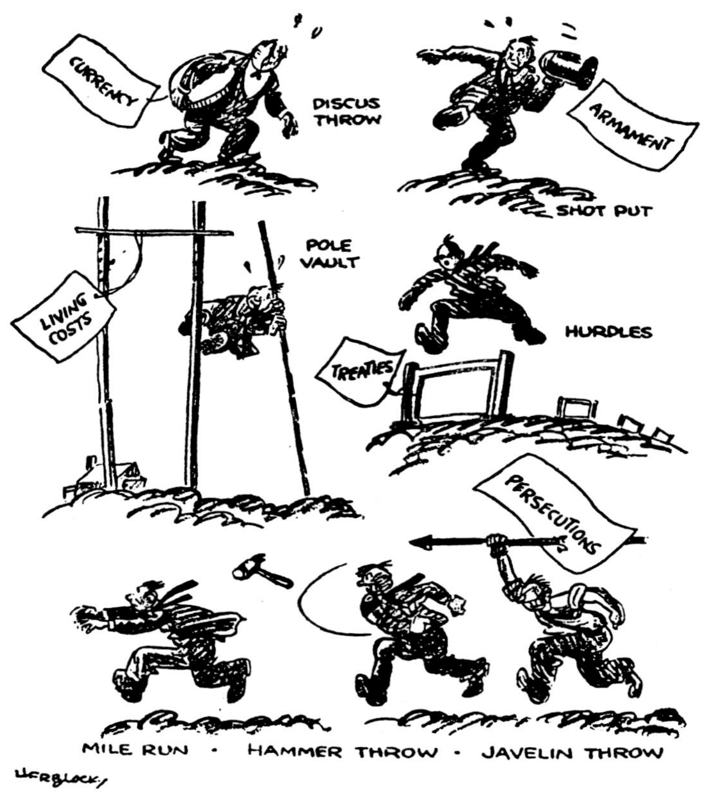

1936

O L Y M P I C S

The American Team

THE AMERICAN OLYMPIC COMMITTEE

HONORARY PRESIDENT

FRANKLIN D. ROOSEVELT, *the President of the United States*

HONORARY VICE-PRESIDENTS

CORDELL HULL, *Secretary of State of the United States*

GEORGE H. DERN, *Secretary of War of the United States*

CLAUDE A. SWANSON, *Secretary of Navy of the United States*

†DR. GRAEME M. HAMMOND, *President Emeritus*

OFFICERS

†AVERY BRUNDAGE, *President*

†FREDERICK W. RUBIEN, *Secretary*

†DR. JOSEPH E. RAYCROFT, *Vice-President*

†GUSTAVUS T. KIRBY, *Treasurer*

REPRESENTATIVES OF ORGANIZATIONS

Amateur Athletic Union of the United States
Judge Murray Hulbert
†Daniel J. Ferris
J. Frank Facey

National Collegiate Athletic Association
Romeyn Berry
†William J. Bingham
Prof. L. W. St. John

National Association of Amateur Oarsmen
†Henry Penn Burke

United States Football Association, Inc.
Dr. G. Randolph Manning

North American Yacht Racing Union
George Emlen Roosevelt

Amateur Fencers League of America
†Leon M. Schoonmaker

National Cycling Association, Inc.
Frank L. Kramer

Amateur Skating Union of the U. S.
Joseph K. Savage

National Ski Association of America, Inc.
Leib Deyo

United States Cavalry Association
†Brig. Gen. Guy V. Henry

Field Hockey Association of America
Henry Kirk Greer

United States Revolver Association
Karl T. Frederick

National Rifle Association
Maj. Gen. M. A. Reckord

Intercollegiate Assn. of Amateur Athletes of America
†A. C. Gilbert

War Department
Major Ross O. Baldwin

Navy Department
Lt. Comdr. C. L. Jacobsen

Ten Members at Large
Dr. Charles W. Kennedy
George W. Graves
Major John L. Griffith
†Dr. John Brown, Jr.
Alfred J. Lill
†Major Patrick J. Walsh
†Fred L. Steers
†Prof. Fred W. Luehring
†William A. Dalton
Frank G. McCormick

Games Committees
Joseph J. Barriskill (Soccer)
J. Lyman Bingham (Basketball)
Joseph O. Bulkley (Ice Hockey)
Dr. I. R. Calkins (Pistol Shooting)
Arnold Eddy (Field Handball)
Joseph T. England (Men's Track & Field)
Emile E. Fraysse (Cycling)
Richard L. Hapgood (Figure Skating)
Judge Frederick L. Hoffman (Baseball)
†Herbert D. Holm (Women's Swimming)
Frank M. Kalteux (Speed Skating)
Martin A. Klein (Women's Track & Field)
C. B. Lister (Rifle Shooting)
†Col. Pierre Lorillard, Jr. (Equestrian)
Carl T. Majer (Canoe)
William Monahan (Rowing)
Roy E. Moore (Gymnastics)
†J. Jay O'Brien (Bobsled)
†Leonard F. O'Brien (Field Hockey)
F. Barnard O'Connor (Fencing)
Prof. Charles A. Proctor (Ski)
Lt. Col. William C. Rose (Modern Pentathlon)
Ernest Stavey (Yachting)
†C. W. Streit, Jr. (Wrestling)
Arch Ward (Boxing)
†Dietrich Wortmann (Weight Lifting)

Past Presidents of Association and Committee
†Dr. Graeme M. Hammond (President Emeritus of American Olympic Assn.)
†Gustavus T. Kirby (1920 American Olympic Committee President)
General Douglas MacArthur (1928 American Olympic Committee President)

Assistant Secretary
†James F. Simms

Assistant Treasurers
A. Jocelyn H. Magrath (Resigned)
†H. Jamison Swarts †Asa Bushnell

†Those in attendance at the Games of the XIth Olympiad.

Committee on Fair Play in Sports

GEORGE GORDON BATTLE — DR. HENRY SMITH LEIPER
Co Chairmen

JOSEPH A. BABOR
HON. RICHARD J. BEAMISH
FRANCIS BIDDLE
DR. FRANZ BOAS
HEYWOOD BROUN
DR. HUGH ELMER BROWN
REV. EDMUND B. CHAFFEE
DEAN E. W. CHUBB
GOV. JAMES M. CURLEY
DR. HARRY EMERSON FOSDICK
DR. JOHN C. FUTRALL
IRVING GEMSON
HON. JAMES W. GERARD
DR. FRANK P. GRAHAM
MARTHA GRUENING
REV. HERMAN J. HAHN
ARTHUR GARFIELD HAYS
FRANCIS A. HENSON
DR. JOHN HAYNES HOLMES
DR. PAUL HUTCHINSON
DR. RAYMOND A. KENT
DR. FRANK KINGDON
FREDA KIRCHWEY
SENATOR JESSE H. METCALF
LUCILLE B. MILNER
RICHARD NEUBERGER
DR. REINHOLD NIEBUHR
DR. ELLEN F. PENDLETON
REV. A. CLAYTON POWELL, JR.
FRANK RITCHIE
REV. MILLARD L. ROBINSON
MERRILL E. ROOT
JOHN A. RYDER
C. W. SAVAGE
WILLIAM JAY SCHIEFFELIN
JACK SHEA
GEORGE N. SHUSTER
LAWRENCE E. SPIVAK
REV. E. V. STANFORD, O.S.A.
NORMAN THOMAS
OSWALD GARRISON VILLARD
DR. E. GRAHAM WILSON
DR. MARY E. WOOLLEY

WILLIAM B. CHAMBERLAIN, Executive Secretary

A Boy Scout collects money for the Olympics at a Princeton invitational track meet.

Getting the Athletes to Germany

The American Olympic Committee formed a transportation committee as early as 1934 to arrange ship passage to Germany for both the winter and summer athletes, plus all railroad and bus transportation in the United States.

All of the large transatlantic steamship lines were asked to submit proposals for the Atlantic crossing. Two alternatives were considered. The AOC reviewed chartering a ship on a flat-rate basis or accepting an offer from the United States Lines to place one of its ships at the disposal of the Olympic committee on a berth-selling basis.

As it would be difficult to tie up a ship for both the voyage and return as well as the two weeks in dock and to know exactly how many births were needed the AOC decided to take the United States Lines' offer.

The company selected the S.S. *Manhattan* to transport both the winter and summer teams. A few winter athletes sailed on the S.S. *Washington* a few days after the *Manhattan* sailed on January 3.

The American Express company was appointed as the official transportation agent for the Olympic committee. It would be in charge of all land tours offered in connection with the Olympic Games.

Four days after the final track and field trials, 383 athletes and officials and 850 passengers, many of them family and friends, sailed from New York. The entire tourist space was reserved for the athletes, managers and coaches and the cabin and third-class space was sold to friends and relatives of the athletes and members of the American Olympic Committee.

Space was allotted on several of the decks for the teams to use for training. By the second day out to sea most of the athletes were going through their training programs almost as they would at home.

On the morning of July 24 the S.S. *Manhattan* docked at Hamburg, Germany, and the team was taken to Hamburg's Rathaus for a welcoming ceremony. Then by train team members arrived in Berlin where another reception was held.

On the return voyage most of the summer team traveled on the S.S. *President Roosevelt*, which sailed from Hamburg on August 19 and docked in New York on August 28.

AMERICAN OLYMPIC COMMITTEE

HANDBOOK

For Officials and Members of the American Olympic Teams

PROPERTY OF

____
Signature

XI OLYMPIAD
BERLIN 1936

THIS BOOKLET IS VALUABLE

KEEP it with your passport or identification card and purse so that it may be available without delay when required.

It contains important information for your guidance while you are a member of the American Olympic Team.

It contains also copies of the various receipts and agreements involved in your relations with the Olympic Committee that you may sign as a member of the team.

READ CAREFULLY

COMPILED BY SPECIAL COMMITTEE:
JOHN BROWN, A. C. GILBERT, JOSEPH E. RAYCROFT.

LETTER OF CONGRATULATION FROM PRESIDENT BRUNDAGE TO THOSE WHO HAVE BEEN SELECTED FOR MEMBERSHIP ON THE AMERICAN OLYMPIC TEAM

PLEASE accept my congratulations on your selection as a member of the Olympic Team which will represent the United States in the Games of the Eleventh Olympiad.

As a member of the Olympic Team, you are entrusted with the responsibility of upholding the American tradition for clean, honest sportsmanlike competition. Everyone with whom you come into contact will unconsciously judge our American athletic system by your personal conduct, both on and off the field of competition. Your demeanor, observation of training rules, skill of performance, and sportsmanship in competition will be closely observed. It is important that you make the most favorable impression.

While a member of the team you are under the immediate direction of your manager and coach. Your hearty cooperation with them and with other officials of the American Olympic Committee in all that has to do with the welfare and success of the team is earnestly requested.

While a member of the Olympic Team you will come in contact with the representatives of the fifty different nations participating in the Games whose ideas and manner of living may seem strange to you. We trust that your relations with them will be marked by dignity and courtesy. The officials and the men who have charge of the Games have been appointed by the International Olympic Committee and the various International Federations. Their authority should be respected accordingly. It is quite obvious that in an event of this kind in order to insure pleasure, enjoyment and fair treatment for all, various rules and regulations must be enforced. These official rules and regulations should be observed by all of us.

The American Olympic Committee has devoted much time and effort to the organization of an Olympic Team and to securing money necessary for its support from many thousands of American citizens. They depend upon the teams to perform in such a way as to bring credit to the United States.

You have the best wishes of the American Olympic Committee for success in your competition and I hope that you will be able to achieve an Olympic championship which is the highest honor in amateur sport.

With entire confidence in your appreciation of these considerations and your cooperation in carrying our joint enterprise to success, I am

Very sincerely yours,

AVERY BRUNDAGE,
President, American Olympic Committee

This handbook was given to every American participant.

BRIEF RÉSUMÉ OF THE ORGANIZATION, FUNCTION AND REGULATIONS OF THE AMERICAN OLYMPIC COMMITTEE FOR YOUR INFORMATION AND GUIDANCE

THE function of the American Olympic Association acting through the American Olympic Committee is to exercise jurisdiction over all matters pertaining to the participation of the United States in the Olympic Games.

The general work of the organization is conducted by the officers, assisted by a general committee consisting of fifty-four representatives of organizations controlling amateur competition in all lines of sport throughout the country.

The active officers are:

PRESIDENT:	Avery Brundage
VICE-PRESIDENT:	Dr. Joseph E. Raycroft
SECRETARY:	Frederick W. Rubien
TREASURER:	Gustavus T. Kirby

There are also a number of important special committees such as finance, administration, etc. Following is a list of the committees that will be most active in handling the affairs of the team during the trip:

ADMINISTRATION: A. C. Gilbert, Chm.

Joseph E. Raycroft	Patrick J. Walsh
Daniel J. Ferris	Frederick W. Rubien
Leon M. Schoonmaker	James F. Simms

Athletes and coaches will present to their respective managers any matters affecting their relationship to the American Olympic Committee. The managers in turn will transact all such Olympic business with the Administration Committee.

TRANSPORTATION: Daniel J. Ferris, Chm.

HOUSING: Leon M. Schoonmaker, Chm.

EQUIPMENT AND SUPPLIES: Patrick J. Walsh, Quartermaster.

POST-OLYMPIC COMMITTEE: Daniel J. Ferris, Chm.

LIST OF TEAMS AND MANAGERS

Sport	*Manager*
Baseball	Leslie Mann
Basketball	Dr. Joseph A. Reilly
Boxing	Roy E. Davis
Canoeing	W. Van B. Claussen
Cycling	Walter Grenda
Equestrian	Brig. Gen. Guy V. Henry
Fencing	John H. Hanway
Field Handball	Dietrich Wortmann
Field Hockey	Leonard F. O'Brien
Gymnastics	Herbert G. Forsell
Modern Pentathlon	Capt. Richard W. Mayo
Pistol Shooting	Major Dean Hudnutt
Rowing	Clement B. Newbold
Soccer	Joseph J. Barriskill
Men's Swimming	Edward T. Kennedy
Women's Swimming	Herbert D. Holm
Men's Track	William J. Bingham
Women's Track	Fred L. Steers
Weight Lifting	Dietrich Wortmann
Wrestling	C. W. Streit, Jr.
Yachting	Owen P. Churchill

IMPORTANT REGULATIONS

The following regulations have been formulated by the American Olympic Committee and should be read CAREFULLY.

1. That no one be permitted to use the name of the American Olympic Association and/or the American Olympic Committee for any purpose without approval of this body.
2. That all members of the American Olympic Team be required to sign a release prepared by the Legal Committee.
3. That athletes while under the jurisdiction of the American Olympic Committee shall not be permitted to do any newspaper or magazine work.
4. That all newspaper and magazine articles written by any manager, assistant manager, coach or trainer during the period from the selection of the team until it is disbanded shall be censored by the President.
5. That the American Olympic Committee do not sanction any commercial tour of any kind.
6. That the American Olympic Committee go on record as disapproving the recognition of all commercial schemes or devices of any kind.
7. That all officers be notified that they have certain duties according to the Constitution, but that included in those duties and powers there is no authority to contract for, or obligate the American Olympic Committee for, expenses of any kind except as authorized by the complete Committee.
8. That all business between members of the American Olympic Team and the Olympic Committee should be through the manager of the team only.

9. That no salaries whatever be paid to any coach or manager out of the funds of the American Olympic Association or American Olympic Committee.
10. That the expense of the American Olympic Team so far as the American Olympic Committee is concerned, starts after the try-outs, the American Olympic Committee to assume responsibility only when the team meets before leaving for the Games and this responsibility terminates when the team is disbanded after its return to New York.
11. That all managers, coaches, trainers and other officials must live with the team if at the expense of the American Olympic Committee.

GENERAL STATEMENT REGARDING YOUR RELATIONS TO THE AMERICAN OLYMPIC COMMITTEE

IT IS obvious that there is a reciprocal responsibility between the American Olympic Committee and the individual who is selected as a member of the Olympic Team.

The American Olympic Committee accepts responsibility for the general welfare of the members of the Olympic teams that compete in the Games at Berlin. This responsibility becomes active at the time the team member joins the official party at the port of embarkation for Europe and is operative, with exceptions to be noted, until the team returns to the home port of the United States, and is officially disbanded.

THE AMERICAN OLYMPIC COMMITTEE HOLDS ITSELF RESPONSIBLE FOR:

a. Transportation, equipment, housing and living expenses from the time the team sails from the United States until its return to the home port.

NOTE: It is understood that if you wish to leave the official party, and approval is granted by the Administration Committee to your written request to do so, for the purpose of touring, exhibition or competition, you assume full responsibility for your expenses during the period between your departure from the official party and your rejoining it at the port of embarkation or at some other point previously agreed upon.

b. Provision for adequate medical care for minor illnesses or injuries that may occur while you are a member of the team; but the Committee will accept no responsibility for the expense of medical care other than that provided by the official medical staff, or for major operations and hospital expenses.

c. The Organizing Committee has made arrangements so that members of the teams can secure accident insurance at a nominal cost.

d. Provision for moral and social welfare, through adequate chaperonage.

RESPONSIBILITY OF THE MEMBER OF THE TEAM

I understand that every individual selected for the team has, as a representative of the United States, a responsibility to the American Olympic Association. Therefore I agree to the following provisions:

a. To report at Pier 60 at the foot of West 20th Street with my papers properly signed (if a minor countersigned by parent or guardian) and in order, in time to check in with the manager of my team so that I will be able to board the ship before 10:30 a.m., Daylight Saving Time, on July 15. Will sign papers at Hotel Lincoln.

b. To maintain strict training during the voyage and until my competition in Berlin is completed.

c. To remain with the team and to return with it to New York unless a special request to do otherwise is granted in writing by an authorized official of the American Olympic Committee (see page 15).

d. To return my uniform and equipment if required by the Equipment Officer.

e. To sign the certificate on the following page.

CERTIFICATE

THIS IS TO CERTIFY that I have read the statements regarding the mutual responsibilities that exist between the American Olympic Committee and myself; that in consideration of my selection as a member of the American Olympic Team, and in recognition of my obligation as an athlete to conform to all the regulations listed in this document, or which may be subsequently adopted by the American Olympic Committee, I accept the conditions as stated and I sign this document in evidence of my willingness and intention to abide by the regulations laid down for the management and conduct of the Olympic Team.

Signed ....

Witness ....

Date ....

SUGGESTIONS AND REGULATIONS FOR THE GUIDANCE OF MEMBERS OF THE AMERICAN OLYMPIC TEAMS

1. You will be wise to provide yourself with overcoat or wrap for use on steamer and during cooler evenings in Europe.
2. Any irregularity or minor physical ailment or injury should be reported immediately to medical headquarters.
3. It is understood of course that all members of the American Olympic Team refrain from smoking and the use of intoxicating drinks and other forms of dissipation while in training.
4. Do not wear white uniform, trousers and shoes before the parade at the Opening Ceremony.
5. Do not take a trunk—use suit cases.

APPLICATION FOR LEAVE OF ABSENCE FROM THE OFFICIAL PARTY

APPLICATION is made by the undersigned for leave of absence from the official party from the

.... day of ...., 1936, to the

.... day of ...., 1936, for the purpose of touring, exhibition or competition. For the latter two give dates and places:

I now expressly agree that in granting me this leave of absence the American Olympic Committee and their agents directly and indirectly shall be relieved and absolved of all and every liability for any damage, expenses or other financial obligation in connection with such leave of absence from the time of leaving to the time of rejoining the official party.

Signed ....
Applicant

Approved ....
(Representing the governing body of the sport in which the applicant competes)

Approved ....
(Representing the American Olympic Committee)

In the event that the applicant is a minor this application must be signed also by his or her parent or guardian unless a letter to that effect has been previously submitted by the minor.

....
Parent or Guardian

(Anyone desiring to leave the official party should make the application before July 20.)

QUARTERMASTER'S RECEIPT FOR UNIFORM AND EQUIPMENT

1. It is agreed and understood by the undersigned that uniform and equipment loaned to me by the American Olympic Committee remain the property of the Committee and are to be returned to the Quartermaster if and when demanded.
2. I agree not to use this uniform or to permit it to be used in any way for advertising purposes or in any other than amateur competition.
3. I received today the following items of equipment:

....

....

....

....

....

....

....

Signed ....

Date ....

QUARTERMASTER'S RECEIPT FOR UNIFORM AND EQUIPMENT

1. It is agreed and understood by the undersigned that uniform and equipment loaned to me by the American Olympic Committee remain the property of the Committee and are to be returned to the Quartermaster if and when demanded.
2. I agree not to use this uniform or to permit it to be used in any way for advertising purposes or in any other than amateur competition.
3. I received today the following items of equipment:

....

....

....

....

....

....

....

Signed ....

Date ....

A. C. Gilbert, chief of protocol

The following is an excerpt from The Man Who Lives in Paradise, *the autobiography of A. C. Gilbert with Marshall McClintock, published by Rinehart & Company, New York. (See page 20 for his biographical sketch.)*

"There was a great deal of controversy before the Olympic Games in Berlin in 1936. Hitler was in power and there was a great deal of persecution of the Jews, so many organizations felt that America should not take part in the games. I was in favor of participation because I felt that it would put the Germans on their best behavior, and I didn't see why we should be prejudiced and act the way the Nazis acted.

"I must say right now that the games were conducted as well as they have ever been, to my knowledge, and in the opinion of many Olympics officials. The German people were kind, considerate, and understanding. The German judges were scrupulously fair. The Olympic village was beautiful and comfortable.

"It was a tremendous job to arrange for transportation and handling of between three and four hundred athletes, men and women, for a trip like this. There were many strong and conflicting personalities and interests, and it was my job not just to handle all the details but to keep everyone happy and in fine spirits. And there were half a dozen problems every day that had to be decided or handled in the most diplomatic fashion. For example, there was our landing in Hamburg, where the people went all out to give a great welcome to the American athletes. A women's organization put on a big buffet, and for this important occasion many of the ladies got out their fine old glassware. When the party was over, and the team was on its way to Berlin, I stayed around, as I usually did, to see that everything was wound up correctly and everything was all right. I inquired of the ladies and they told me that quite a few pieces of fine antique glassware had disappeared.

"I told them how sorry I was and tried to explain that these Americans were not thieves. They were just exuberant young people who were in the habit of picking up anything loose as souvenirs. I said I would see what could be done. When I got to Berlin I called together the managers of all the different teams and explained what had happened, and they went to work. When the men understood the situation and realized that this was valuable stuff they had taken, they did just what I knew they would do—returned every single piece that had been taken. I had it packed up and sent back to the lovely ladies who had been so kind to our team.

"Through these Olympic Games I met many wonderful people, both here and abroad. I also had many interesting experiences, among them a close view of Hitler on numerous occasions, and entertainments by Goebbels and other Nazi bigwigs, giving me a closeup of these strange phenomena that few Americans had.

"In 1940 and again in 1948 I was asked to be *Chef de Mission* of the American team again, but in 1940 I was just getting over a serious illness and in 1948 I did not feel that I could tackle this ever-larger job in view of my other important activities. But I look back on those three Olympic years as great events, as satisfying as that of 1908 when I was a participant and a gold-medal winner instead of a manager."

JOHN MACIONIS '34 GIVES OPINIONS ON OLYMPICS

Olympic Swimmer Maintains "Americans Were Treated Royally" in Germany.

"GERMANS BIG SHOWMEN"

Under Hitler Regime Germany Has Been Made to Take Notice of Its Athletes.

"The Americans were treated royally," stated John Machionis, member of the United States Olympic Swimming Team, to a Mercersburg reporter, when he visited here last week. Macionis graduated from Mercersburg in 1934. While here he broke many pool records and set several world records.

When asked about the Eleanor Holm Jarrett case which caused such a stir in all the newspapers, both English and American, Macionis replied that the Olympic Committee's jurisdiction was justified. All cases were disposed of satisfactorily to the other team members.

Germans Big Showmen

"Everything about the Games was done perfectly," he said. All guests were treated very royally by the German citizens. "The Germans were big showmen," Macionis added. Everything was done to insure the comfort of the athletes. Instead of temporary buildings for the participants, regular houses were built. These will be used for officer's quarters in the future. The stadium was a marvelous piece of work as was the swimming pool.

Germany's 30 Gold Medals

Under the Hitler regime the country has been made to take notice of its athletes. The Olympic games were talked of years before they took place. "Every one is going in heavily for athletics," he added. The results of this are beginning to show. In former Olympic Games the Germans only won one or two places. This year, however, she carried off thirty gold medals against twenty-four for the United States.

John Macionis, '34

At the Third International Swimming Clinic, Held at the Penn A. C. in Philadelphia, Friday Night, September 18, Was Designated Olympic Night in Honor of John Macionis, Who Gave a Swimming Exhibition.

There were capacity crowds to all of the events. People would pay forty cents to watch the trial heats in the mornings. They would bring their lunch with them. At the main events there would be one hundred and ten thousand spectators, mostly German. The Germans thought that Jesse Owens was a super-man. They were flabbergasted at his accomplishments. They never spoke of him as Owens but as the "Negro Owens."

Team Goes to Poland

After the Olympic Games in Berlin the team went to Poland. The Polish swimmers were not very good but promised to be a threat in coming Olympics. There was one main cause of this. Every Polish town of twenty thousand population or over has a municipal swimming pool. Each pool was fifty meters long. This not only gave every Polish youth a chance to become a very good swimmer but also gave them long distance swimming. "That is one thing lacking in the United States," Macionis stated.

Macionis is now a Junior at Yale University. While at Mercersburg in 1933-34 he set several World's Interscholastic records.

FINAL OLYMPIC TRYOUTS

SUMMER GAMES

Sport	*Place*	*Date*
Track and Field	New York, N. Y.	July 11-12, 1936
Decathlon	Milwaukee, Wis.	June 26-27, 1936
50 Kilometer Walk	Cincinnati, Ohio	May 24, 1936
Marathon	Boston, Mass.	April 20, 1936
Marathon	Washington, D. C.	May 30, 1936
Track and Field (Women)	Providence, R. I.	July 4, 1936
Basketball	New York, N. Y.	April 3-4-5, 1936
Boxing	Chicago, Ill.	May 20, 1936
Canoeing	Philadelphia, Pa.	June 27-28, 1936
Cycling (Road)	Paterson, N. J	July 5, 1936
Equestrian	Fort Riley, Kans.	May 23-24-25, 1936
Fencing	New York, N. Y.	Various
Field Handball	New York, N. Y.	June 28, 1936
Field Hockey	Philadelphia, Pa.	June 21, 1936
Gymnastics	New York, N. Y.	June 20, 1936
Gymnastics (Women)	Philadelphia, Pa.	May 9, 1936
Modern Pentathlon	West Point, N. Y. and Rye, N. Y.	June 5-6-7, 1936
Pistol Shooting	Campfire Club, N. Y.	July 7-8, 1936
Rowing	Philadelphia, Pa.	July 3-4, 1936
Rowing (Eight Oared Shell)	Princeton, N. J.	July 4-5, 1936
Soccer	Brooklyn, N. Y.	July 12, 1936
Swimming	Providence, R. I.	July 10-11-12, 1936
Diving	Chicago, Ill.	July 3-4, 1936
Water Polo	Chicago, Ill.	July 3-4-5, 1936
Swimming & Diving (Women)	Astoria, L. I., New York	July 11-12, 1936
Weight Lifting	Philadelphia, Pa.	July 3-4, 1936
Wrestling	Bethlehem, Pa.	April 16-17-18, 1936
Yachting	San Pedro, Cal.	Feb. 22-23-24, 1936
Yachting (Star Class)	Westhampton, L. I., New York	July 10 to 12, 1936
Baseball	Baltimore, Md.	July 1 to 12, 1936

WINTER GAMES

Sport	*Place*	*Date*
Bobsled	Lake Placid, N. Y.	Feb. 11-12, 1935
Figure Skating	New York, N. Y.	Dec. 27-28-29-30, 1935
Ice Hockey	New Haven, Conn.	Dec. 7, 1935
	New York, N. Y.	Dec. 8, 1935
	Rye, New York	Dec. 9, 1935
Ski—Combined Jump and 18 Kilometer Race	Lake Placid, N. Y.	Feb. 12-13, 1935
Ski—18 Kilometer Race	Lake Placid, N. Y.	Feb. 13, 1935
Ski Jump	Salt Lake City, Utah	Mar. 3, 1935
Ski—Combined Downhill and Slalom	Mt. Ranier National Park, Wash.	Apr. 13-14, 1935
Speed Skating	Minneapolis, Minn.	Jan. 13-15-19, 1935

The 1936 United States Olympic Uniforms

Summer Games

The men were outfitted in a double-breasted blue serge coat bearing an emblem on the left breast and six Olympic buttons. They sported white trousers, a white shirt with a red, white and blue striped necktie, a straw hat with blue band and emblem, a white sleeveless "V"-necked sweater trimmed in red and blue with a shield in the center, and white sport shoes and white sox. Blue leather belts bearing the team insignia were also part of the uniform. Each athlete also was furnished an extra pair of blue trousers.

From left to right: Uniforms for basketball, track, yachting and boxing. AP PHOTO

The women wore a blue serge jacket adorned with an emblem on the left breast and two Olympic buttons, a white skirt, white blouse, white shoes and stockings and a white sport hat. They were also supplied with a blue skirt.

The men's uniforms were tailored by Smith-Gray Corporation of New York. This concern sent two tailors at its expense on the S.S. *Manhattan* to make the necessary alterations to the uniforms.

The women's suits were made by Long Mark of New York. The firm of Truly Warner supplied the men's shoes and straw hats. To ensure a perfect fit for each member of the team, it kept a store open until midnight for a three-day period before the departure of the team.

The Marcel Kurtz Corporation donated continental style berets to the athletes.

The white sweaters were furnished by A.G. Spalding & Bros., as were the competitive outfits, for both men and women. The competitive outfit consisted of a white shirt with a red, white and blue satin sash running diagonally, starting from the top right shoulder with Olympic shield on the left breast. White trunks had similar stripes down the sides. Different-styled competitive uniforms were needed for the various teams.

Most of the athletic equipment was obtained through A.G. Spalding & Bros.

The athletes were also furnished with dark blue sweat suits with "U.S.A." red lettering trimmed with white on the front of the shirt. The boxers, swimmers and fencers were supplied with robes.

Left to right: Dee Bøeckmann, Evelyn Ferrar, Gertrude Wilhelmsen and Anne V. O'Brien. AP PHOTO

Winter Games

The men and women competitors wore dark blue, full length double-breasted overcoats made by the Smith-Gray Corporation with the Olympic shield on the left breast and Olympic emblems mounted on six buttons.

Sweat suits with zippers on the trouser legs were also furnished, giving the appearance of ski pants. These were obtained through A.G. Spalding & Bros. The athletes wore caps modeled after the Norwegian winter hat.

Competitors had to furnish their own skates, hockey sticks, pucks, skis, bobsleds and other paraphernalia.

AMERICAN FIRST PLACE WINNERS

HARRIET C. BLAND

KENNETH CARPENTER

RICHARD DEGENER

FOY DRAPER

MARJORIE GESTRING

GLENN F. HARDIN

DOROTHY POYNTON HILL

CORNELIUS C. JOHNSON

ADOLPH KIEFER

FRANK LEWIS

EARLE MEADOWS

JACK MEDICA

— 24 —

TEAM CHAMPIONS—BASKETBALL

IN THE GAMES OF THE XITH OLYMPIAD

RALPH METCALFE

GLENN MORRIS

JESSE OWENS

ELIZABETH ROBINSON

ANNETTE J. ROGERS

HELEN H. STEPHENS

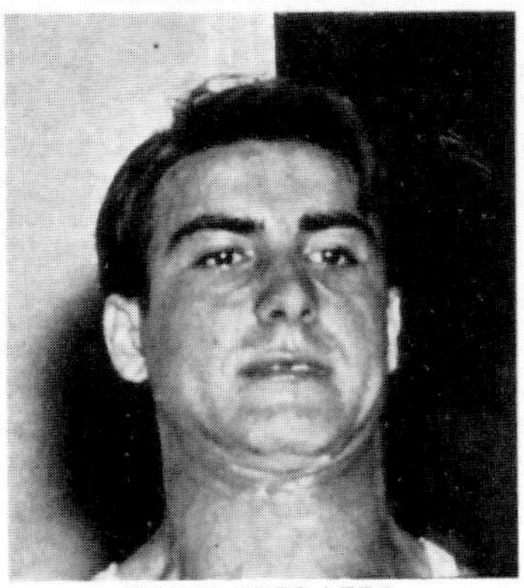
TONY TERLAZZO

FORREST G. TOWNS

MARSHALL WAYNE

ARCHIE F. WILLIAMS

JOHN WOODRUFF

FRANK C. WYKOFF

EIGHT OARED CREW

PHOTOS APPEAR IN RESPECTIVE SPORT SECTIONS

Avery Brundage

A pillar of the American and International Olympic committees for many decades, Avery Brundage was born in Detroit, Michigan, in 1887. A younger brother was born in 1891. His family split up when he was five and the two brothers were raised by aunts and uncles.

Avery got interested in sports early in life and was a track star at the University of Illinois, where he studied civil engineering.

He made the Olympic team in 1912 in Stockholm, participating in the pentathlon (finishing sixth) and the decathlon. Opposing him in the decathlon was the American Jim Thorpe. Realizing that he was far behind in points Brundage dropped out of the decathlon before running the final race, a decision he regretted the rest of his life.

In 1915 he established his own construction company in Chicago and ended up a millionaire, owning real estate in several cities. His official sports affiliation began in 1928 when he was elected president of the Amateur Athletic Union.

He became associated with the American Olympic Committee in the 1920s and was elected second vice-president in 1945 and first vice-president in 1946 of the International Olympic Committee. From 1952 to 1972 he was president of the IOC.

His 20-year reign as president of the IOC was tumultuous—involving racism (South Africa, Rhodesia, etc.), Communist versus non-Communist alliances, nationalism, the expansion of new sports, sites for the games and perhaps the hardest to control, keeping the games purely amateur. He was also accused of being anti-Semitic, pro-Nazi and even at times pro-Communist.

In a much-publicized speech in Madison Square Garden on Oct. 4, 1936, he praised the National Socialists for their opposition to Communism. Addressing the German-American Bund, he spoke intemperately and unwisely: "We can learn much from Germany. We, too, if we wish to preserve our institutions, must stamp out communism. We, too, must take steps to arrest the decline of patriotism." He was denounced as pro-Nazi.

He will be remembered for taking Eleanor Holm off the 1936 swim team and for disqualifying the famed Austrian skier Karl Schranz from the 1972 Winter Olympics. Also he was on the IOC committee that disqualified famous Finnish athlete Paavo Nurmi in 1932 from Los Angeles for allegedly accepting monetary compensation.

Perhaps his most important act as president was to insist that the 1972 Munich Olympics continue even though Palestinian terrorists held the Israeli team members hostage. Both the hostages and terrorists were eventually killed during a failed rescue attempt at the Munich airport.

Brundage was married twice. His first wife died in 1971 and in 1973 he married a German princess, many years his junior, in Garmisch. (She was born in 1936, the year of the Winter Olympics in Garmisch.)

Avery Brundage died in Garmisch in 1975 at age 88. Although a man of controversy, his contributions to sports in the United States and the world are of great significance.

Avery Brundage in his 1912 Olympic uniform. He qualified for both the pentathlon and decathlon in the Stockholm games. He placed sixth in the pentathlon, competing against fellow team member Jim Thorpe, the gold medal winner. He did not finish the decathlon, a decision he would regret the rest of his life. UIA

Avery Brundage in later life. UIA

Remarks of Avery Brundage, President of the American Olympic Committee

The following is a portion of Avery Brundage's report presented in the book "American Olympic Committee Report 1936." In it he reports on the effort to boycott the games, dropping Eleanor Holm from the U.S. team, the 4×100 meter relay, the two "homesick" boxers and the withdrawal of Jesse Owens from Swedish races.

IT IS THE OPINION of those who have long been connected with the Olympic movement in the United States that the 1936 team was the finest and best behaved team we have ever sent abroad. The laurels which it won were well deserved for its performances were perhaps the best ever made by an American Olympic team. The five hundred young athletes of which it was composed made many friends for the United States by their actions both on and off the field of competition. Its members were a credit to the country from which they came and America can well be proud of them.

So many misleading stories and malicious reports have been circulated, however, that it is necessary to review in detail some of the situations which developed in order that the record may be clear. Unfortunately, in hastily assembling any group of four or five hundred individuals from all sections of the country and from every walk of life, no matter how great the care, mistakes will be made. It was found after the team had sailed that some few had been included who did not appreciate that they were honored by being allowed to wear the Stars and Stripes in competition with the champions of fifty other countries. Despite the fact that no other American Olympic team had ever had such superior accommodations or had ever been treated better, these few adopted the attitude that something was owed to them for participating and demanded special consideration of various kinds which it was impossible to give.

Obviously, it is necessary to have rules and regulations for the general good in handling any party of several hundred individuals. These rules and regulations were laid down by the American Olympic Committee, based on its experience at previous Games and without them there would have been utter confusion. Every member of the team before embarking had signed a pledge to observe these rules.

The day after the steamship *Manhattan* sailed from New York City, the team was assembled and the attention of its members was called to the fact that as selected athletic representatives of the United States of America, their every action would be observed by thousands of spectators from all over the world. They were informed that many would judge the United States and its institutions by what they did and what they said, and therefore, that membership on the team carried with it a patriotic obligation to uphold the American reputation for good sportsmanship as well as for athletic achievement. They were told of the regulations which had been adopted for the comfort, pleasure and success of the expedition and they were placed on their honor to do their best for "honor of country and for glory of sport."

The vast majority of the team comported themselves as champions and gentlemen but it finally became necessary by unanimous action of the Committee to drop one individual for continued excessive drinking and insubordination, despite repeated warnings. Suppressing detailed reports from managers, chaperons, coaches, physicians and others, the Committee, with the desire to protect the athlete as much as possible, released only a simple statement that the offender had been dropped from the team for violation of rules. Although there was no other course open, the Committee's action was misinterpreted and became the signal of a torrent of criticism.

Fortunately, the informed section of the public and those who were intelligent enough to read between the lines immediately rushed to the Committee's defense. They remembered the bitter battle which had been waged before the team departed, and recalled that there was a group which was not only unsympathetic but eager to discredit the Committee if possible.

Many of these men were famous athletes in their day and all of them are internationally or nationally known as leaders in the field of amateur sport for a score of years or more. General policies for the administration of the team were laid down by this group, which had the assistance of many subcommittees and a corps of experienced and capable managers and coaches. Never has the American Olympic team enjoyed a more competent and efficient direction.

After the arrival in Berlin it became necessary to send home two members of the boxing team for "homesickness." The "homesickness" was invented to protect the boxers who, while collecting souvenirs, had appropriated several expensive cameras. Since some of the cameras were valued at over seven hundred marks the matter had been referred to the police. The Committee felt it was fortunate to be able to get these men out of the country without trouble.

An erroneous report was circulated that two athletes had been dropped from the American relay team because of their religion. This report was absurd. The two athletes in question were taken only as substitutes. Reference to the results of the final tryouts will show that Owens, Metcalfe, Wykoff and Draper were the first four places. These four men composed the four hundred meter relay team, won the event and broke the world's record. Their performance proved the wisdom of adhering to the rules.

Occasionally in past years, both in the United States and in foreign countries, prominent amateur athletes have declined to participate in events they have regularly entered, after preparations have been made and tickets sold on the strength of their entry, unless they were promised special inducements such as a percentage of the gate receipts or a cash bonus. It therefore became necessary for the Amateur Athletic Union to adopt a rule to discourage this practice. This rule provides that an athlete, who, after he has entered an event, refuses to compete without a legitimate excuse, automatically suspends himself.

After the Olympic Games, American athletes are usually invited to compete in foreign countries. Because these invitations give them a chance to see the world under favorable auspices, the Committee has never objected. These trips are supervised by the A.A.U. or sport governing body concerned. The athletes are not forced to participate—as a matter of fact, they are always eager to do so. Jesse Owens, the outstanding star of the Olympic Games, a boy who conducted himself admirably during the Games despite the fact that he was almost mobbed by the admiring public on every appearance, selected a trip to Sweden. A few days before the event the A.A.U. was informed that Owens did not intend to appear and that he had decided to return to the United Sates with his coach to investigate various commercial offers with the idea of capitalizing on his fame and becoming a professional. This was embarrassing indeed, to the Swedish organizations which, relying on Owens' promise to compete, had made elaborate preparations for his reception. According to the A.A.U. rule referred to above, Owens, of course, suspended himself by this default. In addition, when he announced that he proposed to become a professional, he lost his amateur standing. Although the Olympic Committee had nothing to do with his disqualification, it was subjected to much criticism from uninformed sources.

There was an attempt also to censure the Committee because of the number of managers, coaches, and trainers in the official party. An examination of the roster reveals that three hundred eighty-four athletes and seventy-nine managers, coaches and trainers comprised the American contingent to the Berlin Games. In order to give some recognition to those who had worked so hard to insure the success of the team, a number of individuals were given titles of assistant manager, assistant coach, etc., although they were paying their own way. Of the seventy-nine enumerated above, thirty-eight defrayed their own transportation and housing expenses, including the purchase of official uniforms. The expenses of most of the remaining forty-one were paid by organizations in the sports which they served and the Committee paid from the general fund the expenses of only the administrative staff of ten individuals, including two doctors and a nurse, who gave attention to almost five hundred cases. It is needless to state to anyone who is familiar with the Games and the fact that the results of four years' preparation are crowded into two weeks' times, that the official staff was more than busy from early morning until late at night. The officers and members of the American Olympic Committee not only served without compensation but also defrayed their own expenses to both the Summer and Winter Games.

The Olympic movement embodies such high principles of amateurism and is based on such fine ideals of sportsmanship that it is to be regretted that a wrong impression may have been left by the misrepresentations that were made. The 1936 team was probably the greatest we have ever sent abroad and it was undoubtedly the best behaved and the most efficiently managed. It is an outrage that it should have been slandered because of the shortcomings of a few, which were magnified beyond all proportion. Fortunately, its performances were so outstanding that nothing can detract from its glory.

The five circled Olympic flag travels next to the Orient, and already in Japan preparations are being made to stage the 1940 Games according to the best Olympic traditions. We, too, must stir ourselves and not delay if the United States is to be worthily represented in the Land of the Rising Sun. If once it might have been said that American athletes outclass the world, certainly such a statement is no longer true. Other countries have adopted, and in some instances even improved on American methods and technique, and if the United States is to retain its supremacy we must develop all of our athletic resources and have them at their best at the Games.

Brundage, center, on March 1, 1936, with I.O.C. President Count Henri de Baillet-Latour, left, and Sigfried Edstrom, I.O.C. member. All three of these men were at the 1912 Stockholm games. UIA

Excerpt from Lowell Thomas' Broadcast, July 24, 1936

ON A TRAIN SPEEDING from Hamburg to Berlin today, a committee of grave men sat listening while a young woman made a plea—beauty in tears. They were a special American Olympic Committee. She was Eleanor Holm Jarrett, American Olympic backstroke swimming champion, one of the greatest women swimmers of all times.

This was the third time that the committee was considering the case of Eleanor Holm Jarrett. The first time was in mid-ocean, when they threatened to expel her from the Olympic team, because of infractions of training rules, drinking parties on shipboard. She said she wouldn't do it again, promised to be good. And they said:—"Okay, we'll let it pass this time."

The second time was yesterday aboard ship. Once more the great woman swimmer had broken training rules—a gay champagne party, in which was Charlie MacArthur, the playwright, who was traveling on the boat with his wife, Helen Hayes, the actress. This time the committee was in a stern mood. They wanted to consult the champion mermaid, but found her sound asleep. They took drastic action, expelled her from the team, and ordered her to turn in her blue Olympic uniform.

When the backstroke champion learned that, she asked them to give her a hearing, let her tell her story and make a plea to have the decision reconsidered. That was granted, so today, after the Olympic team had landed at Hamburg and was on its way to Berlin, the committee held session number three with the queen of the water ladies pleading her case.

It was a grave decision that the committee had to reverse or reaffirm. Without Eleanor Holm Jarrett, the chances of the women's swimming team in Berlin are slim indeed—that's how great a champion she is. She started breaking records at 13 as Eleanor Holm. And she's been smashing them ever since—backstroke, 200-meter, one after another. She won easy victories in the 1928 Olympics and in the games of 1932. She was counted on as the American Number One winner in this year's Olympic swim.

She always was singular among women athletes for her grace, her beauty and laughing gaiety. The great Ziegfeld, who glorified the American girl in the Follies, once said of her—that she had the most beautiful figure he had ever seen. She made pictures in Hollywood, and married an orchestra leader. Mirth and jollity were her way—not the severities of athletic training. She once said she trained on champagne and not too much sleep. She would change from an evening gown to a swimming suit and out-swim everybody in the race.

So that was the flashing champion who appeared before the committee today, as the train rolled along to Berlin. She was distracted and in tears. She had told them that if they stuck to their decision and threw her off the team, it would ruin her career. She said she knew she had done wrong in breaking the training rules, but the rules were strange to her. She told them that she never trained for her great victories. She had commonly gone to a party, then into the water—and won the race. She spoke of the Olympic tryouts in New York and said that the night before she had been on a late party with her husband—then gone in and won. She urged that, never following a training system, she had simply been blind about the rigorous discipline imposed on the Olympic team.

The committee listened, and said they would formulate their decision. And they did. Right there on the train, Avery Brundage, President of the Olympic Committee, announced it. And here it is—the expulsion stands. It is reaffirmed that Eleanor Holm Jarrett, champion of women swimming champions, is off the Olympic team. That was made definite and final today.

She is broken-hearted about it, doesn't know whether to stay in Germany or come right back to the United States, or what; —she may petition this Olympic Committee, beg for another chance—vowing she'll never touch another drop. But it's unlikely the Committee will change its decision. Here's one melancholy touch. Eleanor attended the official German reception to the American athletes. One ceremony is a glass of sherry served to each, and drunk in a formal ritual of hospitality. Every American athlete drank his or her glass of sherry—except Eleanor Holm Jarrett. She put hers aside, didn't take a sip.

This affair is a bad blow to American swimming hopes in the Olympics and one cannot help thinking of Lincoln's immortal utterance when they complained to him that General Grant was drinking too much. Lincoln said he wished they'd find out what brand of whiskey Grant drank, because he would like to send a keg of it to his other generals.

The Man Who Invented the Erector Set

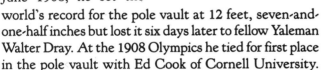

Alfred Casleton (A.C.) Gilbert was a man of many talents. He was born in Salem, Oregon, in 1884. He attended the College of the Pacific and Yale University, where he excelled in gymnastics, wrestling and the pole vault.

In 1907, he tied with four other Yale competitors for the IC4A title. In June 1908, he set the world's record for the pole vault at 12 feet, seven-and-one-half inches but lost it six days later to fellow Yaleman Walter Dray. At the 1908 Olympics he tied for first place in the pole vault with Ed Cook of Cornell University.

Gilbert earned an M.D. degree from Yale but never practiced medicine. He is famous for inventing the popular erector set toy and made a fortune with his toy company, the A.C. Gilbert Company. His American Flyer electric trains rivaled Lionel in popularity.

Gilbert's Olympic experience did not end with the 1908 games. He was a member of the American Olympic Committee from 1924 through 1948 and was on the Executive Committee of the AAU for several years, and a member of its Board of Governors from 1929 to 1954. In 1928, he was the assistant manager of the U.S. team at Amsterdam and worked closely with Gen. Douglas MacArthur, president of the American Olympic Association. In the 1932 and 1936 Olympics he was designated as *Chef de Mission* or team manager.

As he wrote in his autobiography on the '36 games: "It was a tremendous job to arrange for transportation and handling of between three and four hundred athletes, men and women, for a trip like this. There were many strong and conflicting personalities and interests, and it was my job not just to handle all the details but to keep everyone happy and in fine spirits. And there were half a dozen problems every day that had to be decided or handled in the most diplomatic fashion." He was tapped for the cancelled 1940 games and again in 1948 but business interests kept him from the position.

A.C. Gilbert died in 1961 in Boston, Massachusetts.

A New York travel agency advertised the 1936 Olympics in its window. It offered a 60 percent railroad fare reduction and a better price for the U.S. dollar against the Reichmark. NA, GRIO

It appears this photo was taken in New York prior to the Olympics. NA, GRIO

Marjorie Gestring, diving team, left, and Alice Arden, track team, right, on board the *S.S. Manhattan*. ALICE HODGE COLLECTION

Raising the Olympic flag on board the S.S. *Manhattan*, July 4, 1936.

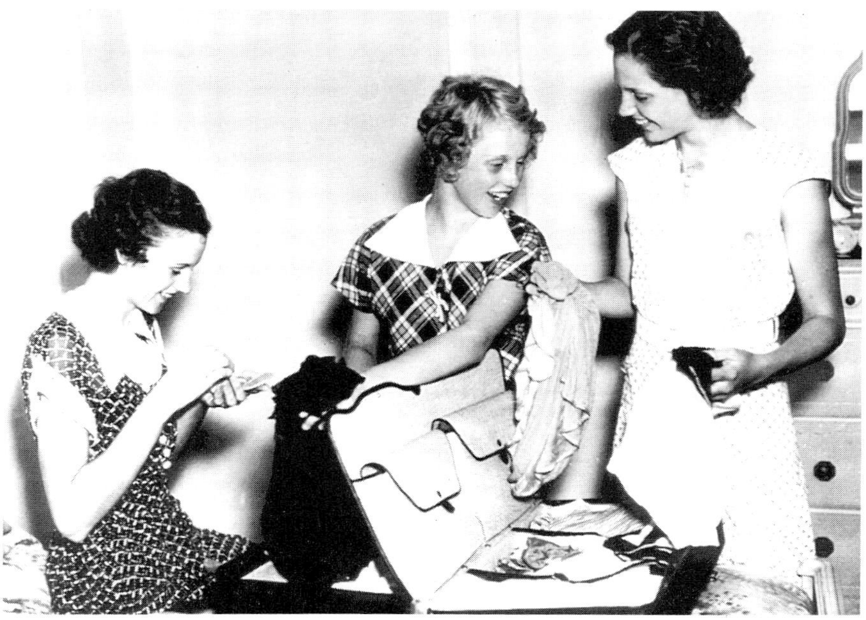

Olympic "child stars" pack up for their first trip to the Olympics. From the left: Kathlyn Kelly, 16, high jumper; Marjorie Gestring, 13, diver, and Elizabeth Ryan, swimmer. AAF

On board the S.S. *Manhattan* team members kept up their rigorous training schedule. Left, Jesse Owens, right, Helen Stephens. AAF

The American team parades through the streets of Berlin on the way to the Olympic Village. NBHF, HERBERT SHAW COLLECTION

The American team arrived at the Berlin railroad station on July 24 and was given a tumultuous welcome by thousands of Berliners. NBHF, STEVE KANIA COLLECTION

The American team arriving at the Olympic village.

A group of American athletes listen to the welcoming address by the commander of the village, Col. von und zu Gilsa, July 24. NBHF, STEVEN KANIA COLLECTION

German Participation

Theodor Lewald

Theodor Lewald, a German, was born in 1860. He was brought into the International Olympic Committee by Coubertin in 1924. It was his idea that a flame should be kindled at Olympia and then carried by relays of torch bearers to light a brazier at the opening ceremony of the Berlin Games in the summer of 1936.

When the Games were allotted to Germany, in May 1931, the International Olympic Committee (IOC) appointed Lewald president of the organizing committee for the summer events.

Lewald's father was a Jew. Under anti-Semitic legislation passed on April 11, 1933, less than three months after assuming control of the government, the Nazis classified as a Jew anybody who had just one Jewish grandparent. Hitler wished to replace Lewald with Hans von Tschammer und Osten, whom he had made state director of sport. However, Count Henri de Baillet-Latour, who had in 1925 succeeded Coubertin as president of the IOC, told Hitler that if Lewald were not allowed to fulfill the function given him by the IOC, then the Games would be taken away from Germany.

Hitler bowed to this ultimatum and in due course walked into the Berlin stadium with Baillet-Latour on his right and Lewald on his left. The three men stood side by side and watched as the last of the torch bearers arrived, carrying the flame, which had in Olympia been kindled by the rays of the sun through a magnifying glass. The torch bearer then lit the brazier which burned until the end of the Berlin Games. Lewald died in 1947.

Theodor Lewald

Reichssportführer (National Sports Leader)

Hans von Tschammer und Osten 1887-1943

by BLAINE TAYLOR

Despite all the publicity given the Olympic Games in the Third Reich before, during and after the events, one of the least known of the top Nazi leaders was the Reichssportführer Hans von Tschammer und Osten. Possibly, this is because he died more than two years before the end of World War II, and thus did not figure in the lists of those tried before the International Military Tribunal at Nuremberg during 1945–46; on the other hand, it is doubtful that he would have been indicted by the Allies as a war criminal, other than the fact that he headed a large Nazi organization throughout most of the regime's 12-year reign.

Writing in *Who's Who in Nazi Germany* in 1982, author Robert Wistrich called him "Secretary of State in the Reich Ministry of Interior and Reichssportführer in Nazi Germany." Von Tschammer und Osten was born in Dresden on Oct. 25, 1887. He joined the Nazi Party in 1929 and in January 1931 became a Stromtroop Colonel in the SA. In March 1932 he was promoted to SA Gruppenführer (Major General) and leader of SA Group Center.

"In March, 1933 von Tschammer und Osten was elected a member of the Reichstag (National Parliament) for the electoral district of Magdeburg. On July 19, 1933, he was appointed Reich Sport Leader by Hitler, and in January 1934 head of the Sport Section of the *Strength Through Joy* movement, the National Socialist recreational organization which was designed to improve the morale of German workers and stimulate their productivity.

"As Reich Sport Leader, von Tschammer und Osten implemented the Nazi policy of boosting German prestige abroad and maintaining public enthusiasm for the regime at home through the promotion of sports. From 1933 onwards all sports were 'coordinated,' and great attention was given to physical training, active participation in sports and endurance tests, at the expense of academic education. Sporting prowess was made a criterion for entrance to schools, for school-leaving certificates and even for certain jobs.

"Nazi sports policy also emphasized the goal of demonstrating 'Aryan' racial superiority in international competition. Under von Tschammer und Osten and his successors, German Jewish athletes were, for example, systematically hindered by being denied adequate facilities and the opportunity to compete, and Jewish sport was first ghettoized and then totally eliminated by the pressure of the police state and its propaganda policies.

"As Head of the Reich Sport Office, von Tschammer und Osten was responsible for the institutionalized system of apartheid which developed, though it was temporarily and hypocritically modified to enable Nazi Germany to stage the Olympic Games in 1936 in Berlin. He died on March 25, 1943," a short time after the surrender of the German 6th Army at Stalingrad, but still at the apex of his own power and that of the Third Reich as well.

A genial von Tschammer und Osten, center, in conversation with Fran Marga Himmler (wife of the Reichführer Heinrich Himmler) and others before the war. NA

Reich Sports Leader Hans von Tschammer und Osten. NA

Carl Diem was the secretary of the German organizing committee for the 1936 Olympics. He had been captain of the German team at the 1912 Stockholm games. In 1920 he founded the Deutscher Hochschule für Leibesüburgen, a university dedicated to the scientific study of sports. Diem survived World War II and was named to the new Federal Republic of Germany Olympic committee in 1951.

Reichführer Adolf Hitler (1889-1945), leader of the German nation.

Booths were set up all over Berlin to provide information to the thousands of visitors to the city. NA, GRIO

The Olympic Bell

To call the world to Berlin, Dr. Theodor Lewald, the president of the German Olympic Committee, commissioned a bell that would be the main trademark of the 1936 Berlin Olympics.

Noted German sculptor Walter E. Lemike was given the job of designing the great bell. Slogans and motifs of Olympianism were inscribed on the bell, including Pere Didon's lycee, "Citius, Altius, Fortius"; the five Olympic rings and an eagle over the Brandenburg Gate (this was to show that the bell was cast for the German Olympics). Around the lip was inscribed, "Berlin 1936" and "Ich rufe die Jugen der Welt" (I summon the youth of the world).

The Bochumer Verein für Gusslahlfabrick A.G. cast the bell in 1933 using 16 and a half tons of steel. Including its yoke, the bell stood almost 10 feet high. It was pitched in the key of E minor.

On Jan. 16, 1936, the massive bell began its journey to the Berlin Olympic stadium from the factory at Bochum in the Rhineland. The German National Railways donated a large tractor and trailer to haul it.

At each stop across Germany, the bell was given a welcome befitting an important government official or returning war hero. Upon the bell's arrival at Potsdam, on the outskirts of Berlin, brass bands played and the bell was paraded through a lineup of thousands of Hitler Youth. The elaborate ceremony was broadcast throughout the nation.

After the Potsdam ceremony the bell was paraded through the "Via Triumphalis" Boulevard to the Kaiser Franz Josef Platz where the manufacturer presented it to Hans von Tschammer und Osten. He declared that the bell "shall not merely summon the youth of the world but shall remind us constantly of those who gave their lives for the fatherland." Even then the bell was presented not only as a symbol of the Olympic games, but as a symbol of the emergence of a new Germany.

A 243-foot tower called The Glockenturm, the highest structure at the sports complex, was erected to hold the bell. On the tower a 12-foot wheel was mounted, which was controlled by an electric motor geared to swing the bell at an exact set time.

The bell was used as a propaganda tool for many months leading up to the games, mainly through photographs showing Hitler standing next to it. After many worldwide protests and threats of boycott by several nations, Hitler and the bell were dropped as promotional icons for the games.

At the end of the war, the bell was buried at the Glockenturmplatz and was not recovered for several years. It now sits on a permanent stand near the south gate of the Olympic stadium. An attempt was made to remove the embossed swastika, but the outline is still visible. The rest of the bell, minus its oak yoke, is still intact.

The finished bell at the Bochumer Verein für Gusslahfabrick A.G. NA, GRIO

After a number of weeks of cooling down, the 16-and-a-half-ton bell, which was cast on Aug. 14, 1936, is out of its mold. It is receiving its finishing touches. Next it will be turned, then it will be readied for its trip to Berlin. Cast-steel bells were long believed to be unfeasible for technical reasons. Jacob Mayer, the inventor of steel mould casting and founder of the Bochumer Association, exhibited three cast-steel bells for the first time at the Paris World Exposition of 1855. Up to 1936 the company produced 100,000 steel bells for customers around the world. NA, GRIO

Miniature Olympic bells made of porcelain were sold as souvenir banks.

Hitler Youth escort the bell through the streets of Berlin on the way to the Olympic Stadium.

The famous bell sits today on a pedestal outside the Olympic Stadium. A large crack developed after the war. An attempt was made to grind out the Nazi swastika symbol but its outline can still be seen.

Postcard view of the Olympic Bell.

The streets throughout Berlin were decorated with the Nazi and Olympic flags.
NA, HH, 242-HB-22037-1

Aerial view of Unter den Linden Street with the Brandenburg Gate in the center. The Reichstag building at the upper right was gutted by fire on Feb. 27, 1933, supposedly by Communist agents. The Tiergarten, the hunting ground of German emperors, is in the upper left.
NA, HH, 242-HD-0326

The family of one of the American black athletes in the Olympic Stadium stands at the opening ceremonies. The Germans are giving the Nazi salute. NA, HH 242-HD-117

Visitors from all over the world attended the Olympic games. NA, HH 242-HD-0420

German youth practicing for the opening ceremonies. NA, HH 242-HB-22104-2

Hundreds of journalists converged on the games from all over the world.
NA, HH 242-HD-120al

Rain fell a few days during the games, but didn't dampen the crowd numbers or enthusiasm.
NA, HH 242-HD-453-4

Soldiers of the S.S. (Schutzstaffel) rest outside the stadium. They were assigned to assist with security at the games. BA

Reichminister Hermann Göring addressing the members of the International Olympic Committee in Berlin before the games began. NA, HH 242-HD-0041

Hitler welcomes members of the Japanese team delegation. NA, HH 242-HD-0324-2

Reich propaganda minister Joseph Goebbels, left, and Hans-Schweitzer Mjölnir, right, inspect the opening of the Olympic art exhibition displayed on the Kaiserdamm, July 1936. BA

A reviewing stand was constructed at the Olympic stadium specifically for Nazi government officials' use.
NA, HH 242-HD-297-1

From left: Theodor Lewald, Hans von Tschammer und Osten, Adolf Hitler and Hermann Göring on the reviewing stand.
NA, HH 242-HD-302-3

Nazi officials are seated trackside. NA, HH 242-HD-616a3

The winners of the women's javelin with Hitler. From left: M. Kwasiewska, Poland, third; L. Krüger, Germany, second; and Tilly Fleischer, Germany, first. NA, HH 242-HD-86

Hitler meets a member of his Hitler Youth on the reviewing stand. NA, HH 242-HD-297-2

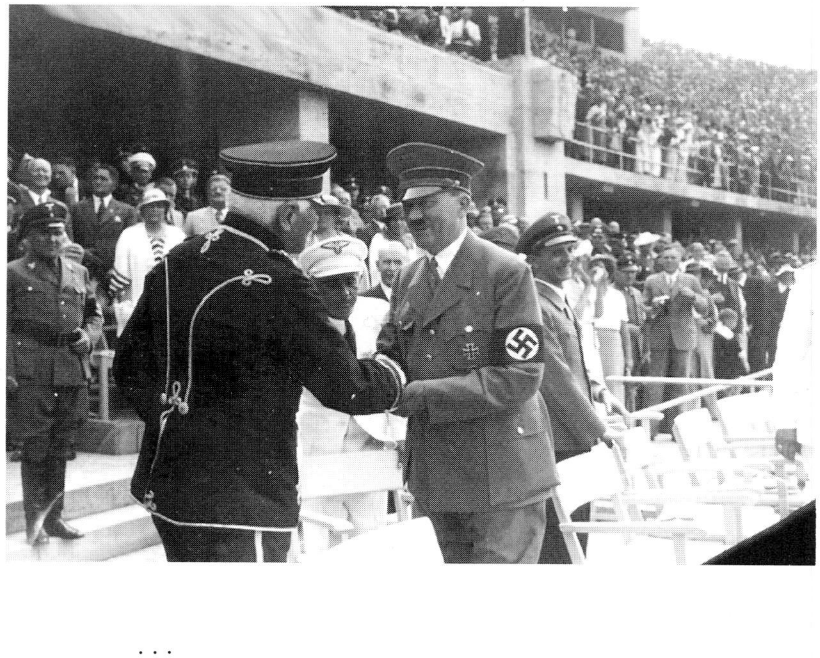

Hitler greets Field Marshall von Mackensen at the reviewing stand. Von Mackensen was a World War I hero credited with saving Berlin from the advancing Russian army. Next to von Hindenburg and von Ludendorf, he was probably Germany's most famous hero. NA, HH-242-HD-0531-1

1936

OLYMPICS

The Sports Facilities

WHEN THE SUMMER games were awarded to Berlin in 1931, a large stadium to host the opening and closing ceremonies and the track and field events was a first priority. A location on a small plateau five miles west of the city center was selected. This was the site of the Deutsche Stadion, built by architect Otto March in 1913 for the cancelled 1916 Olympics. The site was also the Grundewald race course.

Otto March's son Werner was selected to designed the new complex and construction commenced in 1934. Hitler, who had come to power the year before, inspected the site but did not like the architect's idea of using glass screens to enclose the stadium. Albert Speer suggested that natural stone be used instead.

Some 500 firms were involved in the construction with up to 2,000 workers employed on the site each day. Forty-two million reichmarks was spent on the complex. Building materials included 30,500 cubic meters of stone, 17,200 metric tons of rolled iron and 6,000 wagons used to transport the material.

The Olympic Stadium was the center point of the great Reichssportfeld, 325 acres in area. There was space for 110,000 spectators in the upper and lower sections, separated by a wide circular colonnade. The walls of the upper section rose to a height of 48 feet above the surrounding sports field, while the lower ring measured 42½ feet below ground level. The seating accommodations consisted of 72 tiers.

The inner area contained a 400-meter track as prescribed for international events, with seven separate lanes throughout and eight in the straightaway. There were two sets of runways, pits and circles for all field events including six pits for the high jump. The grass plot in the center of the arena was the size of a standard football field. Two tunnels ran under the running track directly to the field, connecting the dressing rooms with the track. On the circular ramp between the upper and lower sections were the dressing rooms for the teams and also shops, concessions, a post office and a first-aid station.

On the south side of the stadium was the grandstand for distinguished visitors and, below it and close to the track, a special judges' box. Above the section for distinguished visitors, there were covered seats and working rooms for the press, with a special press post and telegraph office.

On the top, above the seats, were glass cubicles containing broadcasting equipment used continuously to send reports of the games to all parts of the world and to which from time to time, the winning athletes who had become Olympic champions were taken for interviews.

The core of the sports complex was the aforementioned stadium. The architect chose an oval shape, to ensure the closest possible contact between contestants and spectators. It was divided into an upper and lower part, separated by an access gallery at ground level.

For the lower section the ground was excavated to a depth of 12 meters, while the upper section rose 16.5 meters above the ground access level. The lower ring had 40 rows of seats and the upper one 31 rows.

The open west gate entrance, commanding a view of the Bell Tower which rose 248½ feet, was surmounted by the columns 50 feet high on which the names of the victors were carved in stone before the eyes of the spectators.

Hitler used the viewing stand at the stadium on May 1, 1939, for his May Day address expounding his theory of "Lebensraum," or "living room," in the east (meaning Poland and Russia). He was to put this theory into practice on Sept. 1, 1939, when he invaded Poland.

Toward the end of the war the steel and natural stone stadium housed a field hospital and a factory that manufactured aircraft parts for Blaupunkt.

On April 28, 1945, the stadium area fell to Russian troops. After the war the area was in the British sector and was part of the British military headquarters. Today the stadium has been modernized and is still in use but retains the grand look of its 1930's construction.

Beside the sports stadium were the grandstands of the swimming stadium, with accommodations for 16,000 spectators. The two pools, a diving pool 65 feet square and a swimming pool 65 by 165 feet, were provided with a special plant for filtering and heating the water. The grandstands, with the dressing rooms, concessions and rooms for the press and the managers of the games, were connected by a tunnel with the stadium and grounds of the German Sports Forum. Behind the diving tower, 33 feet high, at the south end of the swimming stadium, was a restaurant with terraces overlooking the swimming pool, while the north end commanded a view of the adjoining recreation grounds.

The rowing events were held on the traditional German regatta course at Grünau, near Berlin. Accommodations were provided in three boathouses for more than 200 boats. The grandstands, together with the adjoining ground, provided room for 20,000 spectators.

The wrestling, weightlifting, fencing and boxing competitions were conducted in the Deutschland Hall, accommodating 20,000 spectators, near the Exhibition Grounds of the City of Berlin. A special cycling stadium was erected near the Deutschland Hall for the cycling races.

The rifle shooting matches were held at Wannsee, near Berlin, which provided more than 150 stands for the competitions with pistols and small-caliber rifles.

The gymnastic competition was conducted in the Dietrich-Eckart open-air theater.

The riders in the equestrian tournament had a field of their own near the stadium with grandstands and accommodations for 7,000 spectators; nearby were sufficient courts for field games and a special hockey stadium. Polo was played on the huge assembly field. The yachting events were conducted on the course in Kiel Bay.

The 1936 Olympic program included, in addition to the sporting events, competitions for the works of living artists in architecture, painting, sculpture, literature and music, in which all nations invited to take part in the celebration of the games could enter. These works were exhibited from July 15 to August 16 in a special Art Exhibition in Fairs Hall VI on the exhibition grounds on the Kaiserdamm.

This report, with minor editing, was taken from the *American Olympic Committee Report, 1936, Games of the XIth Olympiad Berlin, Germany, IVth Olympic Winter Games, Garmisch-Partenkirchen, Germany.*

The Olympic Sports Complex. The Haus des Deutschen Sports was built to house the Olympic administration and training facilities for the German team. It included indoor and outdoor Olympic-size swimming pools, a gymnasium and a special boxing area. It was badly damaged during the war and housed Soviet troops immediately afterwards. It later was repaired and during the Allied occupation was used to house the British Sector Headquarters, the British Military Government and the British Berlin Infantry Brigade.

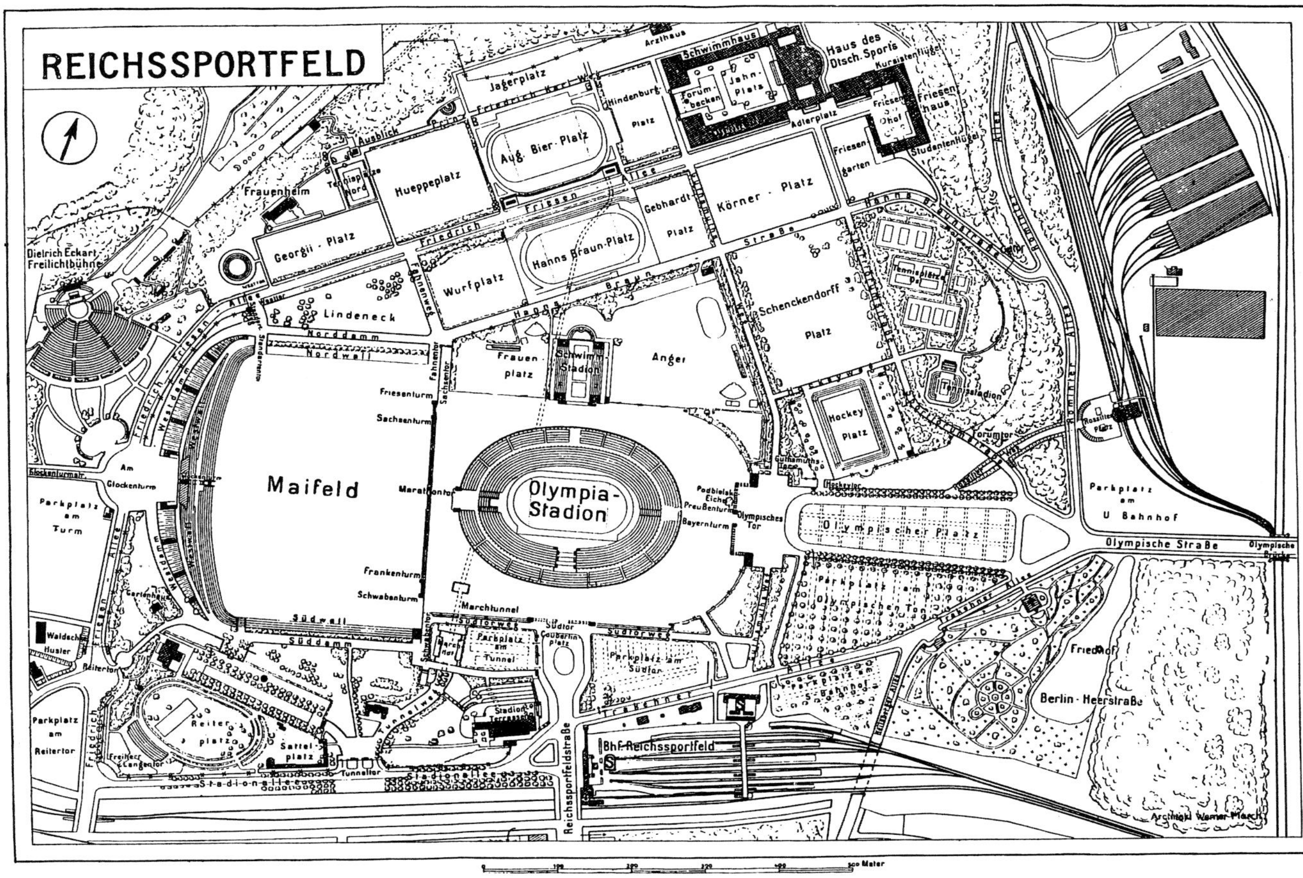

The Reichssportfeld included the following: Olympia Stadium, "Dietrich Eckart" Open Air Theater, Assembly Ground and Polo Field (Maifeld), House of German Sport (top), Swimming Stadium, Bell tower at west end of the Maifeld, Hockey Stadium, Tennis Courts, Equestrian Grounds, Training Fields, Women's Dormitory, and S-Bahn and U-Bahn stations.

Deutschland Hall on Königsweg in Berlin was the site for the wrestling, boxing, fencing and weightlifting competitions.

The massive Olympic Stadium under construction. NA, GRIO

Cornerstone for the Olympic Stadium, "Built under Adolf Hitler 1935." NA, GRIO

Dancing on the cafe terrace adjacent to the Olympic stadium. NA, GRIO

For the 125,000 spectators attending the opening ceremonies a massive parking lot was needed.
NA, HH 242-HD-0060

Looking east out onto the Olympic Plaza through the Olympic gate. LC

Looking west at the stadium with the two towers and Olympic rings forming the Olympic gate. The column on the left was called the Bavarian gate, the one on the right, the Prussian gate.

An automatic release camera was mounted in this balloon gondola to film the events in the stadium.
NA, HH 242-HD-0201-3

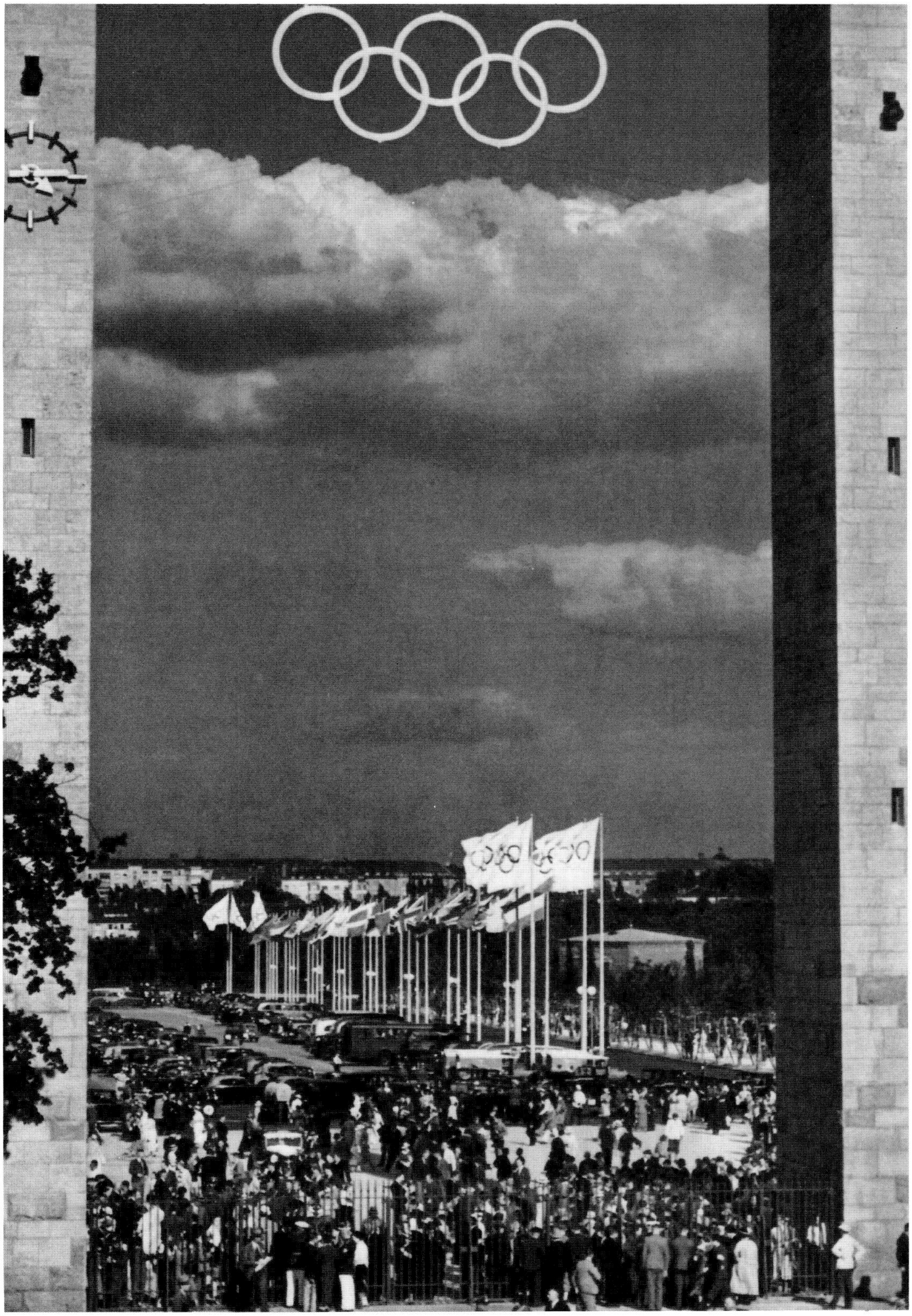

A view through the east entrance to the stadium.

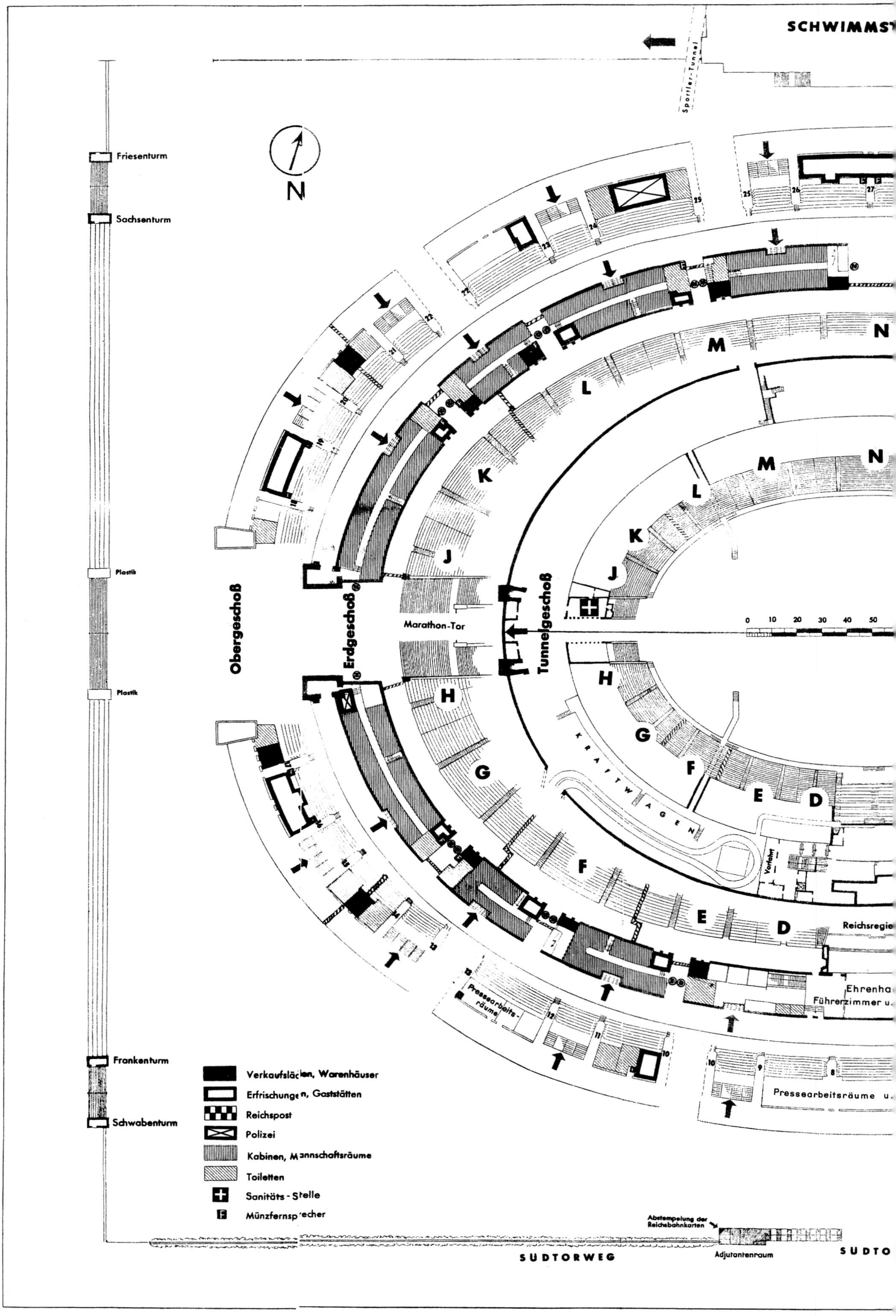

SCHWIMMST
Sportler-Tunnel
N
Friesenturm
Sachsenturm
Plastik
Plastik
Frankenturm
Schwabenturm
Obergeschoß
Erdgeschoß
Tunnelgeschoß
Marathon-Tor
H
G
F
E
D
J
K
L
M
N
KRAFTWAGEN
Vorhalle
Reichsregie
Ehrenha
Führerzimmer u.
Pressearbeitsräume
Pressearbeitsräume u.
0 10 20 30 40 50
Verkaufsläden, Warenhäuser
Erfrischungen, Gaststätten
Reichspost
Polizei
Kabinen, Mannschaftsräume
Toiletten
Sanitäts-Stelle
Münzfernsprecher
Abstempelung der Reichsbahnkarten
Adjutantenraum
SÜDTORWEG
SÜDTO

Olympia-Stadion

Grundriß der einzelnen Stockwerke

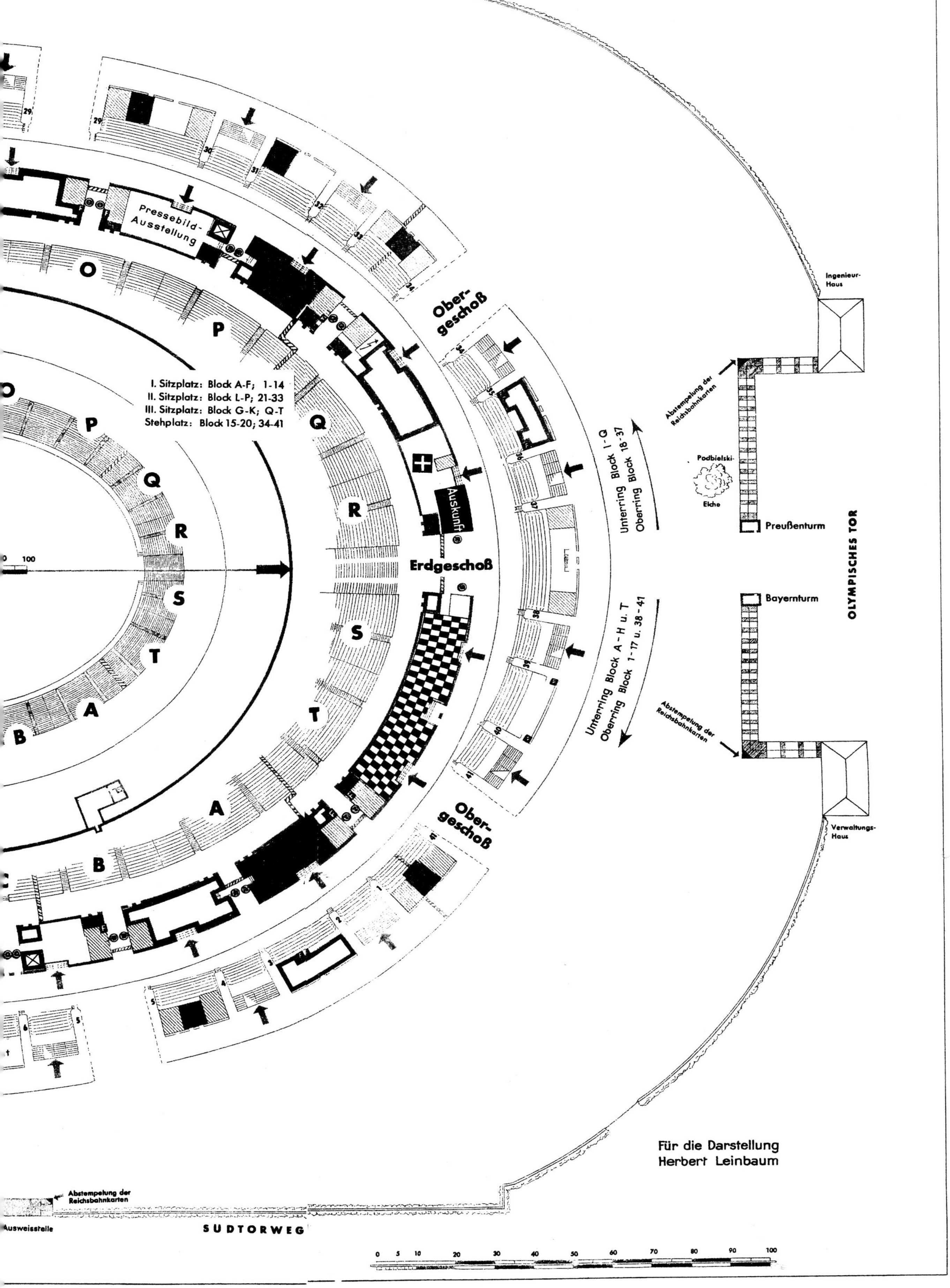

Für die Darstellung
Herbert Leinbaum

Aerial views of the Olympic complex. The top view shows the stadium filled with spectators, looking northeast. The swimming stadium is to the left. The bottom view is looking west with the Maifeld at the top. The hockey stadium is in the lower right and the railroad yard in the lower left. NA, HH 242-HB-22155 and 242-HD-341-4

SHOPS AND STANDS AT THE REICH SPORT FIELD

About 20 shops and two large bazaars for the sale of necessary articles, photographic material, cosmetics, means of protection against sun and rain, stationery, postcards, flowers, badges, souvenirs, newspapers, etc. have been set up along the inner and outer passageways under the stands of the Olympic Stadium. Numerous restaurants and refreshment stands, a first-aid station, and quarters for post offices, the press, radio and police have also been provided on the two levels utilized for this purpose.

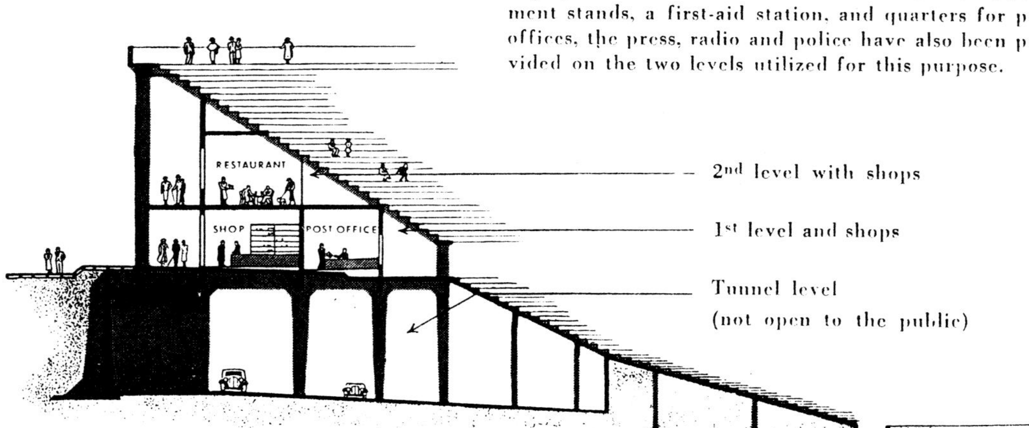

The Olympic stadium with the reviewing stand and press facilities on the opposite tier.

Another view of the complex, looking east. The Maifeld is in the foreground and the Dietrich Eckart Open Air Theater at the bottom left.

Rehearsal for a mass scene for a performance at the world's largest open-air stage – the Dietrich Eckart stage on the Reich-Sport Field. NA, GRIO

Dietrich Eckart was Hitler's anti-Semitic mentor-poet who coined the Nazi slogan "Deutschland Erwache" or "Germany Awake." Eckart died in 1923, but was canonized by the party and the theater was named after him. In 1982 the stage was provided with a tent roof for weather protection. It is now renamed the Waldbühne (Forest Arena).

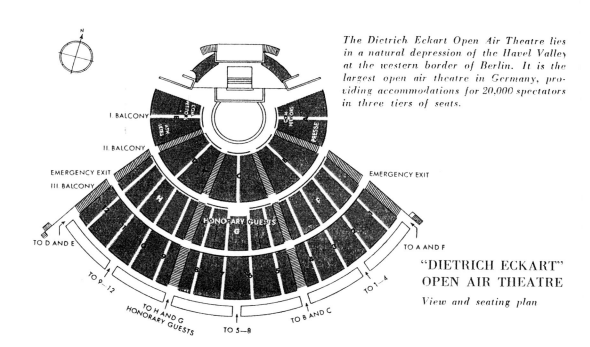

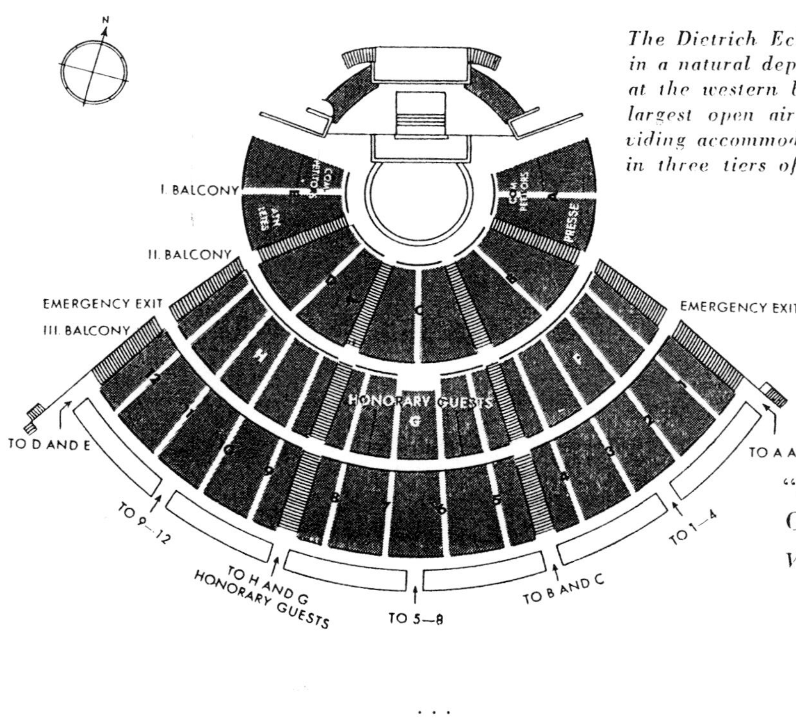

The Dietrich Eckart Open Air Theatre lies in a natural depression of the Havel Valley at the western border of Berlin. It is the largest open air theatre in Germany, providing accommodations for 20,000 spectators in three tiers of seats.

"DIETRICH ECKART"
OPEN AIR THEATRE

View and seating plan

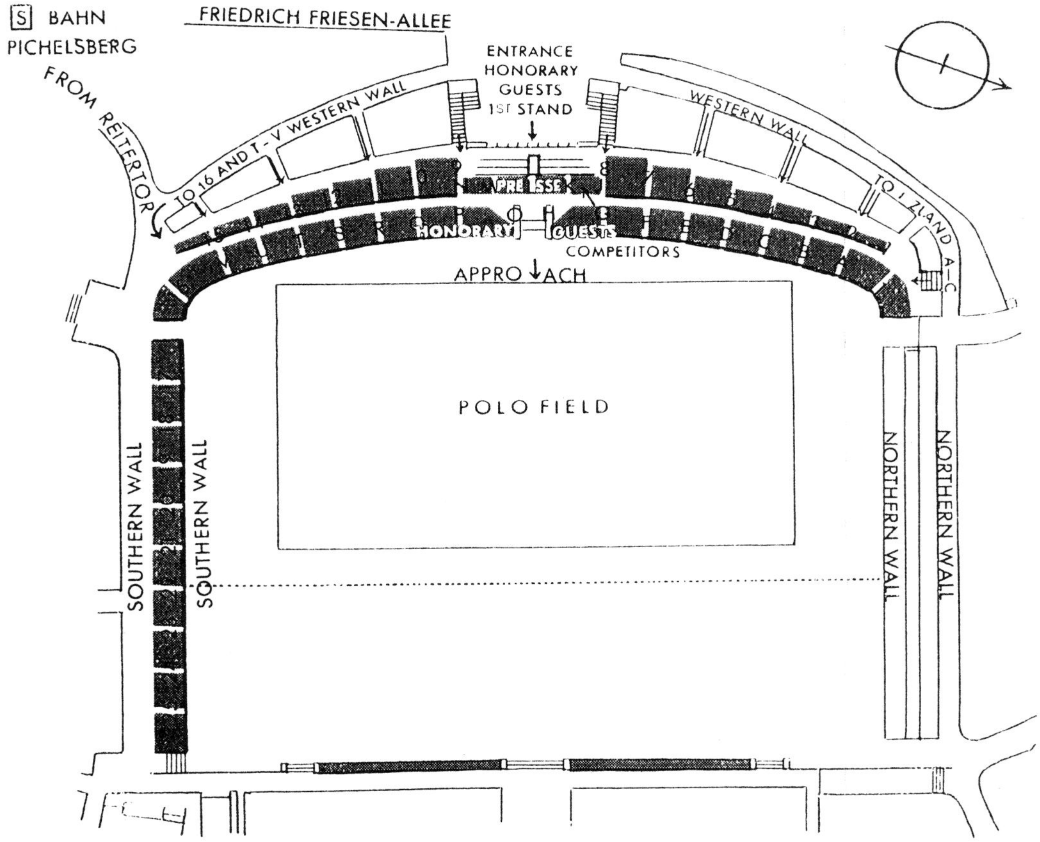

Directly behind the stadium was the Maifeld or sports field, which could hold 250,000 spectators. It was dominated by the Glockenturm bell tower and the Langemarckhalle war memorial to the reserve units formed by students that fought in the Battle of Langemarck on Nov. 10, 1914.

The swimming area north of the Olympic stadium provided for eight 50-meter lanes and a separate 20-meter square diving pool. It had 7,600 permanent seats and could be expanded to hold 16,000. NA, HH 242-HD-368

It is assumed that these women were participants in the opening ceremonies. They are holding horns similar to the Swiss mountain horn.
NA, HH-242-HD-105a2

This spectator holds up a sign that says, "Who sells tickets." NA, HH 242-HD-0478-1

A German band practices for the summer games. They had to master 50 different national anthems for the awards ceremonies for each event. NA 131-GR-219-2

Names of the gold medal winners were carved on large tablets at the stadium. They are still there today. NA, HH 242-HD-0396-2 and 242-HD-0396-1

The new S-Bahn station near the sports stadium. NA, HH 242-HD-006a5

XITH OLYMPIC GAMES, BERLIN, 1936

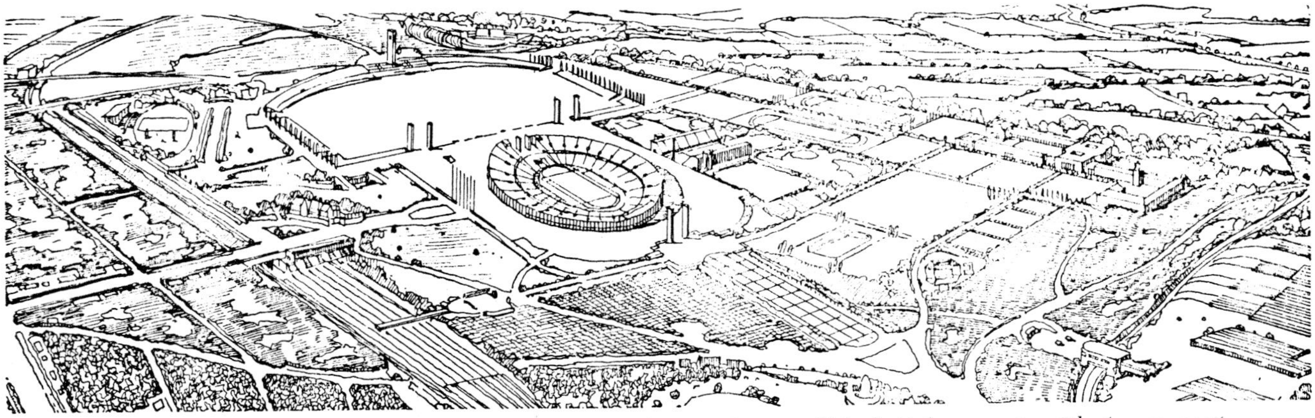

The Reich Sports Grounds, Berlin, where the XIth Olympic Games will be held from 1st to 16th August, 1936

The International Olympic Committee has selected Berlin as the place where the XIth Olympic Games will be celebrated. The Games will be held there from 1st to 16th August, 1936. The Organizing Committee has invited in the prescribed form all sport-loving nations in the world to take part in the competitions and festivals. All the resources of sport and art have been mobilized to contribute to the success of the Games. The whole German nation will extend a hearty welcome to those attending the Olympic Games in Berlin.

PROGRAMME

Saturday, 1st August: Opening Ceremony / Festival Play.

Sunday, 2nd August: Light Athletics / Wrestling / Modern Pentathlon / Fencing / Hockey / Weight-Lifting.

Monday, 3rd August: Light Athletics / Wrestling / Modern Pentathlon / Fencing / Hockey / Weight-Lifting / Football / Polo.

Tuesday, 4th August: Light Athletics / Wrestling / Modern Pentathlon / Fencing / Hockey / Football / Polo / Yachting / Gliding.

Wednesday, 5th August: Light Athletics / Modern Pentathlon / Fencing / Hockey / Football / Weight-Lifting / Polo / Yachting.

Thursday, 6th August: Light Athletics / Wrestling / Modern Pentathlon / Fencing / Hockey / Football / Polo / Yachting / Rifle-shooting / Hand-ball / Cycling.

Friday, 7th August: Light Athletics / Wrestling / Fencing / Hockey / Football / Polo / Yachting / Rifle-shooting / Hand-ball / Cycling / Canoeing.

Saturday, 8th August: Light Athletics / Wrestling / Fencing / Hockey / Football / Polo / Yachting / Rifle-shooting / Hand-ball / Cycling / Canoeing / Swimming / Basket-ball / Gymnastic Display (Sweden).

Sunday, 9th August: Light Athletics / Wrestling / Fencing / Hockey / Yachting / Swimming / Basket-ball / Gymnastic Display (Germany).

Monday, 10th August: Fencing / Hockey / Football / Yachting / Hand-ball / Cycling / Swimming / Basket-ball / Boxing / Gymnastics.

Tuesday, 11th August: Fencing / Hockey / Football / Yachting / Swimming / Basket-ball / Boxing / Gymnastics / Rowing.

Wednesday, 12th August: Fencing / Hockey / Yachting / Hand-ball / Swimming / Basket-ball / Boxing / Gymnastics / Rowing / Riding / Baseball.

rsday, 13th August: Fencing / Hockey / Football / Yachting / imming / Basket-ball / Boxing / Rowing / Riding.

Mond.

figur. *14th August:* Fencing / Hockey / Yachting / Hand-ball / on thening / Basket-ball / Boxing / Rowing / Riding.

Tuesday, 15th August: Fencing / Football / Swimming / Boxing / 11 a.m.

hockey (*th August:* Riding / Final Ceremony.

GROUNDS AND COURSES

Thanks to the decision of the Fuehrer and Reich Chancellor, the Reich Sports Grounds will form a unique arena for the celebration of the XIth Olympic Games. In the heart of the Reich Sports Grounds, which cover an area of 323 acres, lies the German Arena or Olympia Stadium. The inner area, which includes a race track 400 metres long, a playing field and grounds for jumping and throwing competitions, is surrounded by seats for 100,000 spectators. In the middle of the longer southern side are the grand stands for distinguished visitors and the seats for the press. The notice board is at the east gate, while the west gate which is open commands a view across the Festival Meadow to the Bell Tower.

Adjoining the Stadium rise the grand stands of the swimming stadium with accommodation for 18,000 spectators. The two pools, the 65 × 65 feet diving pool and the 65 × 165 feet swimming pool, are reserved for the swimming competitions.

The rowing competitions will be held on the extended traditional German regatta course in Grünau.

The competitions in wrestling, weight-lifting and boxing will be held in the Deutschland Hall accommodating 20,000 spectators, while the riders are provided with a special tournament ground with grand stands in the Reich Sports Grounds.

For the yachting races the well-known regatta course in the Bay of Kiel has been selected.

OLYMPIC VILLAGE

The German Army is building a special Olympic Village for the competitors at the Olympic Games on an especially suitable and picturesque site on the main road to Hamburg, about nine miles from the Reich Sports Grounds. The 3,500 competitors will live there together in 150 separate houses. The Olympic Village also includes a special sports grounds, a practice hall and a swimming pool.

The women will be housed together in a Home on the Reich Sports Grounds.

ART EXHIBITION

The programme of the Olympic Games in 1936 includes, in addition to the sporting events, a competition for the works of living artists in architecture, painting, sculpture, literature and music. The works will be exhibited in a special Art Exhibition from 15th July to 16th August 1936 in Berlin.

YOUTH CAMP

On the occasion of the XIth Olympic Games the youth of Germany are inviting groups of thirty young people from every country. They will live with the same number of German young people in a joint camp and have an opportunity of practising sports and witnessing the Olympic Games.

RELAY TORCH RACE

Fire to light the Olympic fire in the Olympia Stadium in Berlin will be carried by a great relay of 3,000 runners from the ancient scene of the games at Olympia in Greece to Berlin, a distance nearly 2,000 miles, in eleven days.

REDUCED FARES

Railways: The German Railways Co. will grant a *reduction of 60%* on their lines to foreign competitors and visitors attending the XIth Olympic Games in Berlin in 1936. Germans and foreigners domiciled in Germany will be granted a reduction of 33⅓ % on the return fare to Berlin.

Steamers: The usual concessions will be granted on all steamship lines running to Europe. Special concession will be granted by shipping lines running between Europe and the east coast of South America.

Aircraft. The German Luft Hansa and the foreign services associated with it will grant *a reduction of 20%* to visitors attending the XIth Olympic Games on production of the Olympia Stadium Pass.

Autobuses: The autobus companies will organize special trips during the Olympic Games on *favourable terms.*

Circular Tours: It is proposed to grant *reductions of fare up to 60%* for circular tours in Germany which will take place in connection with attendance at the Olympic Games. *Information obtainable from all larger travel agencies.*

ACCOMMODATION IN BERLIN

Sufficient hotels, boarding-houses, hospices and private quarters are available for the *accommodation* of visitors. The price of a bed ranges from 3 to 15 marks; in a number of luxury hotels rooms are available at the usual prices. Quarters on a large scale will be erected for those of simple tastes. Accommodation is guaranteed for all comers. Reservations can be made at any Travel Agency. The "Amtlicher Unterkunftsnachweis für die XI. Olympiade Berlin 1936", 1, Mühlendamm, Berlin C 2, will arrange for accommodation from 1st October 1935 and provide all desired information.

Meals will be served in hotels and restaurants at reasonable rates, and cheap one-dish meals will also be available.

Interpreters are ready to assist visitors to Germany.

PRICES OF ADMISSION

Uniform groups of prices have been arranged for all the events in the XIth Olympic Games from 1st to 16th August 1936. Tickets will be on sale for three classes of seats and for standing room.

A distinction is made between single tickets (for one day and one form of sport), season tickets (for all the days of one kind of sport) and the "Olympia Pass" which entitles the holder to be present at all the events taking place in the Olympia Stadium, i. e. the opening and final ceremonies, the festival play, the eight days of light athletics, the football and handball semi-finals and finals, the last day of the riding and the displays.

ADVANCE BOOKING PRICES

OLYMPIA STADIUM PASS	I Per seat RM	II Per seat RM	III Per seat RM
(For the best seats in each category) .	100.—	60.—	40.—

The Olympia Pass is not issued in the holder's name, and can therefore be used by several persons, but of course not at the same time. The holder has a right to the same place during all the events taking place in the Olympia Stadium. The Pass does not entitle the holder to be present at swimming, rowing, boxing and other events taking place elsewhere.

SEASON TICKETS	I Per seat RM	II Per seat RM	III Per seat RM	Standing room RM
Light athletics	40.—	30.—	20.—	—
Swimming	40.—	30.—	—	20.—
Rowing	40.—	30.—	—	20.—
Boxing	40.—	30.—	—	—
Riding — class I seat in the Olympia Stadium and the Riding Ground	40.—	—	—	...
Riding — Class II seat in the Olympia Stadium and standing room in the Riding Ground	—	25.—	—	—
Football (in the Olympia Stadium. Special tickets must be taken for semi-finals on Berlin grounds)	35.—	25.—	20.—	—
Fencing	35.—	—	—	—
Wrestling and Weight-Lifting	30.—	20.—	—	—
Hockey	25.—	—	—	—
Hand-ball — class I seat in the Olympia Stadium and for semi-finals	25.—	—	—	—
Hand-ball — Class II seat in the Olympia Stadium and standing room at semi-finals	—	15.—	—	—
Gymnastics	15.—	10.—	6.—	—

Season tickets are transferable and entitle the user to be present at all events of the same form of sport. No season tickets are issued for modern pentathlon, polo, rifle-shooting, yachting, cycling, basket-ball and canoeing.

SINGLE TICKETS	I Per seat RM	II Per seat RM	III Per seat RM	Standing room RM
Opening and final ceremonies in the Olympia Stadium, each	15.—	10.—	6.—	3.—
For principal days and finals	10.—	6.—	4.—	2.—
For events on other days. .	6.—	4.—	2.—	1.—

The right to alter the prices is reserved

Olympia Stadium Pass on sale from 1st January 1935. *Season tickets and single tickets* for the opening and final ceremonies and the festival performance on sale from 1st July 1935. *Single (day) tickets* on sale from 1st March 1936.

All earlier orders for tickets will be kept pending until the advance booking begins. The payment for tickets in registered marks is inadmissible under the German Foreign Exchange Regulations. All orders and requests for information will be dealt with by the

Kartenstelle für die XI. Olympiade Berlin 1936, 43, Hardenbergstrasse, Berlin-Charlottenburg 2.

The tickets will be despatched only when the full purchase price plus postage has been received, and then in the order of receipt of the remittances. It is also be possible to order tickets through the leading Travel Agencies.

Guard troops march at the Pariser Platz with some Olympic statues in the foreground.

They don't know it yet, but in a few days these German athletes will win two gold, one silver and one bronze medal. Anni Steuer, Paula Mollenhauer, Milli Reuter, Tilly Fleischer, Gisela Mauermayer and Anny Ondra visiting famous German boxer Max Schmeling.

1936

OLYMPICS

The Olympic Village

HOUSING OLYMPIC ATHLETES in one complex was first introduced at the 1932 Olympics in Los Angeles.

The 130-acre Berlin Olympic village, or "Village of Peace," was constructed by the German army under the direction of Capt. Wolfgang Fuerstner.

The Olympic Village was situated about ten miles from the stadium and fifteen miles from the center of Berlin. One hundred forty buildings were erected in the village, each bearing the name of a German city. The village was laid out in the form of the map of Germany with the main dining-hall representing the City of Berlin. The houses contained 13 bedrooms, each accommodating two athletes in twin beds with showers and toilet at one end of the building and a sitting room at the other. Close to 4,000 competitors were quartered in the Village.

To the right of the circular entrance was a reception hall with an information desk provided for each nation, a restaurant and an outdoor garden. To the left of the entrance were various shops, such as the post office, bank, camera, store, laundry, baggage room, travel agency and sporting goods store, as well as the offices for the administrators of the village.

A large building known as Hindenburg Hall was in the central part of the village, where movies and entertainment were presented nightly. This building also contained a writing room equipped with typewriters, a television room where all of the Olympic events were shown and a large room where church services were held for the various denominations.

The village contained the necessary training facilities including a 400-meter track and field, swimming pool, gymnasium, outdoor basketball court and ample area for all field events. There was a large artificial lake and lawns were attractively laid out and graded.

All of the teams were fed in a central building which contained 38 separate dining-halls. The catering arrangements at the village and at the Friesenhaus where the girls were quartered were in the charge of the North German Lloyd Line. The menus varied from day to day and every reasonable demand was met. On request, lunches were prepared for competitors to take to the various training grounds, preventing the necessity of returning for meals.

Each house had two stewards on duty to assist the athletes. They spoke the native tongue of the guests. Each athlete paid six Reichmarks for lodging and meals.

Attachés from the German army and navy were assigned to the team. Captain Hauptmann and Captain Dierksen looked out for the comfort of the American team.

The Olympic Village was barred to women and no visitors were allowed except those to whom passes were granted. A fence encircled the village, insuring privacy for the athletes.

The Olympic Village where the athletes of all the nations mingled freely together, contributed greatly to the success of the games by helping to cement the bonds of friendship among the competitors.

After the Olympics the buildings were used by the German army. After World War II the area fell within the Soviet sector and was used as a special training center for Soviet athletes.

Note: Captain Fuerstner, who had been in charge of the German army sporting program just before the Olympic athletes arrived in Berlin, was demoted because he was non-Ayran. His replacement was Lt. Col.

Werner von und zu Gilsa. Fuerstner continued as second in command until after the games when out of great despondency he killed himself. The government tried to cover up his suicide by giving him a full military funeral.

This report, with minor editing, was taken from the *American Olympic Committee Report, 1936, Games of the XIth Olympiad Berlin, Germany, IVth Olympic Winter Games, Garmisch-Partenkirchen, Germany.*

At the entrance to the Olympic Village was this Medallion of Gracht showing the Reich eagle and the five Olympic rings.
NA, GRIO

A postcard view of the extensive Olympic Village, located in a birch forest in the western suburbs of Berlin.

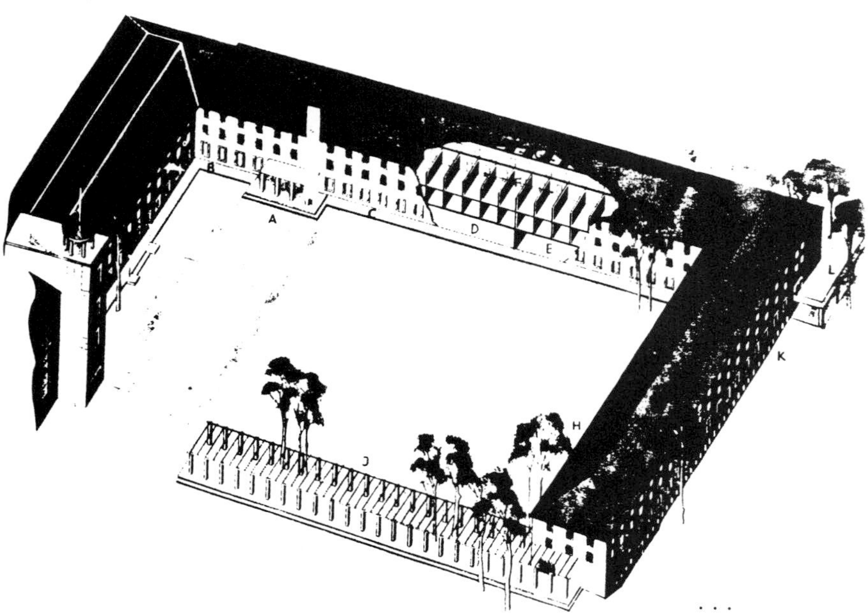

The Women's Dormitory (Fredrich-Friesen-Haus) was located at the north corner of the Reichssportfeld. After the games it served as a dormitory for the students of the Reich Academy for Physical Culture. It was three stories high, quadrangle in form, surrounding a large court. Four hundred women were housed here. (A) Main Entrance, (B) Administration, (C) Reception Hall, (D) Reading Room, (E) Music Room, (F and G) Dormitory Rooms, (H) Dining Room, (J) Refreshment Room, (K) Casino, (L) Terrace.

Training for the hurdles at the Olympic Village. Forest "Spec" Towns is on the left, John Brooks, is on the right. BA

American athletes train at the Olympic Village. Left to right: John Brooks, Mack Robinson, Robert Packard and Foy Draper. BA

Hitler accompanied by General von Blomberg visits the German sprinters at the Olympic village.

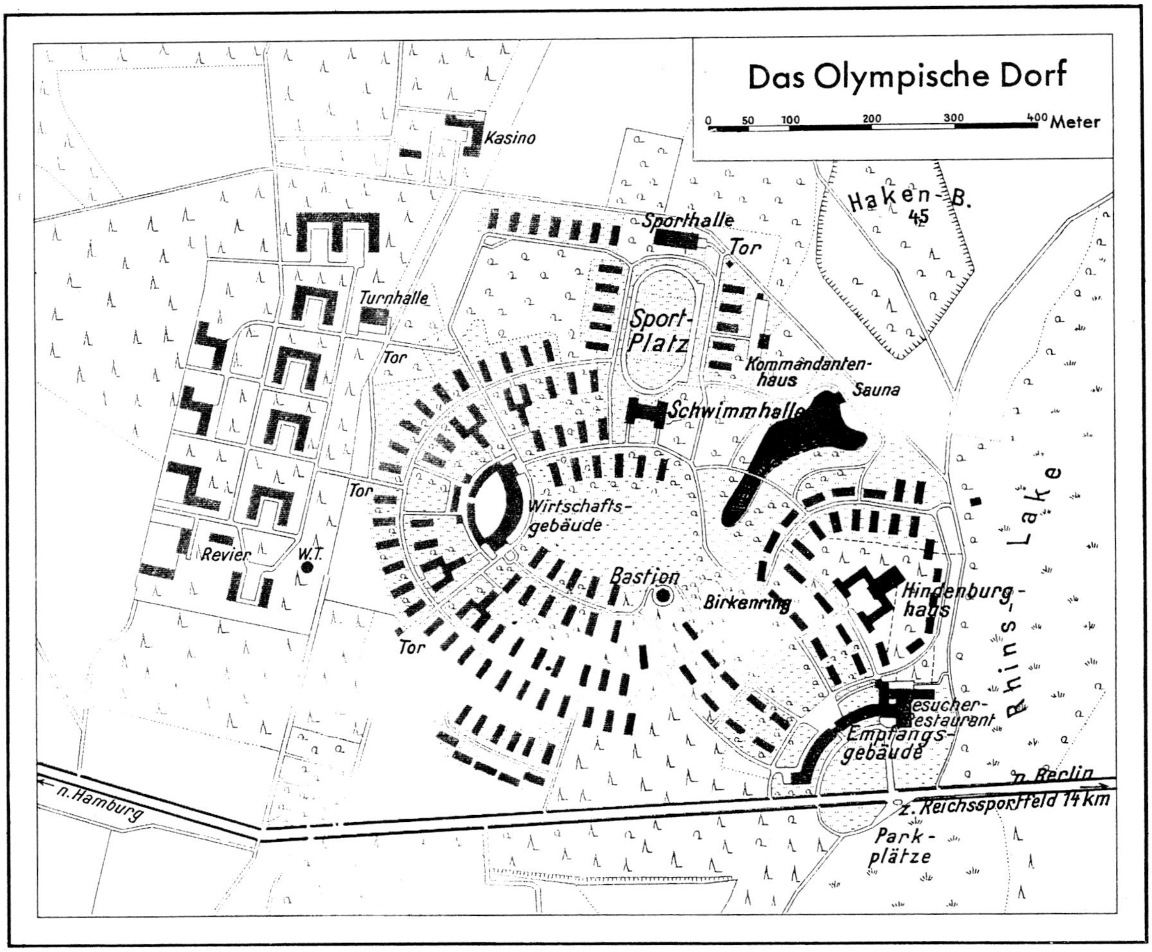

The Olympic Village

The kitchen building was named after the host city, Berlin. Inside were a number of dining rooms, each with its own kitchen and opening out onto a terrace. Laundry rooms were located in the household wings of the building. A refreshment room, the "Bastion," sat on an elevated knoll above the village. Athletes could mingle, drink non-alcoholic beverages and listen to the concerts played in the bandstand located immediately below at the "Birch Ring."

A reception building contained the luggage rooms and customs office, shops, press room, post office, bank, sports department, police, administration headquarters, reception room of the village commandant, information office, Hall of Nations, office of attachés and a visitors' dining room.

Shops in the building consisted of a sporting goods store, a stationery shop, a souvenir shop, a photography shop, a travel office and a fruit and confectionery store. Also in the village complex was a service station for vehicles, first-aid stations, a scales room for weighing weightlifting, wrestling and boxing participants, and a sporting news service.

The German army provided an officer for each team to serve in the honorary capacity of advisor to each nation. In addition about 170 youths of the Voluntary Youth Service lived in the village to render assistance to the athletes both in the village and in Berlin.

GERMAN TOWNS REPRESENTED IN THE OLYMPIC VILLAGE

1 Reception Building
2 Constance
3 Freiburg
4 Baden-Baden
5 Karlsruhe
6 Kaiserslautern
7 Heidelberg
8 Neustadt-on-Hardt
9 Mannheim
10 Hanau (Hospital)
11 Bastion
12 Goslar
13 Kassel
14 Göttingen
15 Wernigerode
16 Hildesheim
17 Hameln
18 Halberstadt
19 Merseburg (Leuna)
20 Bückeburg
21 Halle-on-Saale
22 Detmold
23 Bielefeld
24 Münster
25 Dortmund
26 Duisburg
28 Krefeld
29 Aachen
30 Bochum
31 Essen
33 Wuppertal
35 Marburg
36 Wetzlar
37 Giessen
38 Fulda
39 Darmstadt
40 Frankfort-on-Main
41 Wiesbaden
42 Speyer
43 Worms
44 Nauheim
45 Limburg
46 Solingen
47 Düsseldorf
48 Cologne
49 Bonn
50 Königswinter
51 St. Goar-St. Goarshausen
52 Rüdesheim
53 Mayence
54 Saarbrücken
55 Trier
56 Bernkastel
57 Kochem
58 Coblenz
59 Emden
60 Wilhelmshaven
61 Oldenburg
62 Bremen
63 Heligoland
64 Hamburg
65 Flensburg
66 Schleswig
67 Kiel
68 Rostock
69 Stralsund
70 Rügen
71 Greifswald
72 Schwerin
73 Magdeburg
74 Wismar
75 Lübeck
76 Lüneburg
77 Brunswick
78 Hanover
79 Osnabrück
80 Minden
81 Berlin (Kitchen Building)
82 Household Wing
83 Laundry and Heating Plant
84 Garage
85 Garage
86 Swinemünde
87 Stettin
88 Kolberg
89 Frankfort-on-Oder
90 Neuruppin
91 Brandenburg
92 Wittenberg-on-Elbe
93 Potsdam
94 Lübbenau
95 Guben
96 Dresden
98 Schandau
100 Zittau
101 Dessau
102 Leipzig
103 Freiberg
104 Meissen
105 Bautzen
106 Chemnitz
107 Plauen
108 Tilsit
109 Trakehnen
110 Königsberg
111 Allenstein
112 Tannenberg
113 Elbing
114 Marienburg
115 Schneidemühl
116 Bunzlau
117 Liegnitz
118 Görlitz
119 Sport Hall
120 Oppeln
121 Beuthen
122 Glatz
123 Breslau
124 Hirschberg
125 Neisse (Commandant)
127 Swimming Hall, Sauna
129 Eisenach
130 Erfurt
131 Weimar
132 Jena
133 Naumburg
134 Rudolstadt
135 Meiningen
136 Heilbronn
137 Dinkelsbühl
138 Rothenburg
139 Würzburg
140 Coburg
141 Kulmbach
142 Bamberg
143 Bayreuth
144 Nuremberg
146 Regensburg
147 Passau
148 Berchtesgaden
149 Füssen
150 Oberammergau
151 Garmisch-Partenkirchen
152 Lindau
153 Friedrichshafen
154 Ulm
155 Tübingen
156 Stuttgart
157 Augsburg
158 Munich
159 Hindenburg House
160 Tunnel
161 Purifying Plant

Typical village houses.

Lodging for the rowers and canoeists was close to Grünau at the Köpenick Palace, the Police Officer's School and the Dorotheenschule (school) in Berlin-Köpenick. In Kiel the yachting participants were housed in the Olympic Home, Hindenburgufer, The Imperial Yacht Club, Hotel Bellevue, Christian-Albrechts House of the University, the Deutsch-Nordische Burse and a private residence at Düsternbrook 132.

Afghan athletes "at home" in the Olympic Village.

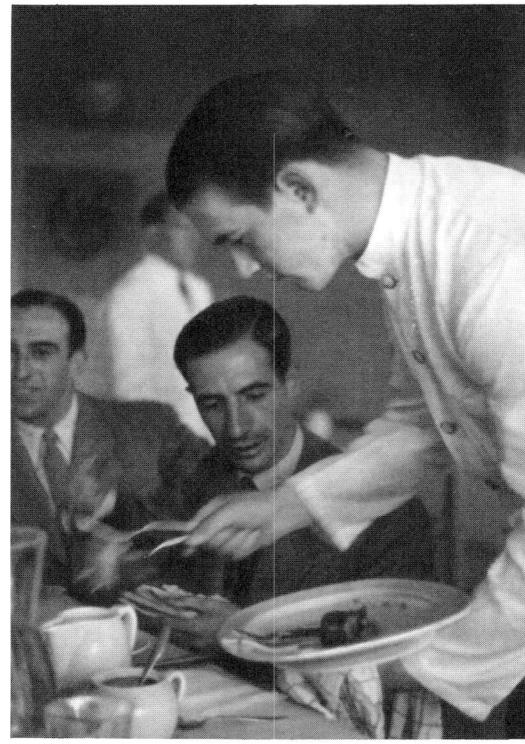

In the village athletes of every race and nation found homes where they live and eat according to their native customs.

Athletes from all over the world could mingle with one another and learn about customs from other countries.

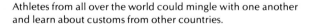

Jack Torrance, a 304-pound policeman from Baton Rouge, Louisiana, was the world record holder in the shot put. He is shown here practicing at the village. Unfortunately he was out of shape and finished in fifth place.

1936

OLYMPICS

The Opening Ceremonies

This report, with minor editing, was taken from the *American Olympic Committee Report, 1936, Games of the XIth Olympiad Berlin, Germany, IVth Olympic Winter Games, Garmisch-Partenkirchen, Germany.*

THE OPENING CEREMONIES of the Games of the XIth Olympiad were celebrated with more than 5,300 athletes from 51 nations participating, all in distinctive uniforms and many in native garb. Leaden skies and occasional showers failed to dim the riot of color, music and ceremonial pageantry.

Outside the stadium, on the huge assembly field, unseen by the vast crowd which filled every seat in the arena, the athletes formed for their entrance. The medley of bright colors caused by the intermingling of groups from many nations, slowly formed into well ordered lines of four abreast. Newcomers to Olympic competition, the great majority endeavored to control their excitement, while the veterans who had marched in other ceremonies tried to hide their emotion.

The arrival of Chancellor Adolf Hitler, Count Henri de Baillet-Latour, President of the International Olympic Committee; Dr. Theodore Lewald, President of the Organizing Committee of the Games of the XIth Olympiad, and the members of the International Olympic Committee, was signaled by a trumpet solo from the huge tower located at the west end of the stadium and was taken up by the orchestra conducted by Richard Strauss and a chorus of 10,000 voices that burst out with "Deutschland uber Alles" and "Horst Wessel." [*Editor's note:* Horst Wessel was a member of the Nazi party who was killed in 1930, supposedly by a Communist and was made a martyr by the party.] This was followed by the chorus' rendition of the Olympic Hymn. The Olympic bell with the motto "I Call the Youth of the World" began to slowly toll.

The pageant unfolded itself in a precise movement on a time schedule. The athletes started their march into the stadium, circled the 400 meter track and lined up in columns on the grass infield. Greece, the originating country, led the parade. Greece was followed by Egypt, Afghanistan, Argentina, Australia, Belgium, Bermuda, Bolivia, Brazil, Bulgaria, Canada, Chile, China, Colombia, Costa Rica, Denmark, Estonia, Finland, France, Great Britain, Haiti, Holland, Iceland, India, Italy, Japan, Yugoslavia, Latvia, Lichtenstein, Luxemburg, Malta, Mexico, Monaco, New Zealand, Norway, Austria, Peru, Philippines, Poland, Portugal, Romania, Spain, Sweden, Switzerland, South Africa, Czechoslovakia, Turkey, Hungary, Uruguay, United States and Germany as the host nation, last.

[*Editor's note:* Fifty-one nations participated. Russia would not send a team until 1952. Germany and Japan did not compete in another Olympics until 1952.

The Airship *Hindenburg* flew low over the Olympic Stadium carrying the Olympic flag. Each group was preceded by a standard bearer carrying a banner denoting the nation and followed by another bearing the national colors. Alfred Jochim was given the honor of being the flag bearer for the United States, accompanied by James W. O'Connor and Fred Lauer, color guards, all three athletes being members of four Olympic teams. [*Editor's note:* Alfred Jochim was on the gymnastics team and seven-time winner of the American all-around championship. O'Connor and Lauer were on the water polo team.] All flags were dipped as they passed the reviewing stand, with the exception of the Stars and Stripes, following the military custom of dipping the flag only to the President of the United States. The huge German band played without interruption the ever-changing tunes of the national anthems of all participating countries.

The French team of 250 appeared in blue berets, blue coats and white trousers; Bulgaria goose-stepped past the reviewing stand; the Afghans and Indians wore their native turbans; the Argentines, Australians and Chinese in naval caps, cricket caps and straw hats respectively. The English team made a very presentable appearance in navy blue coats, straw hats and white trousers; the Canadian group with red blazers and white trousers; Japan, with one of the largest delegations at the Games, in straw hats, blue coats and white trousers; the Egyptians in red fezes and the Italian athletes in Fascist caps. The American team of 383, led by President Avery Brundage followed by officers Dr. Graeme M. Hammond, Dr. Joseph E. Raycroft, Frederick W. Rubien and Gustavus T. Kirby, wore white trousers, blue coats with the Olympic emblem embroidered on the left breast, straw hats with the small Olympic emblem on the band, white shirts, red, white and blue neckties and white sport shoes and socks. The women athletes from the United States were dressed in blue tailored jackets, white skirts and white felt hats, white blouses, white shoes and hose. The greeting to the American team was noisily enthusiastic both on entry and leaving the stadium.

Most of the nations gave the Olympic salute as they passed the reviewing stand (right arm stretched out sidewise from shoulder). The American team turned eyes right and placed their hats over their hearts as they marched by.

The German team marched into the stadium with military precision, dressed in white suits with yachting caps. On account of the large number of competitors, the United States and Germany paraded eight abreast.

Each contingent having completed its march round the stadium, lined up on the field in deep columns behind its insignia and flag, facing the Tribune of Honor. The International Olympic Committee and the Organizing Committee then formed themselves into a semi-circle facing the athletes. Dr. Theodore Lewald, speaking in German for twenty minutes, extended a hearty and sincere welcome to the athletes.

Chancellor Hitler opened the games with the following message: "I proclaim the Games at Berlin in celebration of the Eleventh Olympiad of the modern era open."

With the welcome concluded, a fanfare was sounded by sixth trumpets and from a distance a battery of cannons roared eleven times denoting the Eleventh Olympiad. The Olympic flag was slowly raised to the central mast. Suddenly, from 100 ramparts, the flags of the participating nations interspersed with Olympic flags of equal

As Hitler entered the stadium his "Standarte des Führers" (flag) is hoisted for all to see.

Famous distance runner Paavo Nurmi, the "Flying Finn," came to the opening ceremonies. He set 29 world records at distances from 1,500 meters to 20,000 meters.

size, were raised in perfect unison. Three thousand doves were released on their symbolic mission to tell the world that another Olympiad had begun.

At this moment, an athlete appeared high on the east end of the stadium in a white athletic uniform, the last of 3,300 relay runners who carried the Olympic fire. Each youth carried the torch a distance of one-half mile and the total distance covered was approximately 1,837 miles. The torch was lit with a burning glass at Olympia in Greece and appropriate ceremonies were held in all of the towns through which the race was staged. The torch bearer gracefully ran down the stadium steps, sped over the straightway, leaving a trail of blue smoke behind him, and raced up the stairs at the west gate where he lit the Olympic torch. The Olympic torch on top of the stadium wall burned during the duration of the games.

The flag bearers advanced to the center and formed a semi-circle, facing the International and Organizing Committees. With all athletes joining in, Rudolf Ismayr of the German weight lifting team, pronounced the Olympic Oath as follows: "We swear that we will take part in the Olympic Games in loyal competition, respecting the regulations which govern them and desirous of participating in them in the true spirit of sportsmanship for the honor of our country and for the glory of sport." All of the athletes raised their right hands in assent.

The Opening Ceremonies climaxed two years of preparation on the part of Germany, the like of which had never before been attempted. Six miles of Olympic highway from Lustgarten through Unter den Linden was a long avenue of color. At every 50 feet on either side of the street were flag poles 50 feet in height, flying the flags of the participating nations. More than 100,000 members of the Hitler Youth lined the streets for the final stages of the torch relay, in addition to about 2,000,000 Germans who were unable to obtain tickets for the games. The entire German nation caught the spirit of the Olympic Games. At approximately every eighth mile along the highway loud speakers were installed which kept the crowed informed of what was going on.

The administering of the Olympic Oath was a fitting climax and immediately thereafter the march of the athletes took place in reverse order, bring the ceremony to a close.

Hitler and an entourage of International Olympic Committee members and Nazi government officials enter the stadium during the opening ceremonies. LC

The *Hindenburg* over the Olympic Stadium during the opening ceremony.
AP PHOTO

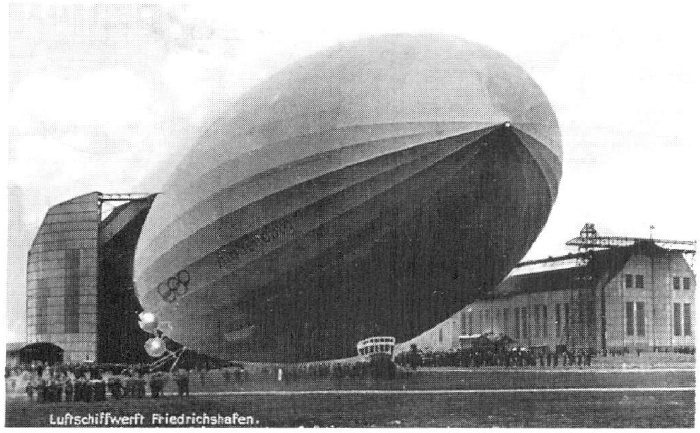

The *Hindenburg* LZ129

The largest airship ever built, 803 feet in length and 131 feet in diameter, was named for the late German president Paul von Hindenburg, and launched at Friedrickshafen in March 1936. Because of the American ban on the export of the inflammable gas helium, the *Hindenburg*'s crew filled its gasbags with 7,062,100 cubic feet of hydrogen.

On two decks inside its hull just aft of the control gondola, 50 people could live in the style and comfort of a grand hotel. Its first flight across the Atlantic to the United States was in May 1936. On its sides were painted the five interlocking multicolored rings symbolizing the 1936 Berlin Olympics.

In August 1936 the great airship soared above the Olympic Stadium in Berlin, emphasizing Germany's predominance in this form of transportation.

In one of the most famous disasters ever captured on film and radio, the *Hindenburg* caught fire and was destroyed while approaching its mooring mast at Lakehurst, New Jersey, on May 6, 1937. Thirty-five of the 97 passengers and crew died.

Above: *LZ 129* over the Brandenburg Gate. NA, HH 242-HO-00578

Above right: *LZ 129* at its base at Friedrickshafen.

Below: Another view of *LZ 129* over the Olympic Stadium on August 1. NBHF

ORGANISATIONS-KOMITEE FÜR DIE XI. OLYMPIADE
BERLIN 1936 E.V.

BERLIN-CHARLOTTENBURG 2 · HARDENBERGSTRASSE 43III

DIRECTIONS FOR THE OPENING CEREMONY OF THE XIth OLYMPIAD BERLIN 1936

ON SATURDAY, AUGUST 1st 1936
IN THE STADIUM AT THE REICH SPORTS FIELD

DIRECTOR OF THE PROCESSION:
Major *Feuchtinger*

Alfred Jochim, center, flag bearer with color guards, Wallace O'Conner, left and Fred Lauer, right – all veterans of four Olympiads.

The active participants of all nations will take part in the opening ceremony. The national teams will be led by their officials.

From 1.15 p. m. The participants mount the special omnibusses in the Olympic Village.

Those lodged in the Olympic Village will be transported to the Bell Tower via Staaken, Heerstraße and Glockenturmstraße.

The order of departure for the different nations will be given out by the National Army Transportation Division in the Olympic Village.

1.01 p. m. Departure of the rowers living in Grünau from the Köpenick Station. The participants enter and leave the Municipal Railway in Köpenick at Ladestrasse.

1.57 p. m. Arrival at the Reich Sports Field.

1.00 p. m. Arrival of the Saluting Company at the Maifeld.

From 2.15 p. m. Arrival of the teams at the Bell Tower.

2.30 p. m. Arrival of the women participants from "Friesenhaus".

The south and north stands at the Maifeld will be at the disposal of the participants.

3.15 p. m. Arrival of the Honour Bataillion of the National Army at the Bell Tower.

3.30 p. m. The ranks of the officials and active participants form upon the Maifeld according to Plan 1. The team leaders will arrange their national teams in the space designated for them by means of special placards. The participation of the attachés of the various nations is optional.

Plan 1.

Order of arrangement for the national groups, right to left: One pace in front of the right wing, the national flag. Behind, the officials, women and men. If the national teams include military groups (pentathlon and equestrian competitors) who are in uniform, these should stand between the women and men.

3.35 p. m. Arrival of the International Olympic Committee and Organizing Committee at the Bell Tower.

The International Olympic Committee and Organizing Committee pass through the Bell Tower and take their places at the Maifeld according to plan 1.

3.48 p. m. Arrival of the Führer and the Reich Minister of the Interior at the Bell Tower. Immediately following, in spection of the Honour Batallion of the National Army before the Bell Tower.

3.51—3.54 p. m. The Führer inspects the Battalion of Honour.

Hitler gives an informal Nazi salute as he arrives to officially open the games. The clock on the tower at right has struck noon. NA, HH

3.55 p. m. The Führer enters the Maifeld.

The Führer is greeted by the Presidents of the International Olympic Committee and the Organizing Committee.

Announcement of the Saluting Company.

Reception of the International Olympic Committee and the Organizing Committee by the Führer.

ca. 3.56 p. m. At the end of the reception the trumpeters stationed on the towers of the Marathon Gate play the Olympic Fanfare of 1936, composed by Major Paul *Winter*.

The Führer proceeds towards the Stadium, passing through the ranks of participants and officials and followed by the International Olympic Committee and the Organizing Committee.

4.00 p. m. The Führer, the International Olympic Committee and the Organizing Committee enter the Stadium.

As soon as the Führer reaches the steps of the Marathon Gate, the trumpeters on the towers of the Marathon Gate cease playing, and the trumpeters on the Announcement Tower sound the Festive Fanfare composed by Professor *Schmidt* until the Führer has reached the lower steps.

Then the large orchestra plays the "March of Allegiance" by Richard Wagner under the direction of Prof. Dr. *Havemann* until the Führer, the International Olympic Committee and the Organizing Committee have entered their loges.

4.05 p. m. The Führer, International Olympic Committee and Organizing Committee enter their loges.

When the Führer is seated, the German national hymns, "Deutschland" and "Horst Wessel-Lied" are played.

4.09 p. m. Prelude by Herbert *Windt*.

4.12—4.12½ p. m. At the command, "Raise the colours!", a company from the Reich Naval Corps hoist the flags of all participating nations on the various flag staffs at the Stadium.

4.12½—4.13½ p. m. The ringing of the Olympic Bell heralds the opening of the Games.

4.13½ p. m. By this time the teams have traversed the Maifeld and stand at the mouth of the tunnel ready to enter the Stadium.

A German placard carrier will be allotted to each nation. The placards will bear the names of the countries in the German language. The nations will march in alphabetical order (according to German spelling) with Greece at their head.

4

Hitler and his officials pass through the Brandenburg Gate on the way to open the games.

. . .

Famous German composer Richard Strauss wrote the official music, "Olympic Hymn," for the games.

Rudolf Ismayr, German weightlifting champion, pronounced the Olympic oath.

	Width of the ranks of the nations in the parade:
1. *Griechenland (Greece)*	3
2. *Ägypten (Egypt)*	3
3. *Afghanistan (Afghanistan)*	3
4. *Argentinien (Argentina)*	3
5. *Australien (Australia)*	3
6. *Belgien (Belgium)*	4
7. *Bermuda (Bermuda)*	2
8. *Bolivien (Bolivia)*	2
9. *Brasilien (Brazil)*	3
10. *Bulgarien (Bulgaria)*	3
11. *Chile (Chile)*	3
12. *China (China)*	3
13. *Columbien (Columbia)*	2
14. *Costa Rica (Costa Rica)*	2
15. *Dänemark (Denmark)*	3
16. *Estland (Estonia)*	3
17. *Finnland (Finland)*	3
18. *Frankreich (France)*	6
19. *Großbritannien (Great Britain)*	5
20. *Haiti (Haiti)*	2
21. *Holland (Holland)*	3
22. *Indien (India)*	3
23. *Island (Iceland)*	3
24. *Italien (Italy)*	4
25. *Jamaica (Jamaica)*	1
26. *Japan (Japan)*	5
27. *Jugoslawien (Yugoslavia)*	3
28. *Kanada (Canada)*	3
29. *Lettland (Latvia)*	3
30. *Liechtenstein (Liechtenstein)*	3
31. *Luxemburg (Luxemburg)*	3
32. *Malta (Malta)*	3
33. *Mexiko (Mexico)*	3
34. *Monaco (Monaco)*	2
35. *Neuseeland (New Zealand)*	2
36. *Norwegen (Norway)*	3
37. *Österreich (Austria)*	6
38. *Panama (Panama)*	2
39. *Peru (Peru)*	3
40. *Philippinen (The Philippine Islands)*	3
41. *Polen (Poland)*	3
42. *Portugal (Portugal)*	3
43. *Rumänien (Rumania)*	3
44. *Schweden (Sweden)*	4
45. *Schweiz (Switzerland)*	6
46. *Spanien (Spain)*	3
47. *Südafrika (South Africa)*	3
48. *Tschechoslowakei (Czechoslovakia)*	4

5

	Width of the ranks of the nations in the parade:
49. *Türkei (Turkey)*	3
50. *Ungarn (Hungary)*	6
51. *Uruguay (Uruguay)*	2
52. *Vereinigte Staaten (The United States)*	8
53. *Deutschland (Germany)*	8

The order of the national groups should be as follows:

a) Officials
b) Women
c) Military groups, if in uniform (the German pentathlon athletes and horsemen will march in uniform)
d) Men

The nations will march to the tunnel at the directions of those in charge of the order of the procession.

4.14 p. m. At the command, "Participants, march!", the nations enter the Stadium, the spacing between the different nations being regulated at the mouth of the tunnel. A space of 5 metres should be maintained between the placard carrier and the flag-bearer. The distance between the last row of a national group and the placard carrier of the following group should be 20 metres.

After the entrance through the mouth of the tunnel, the national groups will march along the running track of the Stadium past the Loges of Honour and down the eastern side to the northern side, where they make a turn to the south. The march up to the position before the Loges of Honour will start from here, each nation making a left turn towards the position designated for it by a placard.

The Executive Head of the German Reich, Leader and Reich Chancellor Adolf Hitler, the *International Olympic Committee* and *Organizing Committee* will be saluted by each team marching past the Loges of Honour through a lowering of the flags.

Each national group will salute according to the custom of its country. Members of the Voluntary Youth Service will be posted at the spots where the salute should begin and end.

The public will salute the flags.

The officials and active participants will arrange themselves in rows according to the size of each national group:

Greece	in rows of	2
Egypt	in rows of	2
Afghanistan	in rows of	2
Argentina	in rows of	2
Australia	in rows of	2
Belgium	in rows of	4
Bermuda	in rows of	2
Bolivia	in rows of	1
Brazil	in rows of	2
Bulgaria	in rows of	3
Chile	in rows of	2
China	in rows of	2
Columbia	in rows of	2
Costa Rica	in rows of	1
Denmark	in rows of	3
Estonia	in rows of	2
Finland	in rows of	3
France	in rows of	6
Great Britain	in rows of	5
Haiti	in rows of	1
Holland	in rows of	3
India	in rows of	2
Iceland	in rows of	2
Italy	in rows of	4
Jamaica	in rows of	1
Japan	in rows of	5
Yugoslavia	in rows of	3
Canada	in rows of	3
Latvia	in rows of	2
Liechtenstein	in rows of	2
Luxemburg	in rows of	2
Malta	in rows of	2
Mexiko	in rows of	2
Monaco	in rows of	2
New Zealand	in rows of	2
Norway	in rows of	3
Austria	in rows of	6
Panama	in rows of	2
Peru	in rows of	2
The Philippine Islands	in rows of	2
Poland	in rows of	3
Portugal	in rows of	2
Rumania	in rows of	3
Sweden	in rows of	4
Switzerland	in rows of	6
Spain	in rows of	3
South Africa	in rows of	2
Czechoslovakia	in rows of	4
Turkey	in rows of	3
Hungary	in rows of	6
Uruguay	in rows of	2
The United States	in rows of	8
Germany	in rows of	8

Plan 2. After the procession, the flag-bearers will stand on a previously marked line at a distance of 5 metres from their national groups, the right and left wings and the front rows of which will be designated by markings in the national colours of the nations.

The placard carriers in their turn will stand at a distance of 5 metres from the flag-bearers of the national groups. The lines for the flag-bearers and placard carriers are clearly designated (plan 2).

Hundreds of German youth perform gymnastics during the opening ceremonies.

4.55 p. m. The words of Baron de Coubertin are repeated over the loud speaker: "L'important aux Jeux Olympiques n'est pas d'y gagner, mais d'y prendre part, car l'essentiel dans la vie n'est pas tant de conquérir, que de bien lutter."

(The important thing in the Olympic Games is not winning but taking part. The essential thing in life is not conquering but fighting well.)

In the meanwhile the International Olympic Committee and the Organizing Committee (IOC right, OC left) have arranged themselves in a half circle near the speaker's stand. The President of the Organizing Committee of the XIth Oympiad, Berlin, 1936, His Excellency, Dr. Lewald, mounts the speaker's stand and delivers the address of welcome.

5.03 p. m. The Führer proclaims open the Games of Berlin celebrating the XIth Olympiad of the modern era.

5.03 – 5.05 p. m. At the command, "Hoist the flag!":

a) The Olympic Flag will be hoisted,
b) Salutes will be fired by the artillery squad,
c) 30,000 carrier pigeons will be released,
d) Fanfares will be played by the trumpeters.

5.05 p. m. The Olympic Hymn by Richard Strauss under the direction of the composer.

5.11 p. m. The last torch relay runner enters the Stadium at the East Gate, runs down the southern track to the West Gate and lights the Olympic Fire.

5.15 p. m. The Marathon winner of the Olympiad of 1896, Louis, hands over to the Führer the olive branch from Athens.

5.18 p. m. At the command, "Advance the flags!", the flags of the nations will be assembled in a half circle around the speaker's platform, the flags pointing to the Loges of Honour. Nations from Greece to Japan will stand to the left of the speaker's platform, and those from Yugoslavia to the United States, to the right of the platform.

The German flag-bearer and an active German participant step forward to take the Olympic Oath. The flag-bearer stands at the left of the speaker's platform, facing the Loges of Honour. The active participant mounts the speaker's platform and raises the right hand to take the Olympic Oath, while with the left hand he grasps the German flag, which the flag-bearer holds up to the platform. The active participant will be chosen by the German Olympic Committee.

The command, "Sink the colours!", will be given before the Oath is taken, at which the flags will be lowered.

5.21 p. m. The Olympic Oath is taken by the active German participant, who repeats **aloud:**
"We swear that we will take part in the Olympic Games in loyal competition, respecting the regulations which govern them and desirous of

8

Baron Pierre de Coubertin was in Lausanne during the games. The following message from him was broadcast via phonograph record to the crowd: "The important thing at the Olympic Games is not to win, but to take part, just as the most important thing about life is not to conquer, but to struggle well."

Hitler spoke to the crowd: "I announce as opened the Games of Berlin, celebrating the eleventh Olympiad of the modern era."

participating in them in true spirit of sportsmanship for the honour of our country and for the glory of sport."

5.22 p. m. Music: "Händel's "Hallelujah" Chorus". Direction: Prof. Bruno *Kittel.*

5.26 p. m. The International Olympic Committee and the Organizing Committee take their places.

At the command, "Raise the colours!", the flag-bearers, having raised the flags, return to their national groups.

5.29 p. m. Following the directions of the marshall, the nations march out in the same order as they entered the Stadium. Each nation will follow the national group standing directly to the right of it, observing that the required 20 metres' distance is maintained between the last row of the foregoing national group and its own placard carrier. The nations will march to the running track and then turn right (to the west). The parade to the Maifeld will take place without greeting through the tunnel exit. Having reached the Maifeld the participants will disperse and return to the omnibusses. The team leaders will be informed by the National Army Transportation Division where the omnibusses are standing.

The women will return to their dormitory, "Friesenhaus", on foot.

The teams lodged in Grünau will head for "Reichssportfeld" Station, from which a train bound for Grünau will leave at 6.22 p. m. Arrival in Köpenick, 7.15 p. m.

6 p. m. The Führer leaves the Stadium when the parade is finished.

Concluding fanfars by Paul *Winter.*

Major *Feuchtinger.*

The musical side of the Olympic festivities is under the direction of the Reichsmusikkammer (Organizing Director, E. Kalanke).

9

Plan 1

Formation of the national teams for the Parade at the Maifeld on August 1st, 1936, at 3.30 p.m.

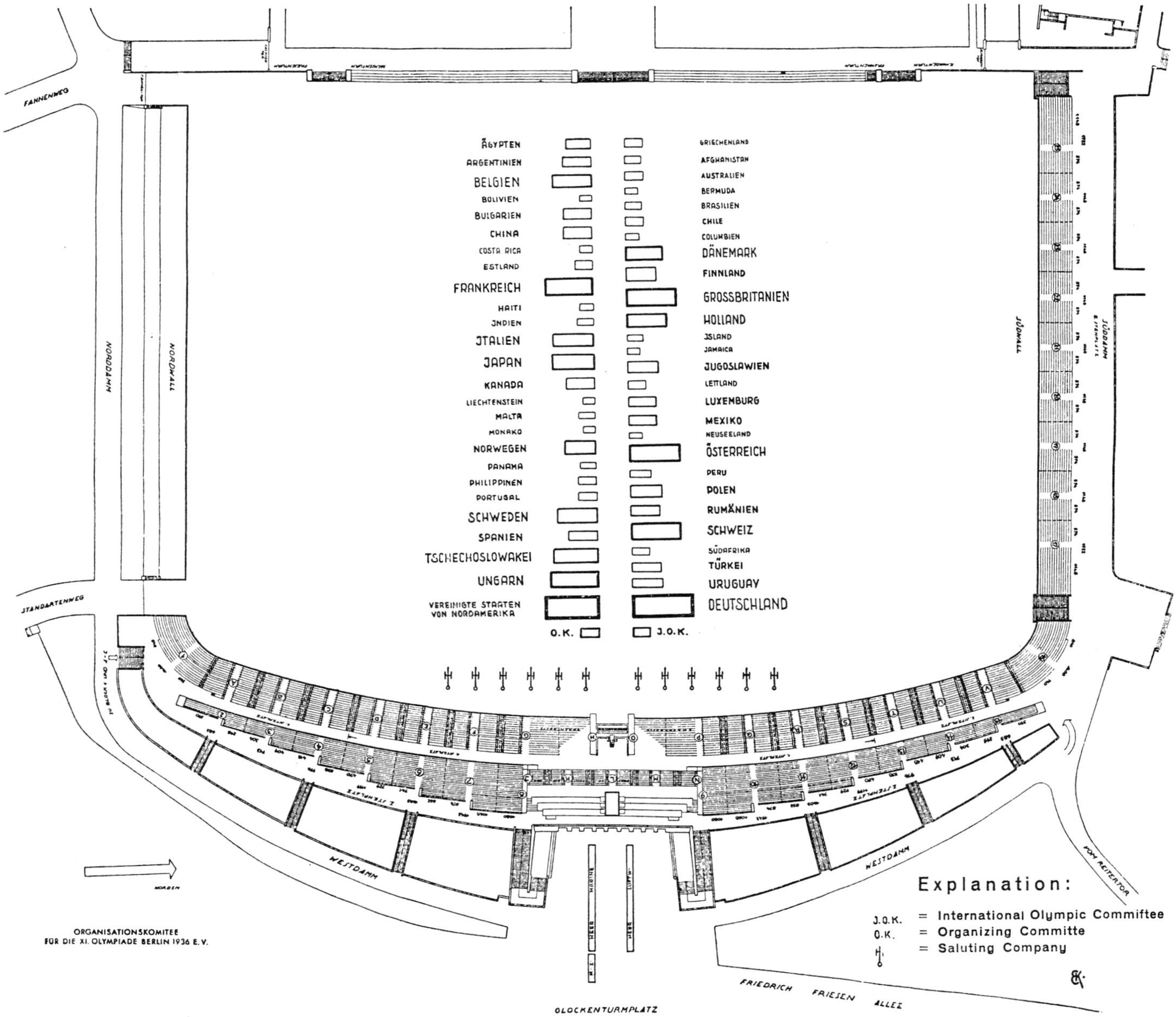

Einmarschweg und Aufstellung

Plan 2

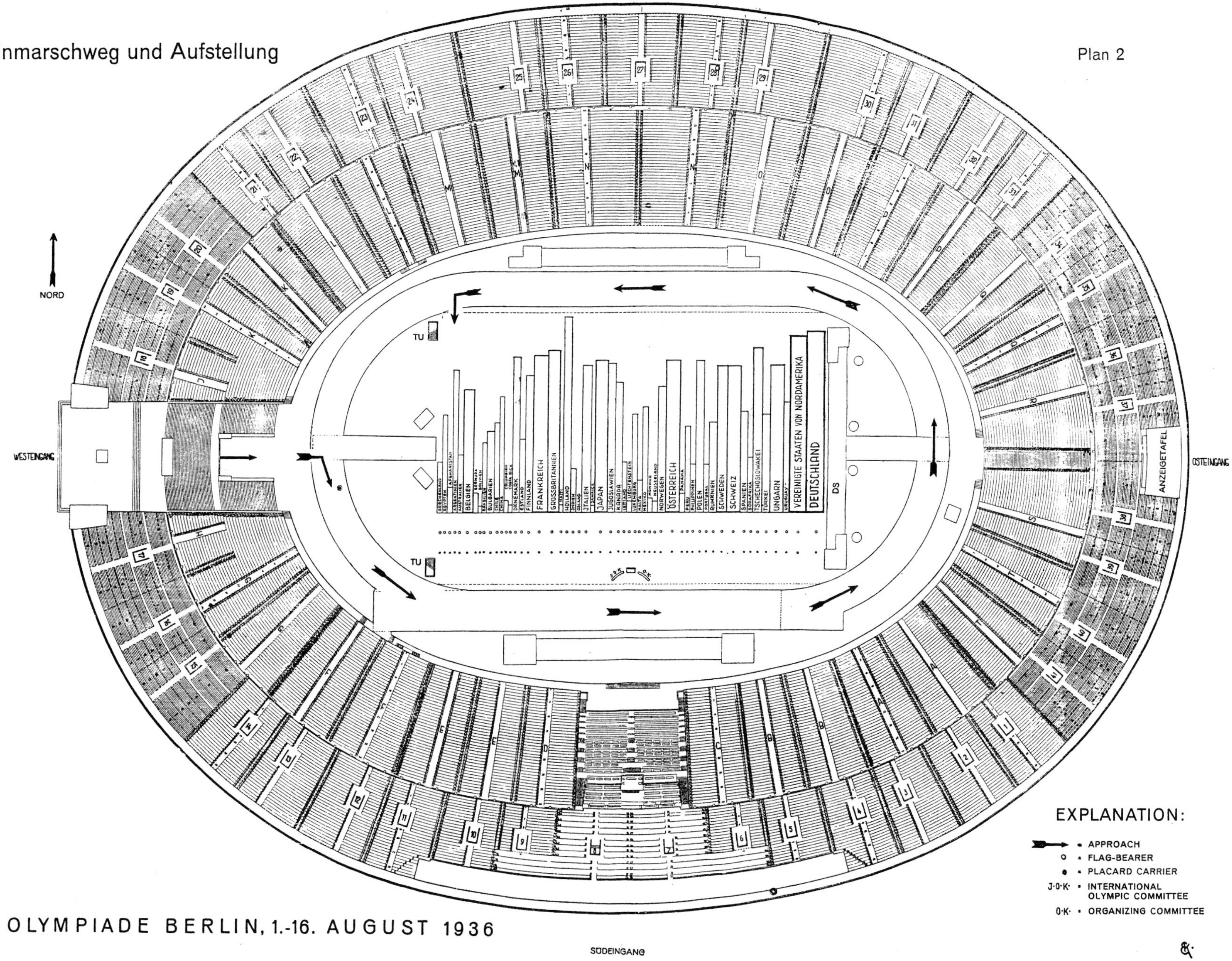

XI. OLYMPIADE BERLIN, 1.-16. AUGUST 1936

The Torch Relay Run

According to Olympic protocol, the Olympic flame must burn during the period of the games. The International Olympic Committee at its meeting in Athens in 1934 decided that the flame should be brought from Olympia in Greece to Berlin by a series of runners, each carrying a torch lit one to another.

More than 3,000 runners, each covering a distance of one kilometer, participated. The torches for the run were especially manufactured by the Krupp Works from Nirosta steel and each burned for 10 minutes.

The route took the runners through Greece, Bulgaria, Yugoslavia, Hungary, Austria, Czechoslovakia and Germany. The Olympic flame was ignited at a special ceremony at Olympia in Greece on July 20, 1936, at noon. The relay had been arranged so that the final runner would arrive at the Olympic stadium in Berlin on August 1 at 4:00 p.m. during the opening ceremony.

At each stop along the route a celebration was held and each runner received a diploma and was allowed to keep the torch as a souvenir of the historic event.

The last runner arrived at the Berlin Lustgarten on Saturday, August 1, at 12:30 p.m. The route took the torch through Tempelhof Berliner Strasse, Belle-Alliance Strasse, Wihelmstrasse, Unter den Linden to the steps in front of the Old Museum. From the museum the flame continued at 3:30 p.m., passing through Unter den Linden, the Brandenburger Tor, Charlottenburger Chaussee, Bismarckstrasse, Kaiserdamm, Reichsstrasse, and Olympische Strasse to the eastern gate of the Olympic stadium.

German runners carried the flame by relay to Kiel, where it burned on a Hanseatic sailing ship during the yachting regatta in Kiel Bay. The run started on Sunday, August 2, at 4:45 p.m. in the Olympic stadium and proceeded through Nauen, Kyritz, Pritzwalk, Parchim, Schwerin, Gadebusch, Lübeck and Ploeu. The last runner arrived in Kiel on Monday, August 3, at 10:00 p.m.

The Olympic flame was also carried by relay runners from the Olympic stadium to Grünau on August 7, the site of the rowing and canoeing competitions. The flame burned from the Bismarck Tower on the Müggelberge during the events.

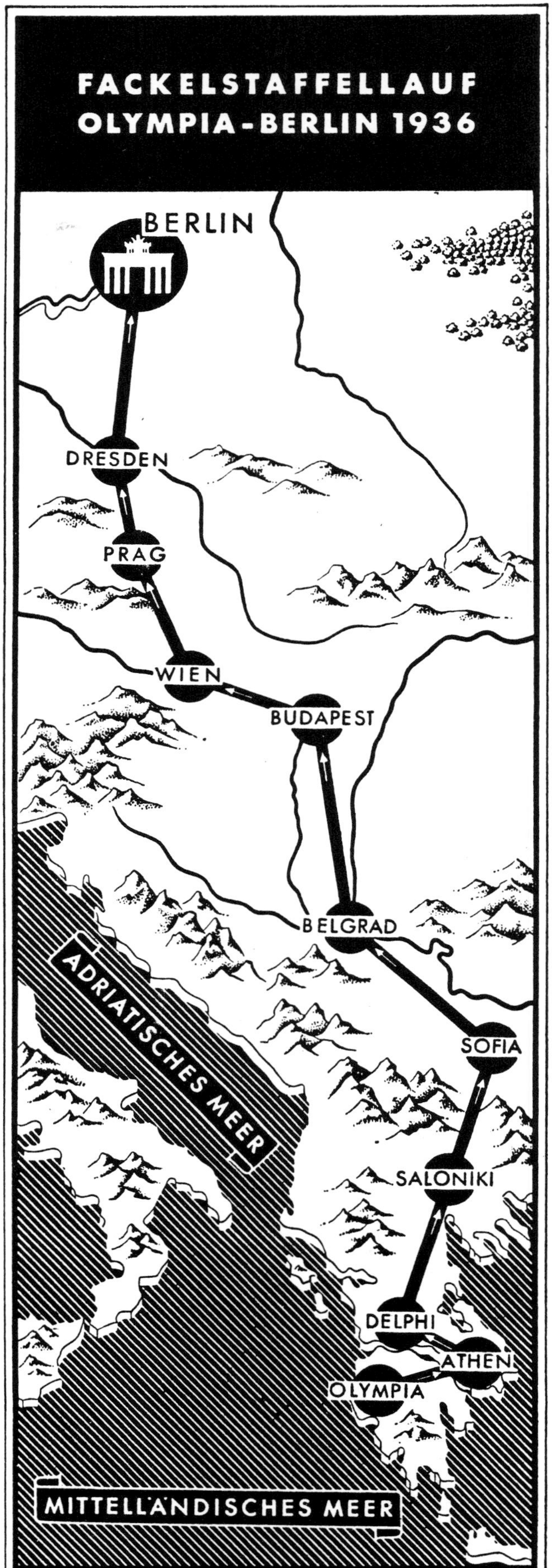

of the torch run rehearse for the flame lighting
Acropolis in Athens. LC

At Olympia, in Greece, the Olympic flame is lit by the sun.

The torch has just passed through the Brandenburg Gate on the way to a ceremony at the Old Museum just down Unter den Linden Street. NA, HH 242-HO-00

The Olympic torch was carried by more than 3,000 runners from Greece to Berlin. NA

At noon on Aug. 1, 1936, at Marienfelde on the outskirts of Berlin, a runner named Clar from the Athens Sports Club has just handed over the Olympic torch to the German relay team, whose members will carry it to the center of the capital. BA

The last of the more than 3,000 runners lights the Olympic flame to open the games.

The last of the runners enters the stadium. NA, HH 242-HB-22108

The last runner with the torch arrived at the Berlin Lustgarten and ran to the steps of the Old Museum for a ceremony. From here the torch was carried to the Olympic Stadium.

The Olympic torch is carried by canoe to Grünau on August 7.
NA, HH 242-H0-234

The Olympic flame burned from the Bismarck Tower on the Müggelberge during the water events at Grünau.

Thousands of spectators give the Nazi salute at the opening ceremonies in the Olympic stadium.

Olympia-Sonderdienst 1
Einzelpreis 10 Pf., auswärts 15 Pf.

„Freiheit und Brot!"

Olympia-Sonderdienst 1
München, Samstag, 1. August 1936

VÖLKISCHER BEOBACHTER

Kampfblatt der national-sozialistischen Bewegung Großdeutschlands

Die XI. Olympischen Spiele von Adolf Hitler eröffnet

Entschluß des Führers: Deutschland nimmt die Ausgrabungen in Olympia wieder auf - Das Olympische Feuer brennt in der Reichshauptstadt - Jugend marschiert im Lustgarten auf - Die Reichsregierung empfängt das Internationale Olympische Komitee

Der 1. Tag

Die von der ganzen Welt mit größter Spannung erwartete Eröffnung der XI. Olympischen Spiele nahm morgens 7.35 Uhr mit dem großen Wecken der Wehrmacht ihren Anfang. Um 9.15 Uhr hatten sich bereits die Mitglieder des Internationalen Olympischen Komitees und des Organisationskomitees im Hotel Adlon Unter den Linden versammelt, um dann zum Festgottesdienst im Dom und zur Hedwigskathedrale zu fahren.

Während des Gottesdienstes sammelten sich in den Seitenstraßen die Jugendverbände, um ebenfalls zum Lustgarten zu marschieren und dort an der großen Jugendkundgebung teilzunehmen.

Nach dem Gottesdienst begaben sich die Mitglieder des IOK. und OK., von der begeisterten Menge stürmisch begrüßt, zum Zeughaus, wo inzwischen ein Ehrenbataillon der Wehrmacht, aus zwei Kompanien der Luftwaffe und der Kriegsmarine bestehend, zur Heldenehrung angetreten war.

Graf de Baillet-Latour schritt mit dem Kommandanten von Berlin die Ehrenfront ab und unterdessen brachten zwei Jungen des olympischen Ehrendienstes den großen Kranz herbei, den die Mitglieder des IOK. und OK. zur Ehrung unserer Toten des Weltkrieges am Ehrenmal niederlegten. Anschließend folgte der Vorbeimarsch des Ehrenbataillons, das die Tradition des alten Heeres verkörpert, am Ehrenmal.

Sodann begaben sich die Mitglieder des IOK. und des OK. durch das Spalier der Menschenmauern zum Empfang nach dem Alten Museum, wo sie von dem preußischen Ministerpräsidenten Generaloberst Göring herzlich begrüßt wurden.

Um 12 Uhr marschierten dann 28 600 Mitglieder der Jugendverbände im Lustgarten auf. Hier fand die große Jugendkundgebung statt, auf der der Reichsjugendführer Baldur von Schirach die Jugend der ganzen Welt begrüßte. Anschließend sprachen dann noch der Reichssportführer von Tschammer und Osten, der Reichserziehungsminister Rust und Reichsminister Dr. Goebbels.

Nachdem sich die Erwartung und die Erregung der unübersehbaren Menschenmenge zu fieberhafter Höhe steigerte, traf dann gegen 1 Uhr das olympische Feuer im Lustgarten ein, worauf mit der olympischen Flamme die Feuer auf den Altären im Lustgarten entzündet wurden, die nunmehr von der Hitler-Jugend bis 16 Uhr gehütet wurden. Damit fand die Jugendkundgebung ihr Ende und die Mitglieder des IOK. begaben sich über die Linden in die Wilhelmstraße zur Reichskanzlei, wo sie vom Führer empfangen wurden.

Am Nachmittag fuhr dann das IOK. und das OK. um 3 Uhr von der Wilhelmstraße über die Froststraße zum Reichssportfeld.

Den Höhepunkt des Festes bildete dann der weihevolle Akt der Eröffnung der XI. Olympischen Spiele Berlin 1936 um 4 Uhr durch den Führer.

Abends um 9 Uhr fand sich dann eine vieltausendköpfige Menschenmenge zum großen Festspiel im Olympia-Stadion ein.

Die auserwählte Jugend von 53 Nationen leistet den Olympischen Schwur

Drahtbericht unseres Mitarbeiters Roland Strunk

Mutter, o, du des goldgekrönten Kampfspiels, Olympia, du Herrscherin der Wahrheit...

(Pindar, Olympische Ode)

Das Fest des Zeus ist wiederum nahe, aller Streit soll ruhen, jeder Waffenlärm schweige, frei mögen auf allen Land- und Wasserstraßen die Pilger heranziehen zu der gastlichen Schwelle.

Mit diesem Ruf luden die Gesandten des alten Hellas die Völker der Antike zur Weihestätte am Alpheios.

Ihre Stimmen sind längst verhallt. Jahrhunderte begruben Olympia, den hellenischen Friedensstein an den sonnigen Gestaden Arkadiens. Hellas ging zugrunde — der olympische Geist aber lebe weiter.

Die Idee eines Franzosen, die Liebe und Ausdauer deutscher Gelehrter haben den heiligen Kampfplatz der griechischen Antike dem Licht der Sonne wiedergegeben. Neuerstanden schwang sich die Idee des friedlichen Wettstreits in festlicher Form von Nation zu Nation, wenngleich der Ruf der olympischen Sendboten nun nicht mehr Streit- und Waffenlärm zum Schweigen bringen konnte. Es war, als fehlte dem neuerweckten olympischen Geist der Funke des heiligen Feuers, erdacht und entzündet, um hineinzuleuchten in die Abgründe des Hasses und zu überstrahlen die dunklen Mächte der Zwietracht.

Heute, wo in den festlichen Pylonen der XI. Olympischen Spiele ein ganzes von Friedenssehnsucht und Friedenswillen erfülltes Volk als Gastgeber und Rufer steht, hat die symbolische Geste des Führers dieses Volkes im heiligen Hain am Alpheios die Flamme entzündet, die, getragen von der rastlosen Sehnsucht eines kampfmüden Menschengeschlechts von den Gestaden Arkadiens ans Herz Europas in den Mittelpunkt der olympischen Kampfbahn, ins Deutsche Reich eilt.

Noch ist die Feuerschale kalt, die Flamme, begleitet vom hochherzigen Jubel einer ahnungsvoll erkennenden Nation, ist eben jetzt auf ihrem Wege knapp vor dem Ziele. Das weite Rund der gigantischen Kampfbahn, bald umlodert von der Glut der Flaggen, ist erfüllt vom Brausen und Dröhnen der Unzähligen, die „frei auf allen Land- und Wasserwegen zu der gastlichen Schwelle kamen, müde des Streits und Waffenlärms", und es ist uns, als wäre dieses Dröhnen der geisterhafte Hall unsichtbarer, zu dieser noch kalten Schale eilender Läufer, deren Hände die Funken und Flammen aus allen Bezirken unserer Erde herantragen, um sie nie mehr erlöschen zu lassen — die Flamme des Friedens.

Die sittliche Idee der reinen, stillen Flamme, des einfachen Ehrenkranzes zutiefst erfaßt zu haben, ist demütiger Stolz des Volkes, das heute über alle Grenzen hinweg den Glockenruf zum Friedensfest schallen läßt. Es ist, als schwebe diese Stätte, getragen von silbernen Flügeln des Lichts, hoch in einer reinen Atmosphäre, Thingplatz der Jugend der Welt — damit sie in Schönheit und Kraft, heraustretend aus der Vielfalt und dem Chaos, ihren heiligen Willen kundtue für den Beginn einer besseren, sittlicheren Epoche unseres Geschlechts.

Die Jugend der Welt folgte dem Ruf; 53 Nationen werden in wenigen Minuten, vertreten durch ihre gläubigste Jugend, Antlitz und Schwurhand ins olympische Licht heben, denn die weise Gültigkeit dieser Sinngebung, dieses von allen Kräften des Herzens und des Leibes getragenen Vorwärtseilens zum sieghaften Ziel, soll nicht nur die Kampfbahn, sondern das gigantische Stadion der Erde erfüllen. Olympia, du Herrscherin der Wahrheit.

Die weite Granitschale, überdimensional, ist fast gefüllt. In ihrem Körper hellgrün die noch nicht betretene Kampfbahn, der Rasen. Im leuchtenden Braunrot die Kampfbahn. Die Ränder in diesem ungeheuren Rund ragen in den graublauen Himmel, über den soeben das Luftschiff „Hindenburg" majestätisch mit leise laufendem Motor seine Runden zog.

Unter dem Klang des einsetzenden feierlichen Glockengeläutes, begrüßt von dem Jubel der Hunderttausend, stieg, begleitet von Offizieren des Reichsheeres, in der malerischen Tracht seiner Heimat,

Spyridon Louis, der erste Marathonsieger, mit dem heiligen Zweig aus Olympia, den er dem Führer überreichen will,

mit blauweißen Schleifen seines Landes geschmückt, die Treppen vom Marathontor herunter. Dahinter, durch den Schacht dieses Tores, kann man auf der weiten Rasenfläche des Maifeldes die hellblauen und dunklen Karees der Olympia-Kämpfer aller Länder im Aufmarsch sehen. Weit blähen sich im Winde die weißen Flaggen. Von Minute zu Minute fühlt man die Spannung steigen, die dieses gewaltige Rund mit Elektrizität durchbebt.

In den Fernschreibern und Sprechmaschinen der internationalen Presse, hinter gläsernen Schutzscheiben rasseln Telephone und Schreibmaschinen. Noch sind die meisten Plätze der Ehrentribünen und die Plätze der Führerloge leer, doch ringsum drängt sich, geladen von Spannung und Erwartung, das rauschende Oval der Arena, seltsam kontrastiert von der noch ruhenden Kampfbahn.

Das Eintreffen des Führers

Rechts und links hinter der Führerloge auf den erhöhten Granitblocks bereiten Männer der Kriegsmarine die Standarte des Führers und eine Olympia-Standarte zur Hissung vor. Und nun, noch weit vor dem Marathonthor, beim unsichtbaren Glockenturm muß der Führer eingetroffen sein. Von den Türmen des Marathontores lösen feierliche und ernste Fanfarenklänge. Sie zeigen an, daß der Führer beim Glockenturm eingetroffen ist.

Auf der Plattform dieser Türme stehen die Ehrenformationen des Heeres, der Kriegsmarine und der Luftmacht. Draußen auf dem Maifeld in feierlicher Aufstellung die Olympiateilnehmer und die Sportstudenten, durch deren Reihe schreitend der Führer nun jeden Augenblick erscheinen muß.

Nun klingt rauschender Beifall auf, noch gedämpft durch die Mauern, die uns von dem Anblick des Führers trennen. In die Hunderttausend kommt Bewegung, und jetzt, links von der noch leeren Flammenschale, umgeben vom Internationalen Olympischen Komitee, deren goldene Ehrenketten über den dunklen Anzügen leuchten, zu seiner Linken den Präsidenten des Internationalen Olympischen Komitees, Baillet-Latour, zu seiner Rechten Exzellenz Lewald, langsam schreitend, in der Entfernung nur durch seine charakteristische Haltung zu erkennen: der Führer des deutschen Volkes. Hinter ihm in tiefer Gruppe das Olympische Komitee, Offiziere der Wehrmacht, die schwarzen Uniformen der SS.

Langsam schreitet der Führer die Treppe am Olympischen Tor in das tiefe Rund der Kampfbahn herab. Auf der Sandbahn, wie ein kleines verlorenes Vergißmeinnicht in Blau die Gestalt eines kleinen Mädchens, ein Blondkopf, der mit tiefem Knix dem Führer mit rührender Gebärde den Blumenstrauß des Willkommens reicht. Leise streicht die Hand des Führers über die Wange des Kindes, das an der Hand des Grafen Baillet-Latour dem Führer auf seinem Weg zu seinem Platz folgen darf.

Die Führerstandarte in sattem Purpur mit Gold steigt langsam neben der Olympiaflagge hoch, die Heroldsfanfaren klingen majestätisch und hell gegen den Himmel.

Rudolf Heß ist dem Führer entgegengegangen und begrüßt ihn. Die gesamte Reichsregierung in der Regierungsloge hat sich erhoben, und nun schlägt über diesen Raum, der gefüllt von einer tiefen, alles erfassenden Erregung, der brausende Jubel der Ungezählten, nicht endenwollend, sich steigernd. Hunderttausend Arme sind hochgereckt zum Deutschen Gruß. Das Deutschlandlied, das den Führer, bereits stehend in seiner Loge, begrüßt, das Horst-Wessel-Lied.

Und jetzt in der plötzlich eintretenden Stille der Wechselgesang zwischen Fanfaren und dem Chor. Ernst und feierlich sind die Klänge, ernst wie der Himmel, der sich über uns wölbt, ernst wie der herrliche Wille all derer, die ihren Führer und des Reichs Gäste umgeben, die hier versammelt sind, um zu sehen, wie das Reich vor dem Urteil der Welt, die heute auf uns blickt, bestehen wird, weil es bestehen muß.

Der Einmarsch der Nationen

In ehrfürchtigem Schweigen, das nur der Klang der olympischen Fanfaren umrahmt, steigen die 52 Flaggen der Weltnationen an den Fahnenmasten empor. Und dann betritt die Jugend der Welt die Kampfbahn der olympischen Kampfstätte.

Voran Griechenland, neben dem Führer dieser Gruppe der erste Olympiasieger, der griechische Bauer Spiridon Louis, der dem Führer den Ölzweig überreichen soll. Dahinter Ägypten, blauweiß die Uniform mit rotem Tarbusch. Afganistan, die schwarz-rot-grüne Flagge senkt sich vor der Führerloge. Argentinien mit weißen Mützen und blauen Jacken. Australien, stahlgrün, Belgien in schlichtem Grau mit hellen Strohhüten, die sich auf Kommando vor der Führerloge senken. Bermudas schneeweiß, die kleine Gruppe der 5 Sportler mit Tropenhelmen. Jede einzelne Gruppe begleitet von einem Filmwagen. Bolivien in Weiß, Brasilien in Hellblau, Bulgarien in blauen Jacken und weißen Hosen. Chile mit auffallend starkem Mannschaftsfeld. China erstmalig mit 69 Mann zum olympischen Kampf angetreten. Kolumbien, Costarica, Dänemark und Estland, Finnland, Frankreich, brausend begrüßt, besonders herzlich empfangen von einem Volk, das nicht nur als Gastgeber, sondern aus ehrlicher Überzeugung heraus die jahrhundertlange Fehde vergaß und mit erhobner Grußhand die Friedenshand darbietet. England, Haiti, Holland, das Land der Olympiade Amsterdam 1928, Indien mit Turbans, Irland in Blaugrau, und nun, umrauscht in einem immer mehr anschwellendem Jubel Italien, voran die Balilla in schwarzen Hemden, dahinter das starke Feld der Sportmannschaft in Blau und Weiß. Japan, eine der stärksten Sportnationen, das Land der nächsten Olympischen Spiele. In diesem Augenblick schwenken im Block uns gegenüber, wo wahrscheinlich die japanische Kolonie sitzt, japanische Sonnenflaggen. Jugoslawien in Kornblumenblau, Kanada in leuchtend Rot, Lettland schneeweiß.

Einstweilen haben die schon am Führer vorbeidefilierten Gruppen in der Mitte der unendlichen Rasenfläche Aufstellung genommen. Voran die weiße Mauer der Namensträger, dahinter die Flaggenträger, und dann, fast erinnernd an die vielfarbenen Tulpenbeete Hollands, die Blocks der verschiedenen Nationen.

Dann Liechtenstein, Litauen, Malta. Die englischen Dominions und Kolonien unter eigener Flagge marschierend, Mexiko in Weiß, die kleine Gruppe Monaco in weißen Baskenmützen.

Der Führer steht während des ganzen Vorbeimarsches, grüßt jede einzelne Gruppe, links von ihm der italienische Kronprinz, rechts der Präsident des Internationalen Olympischen Komitees. Weiter geht der feierliche Anmarsch durch das Marathontor, begleitet vom brausenden Jubel der Menge

— Neuseeland, Norwegen, und nun umrauscht von einem Beifall, der nicht steigerungsfähig erscheint, Österreich. Tadellos sieht diese Gruppe aus, schwarz-weiß. Auffallend stark die Gruppe der Offiziere. Peru, die berühmten Schwimmer der Philippinen, die Polen in Rot, Portugal, Rumänien, Schweden, letzteres mit hellen Heja-Rufen des schwedischen Blocks begrüßt. Dahinter die Schweiz — voran der berühmte Fahnenschwinger, der die rote Flagge mit dem weißen Kreuz hoch in die Luft wirbelt und wieder fängt. Südafrika, die Tschechoslowakei, die Türken und Ungarn — auch hier auffallend die Menge der Offiziere. Der Beifall geht dem tadellosen Bild, das diese Sportler hinter der rot-weiß-grünen Fahne zeigen. Uruguay, die Vereinigten Staaten von Amerika, aus dem amerikanischen Block mit Pfiffen und Zeichen amerikanischen Beifalls begrüßt und dann als letztes das Gastland, Deutschland, ein fast endloses Feld in blendendem Weiß. Und als unsere Olympiakämpfer um die Bahn ziehen, begleitet sie von den Hunderttausend stehend mitgesungen das Deutschlandlied und das Lied der Bewegung.

Die Olympia-Mannschaften stehen versammelt,

Exzellenz Lewald

begrüßt die Teilnehmer im Namen des deutschen Komitees und wünscht den Spielern einen ritterlichen Verlauf. Er führte aus:

Mein Führer!

Im Namen des Organisationskomitees für die XI. Olympiade Berlin 1936, habe ich die Ehre, Sie als den Schirmherrn der Olympischen Spiele in Berlin in diesem herrlichen Stadion, das nach Ihrem Willen geschaffen ist, in Dankbarkeit und Ehrerbietung zu begrüßen.

Was könnten die stärksten Worte der Begrüßung und des Dankes an einzelne heute uns hier sagen, das nicht überklungen würde von dem ungeheuren Eindruck dieses gewaltigen Raumes mit seinen edlen Maßen, von der kraftvollen Schönheit dieser jungen Mannschaften zu unseren Füßen. So bitte ich alle die vielen bedeutenden und wertvollen Männer und Frauen, die in Deutschland und in allen anderen Ländern der Erde die Abhaltung dieser Spiele ermöglicht haben und Sie alle, die mit Ihrer Anwesenheit zur Weihe,

Kronprinz Umberto von Italien, Prinz Paul von Griechenland und der Erbprinz von Schweden beim Führer

Berlin, 1. August

Seine Königl. Hoheit Kronprinz Umberto von Italien stattete heute vormittag dem Führer und Reichskanzler einen Besuch ab.

Später empfing der Führer und Reichskanzler seine Königl. Hoheit den Prinzen Paul von Griechenland und anschließend hieran den aktiv an den Olympischen Spielen teilnehmenden Erbprinzen von Schweden, seine Königl. Hoheit Prinz Gustav Adolf.

Das olympische Feuer in Berlin

Die olympische Fackel leuchtet auf deutschem Grunde

Nun haben wir rd. 300 Stunden Tag und Nacht über 3000 km weit die olympischen F[illegible] größer begleitet. Wohin wir kamen, [illegible] ihren die Gottesgeist, Jubel, Vaterlands- [illegible] aufgehen in der olympischen [illegible] wir es schöner nicht hätten wünschen können.

Der Jugend der Welt gehört die Zukunft.

Das ist die Quintessenz des Fackellaufes. Ihr Idealismus, ihre Sportbegeisterung werden festere Brücken für die Weltverständigung und einen sicheren Frieden schlagen als alles andere.

Unvergeßlich die ungeheueren Eindrücke der Tausende von Läufern. Auf dem Balkan waren es die Hitze und der Staub, der bei den oft großen Steigungen das Letzte von den Läufern verlangten. In den anderen Ländern war es das unheimlich scharfe Tempo, das die ehrgeizigen Sportler angesetzt haben, in der Tschechoslowakei die Sorge, die heilige Flamme unversehrt in die Hände des Nachbarlandes zu bringen. Da standen die Jungens oft stundenlang in stockfinsterer Nacht, mutterseelenallein ihre Blicke nach vorn gerichtet, bis um die Kurve die Fackel erschien. Ihr Kamerad kam. Wieder andere fuhren kilometerweit mit ihren Fahrrädern, liefen zu Fuß, kamen auf Pferdekutschen, um ihre Posten zu besetzen. Ergreifend eine Szene, die ich in Mazedonien beobachtete. Im Schatten einer Hecke stand ein Vater, seinen kleinen Jungen auf den Knien, die Fackel in den Händen. Andächtig lauschte der Junge den Worten seines Vaters. Was wird er ihm wohl erzählt haben. Wie schön das Leben ist, wie herrlich der Sport, wie hehr die Aufgabe, für sein Vaterland zu kämpfen. Auch Läufer sahen wir bei Weihestunden, das Gesicht schmerzlich verzerrt, das Magnesium der Fackel, vom Wind abgetrieben, tropfte auf ihren nackten Arm. Und doch hielten sie aus. Man sang die Nationalhymne.

Und nun sind wir wieder bei den Fackelläufern — nach einigen Stunden Ruhe stießen wir zwischen Luckenwalde und Groß-Beeren auf die Olympia-Läufer. Noch waren die Straßen spärlich von Zuschauern besetzt. Je weiter wir aber nach Groß-Berlin kamen, desto mehr erkannten wir: Heute hat es nur wenige Kurmärker selbst in ihren idyllischen Dörfern gehalten. Alles ist nach Berlin geeilt, die XI. Olympischen Spiele riefen.

Nicht, daß wir die jubelnden Empfänge irgendeiner Nation schmälern wollten, nein, dafür erlebten wir überall zu offene Herzlichkeit, Gastfreundschaft und ehrliche Begeisterung. Aber fragen wir die Tschechen oder die Griechen, die in ihren großen Omnibussen hierher geeilt waren, und hinter dem Fackelläufer den Siegeseinzug in die Reichshauptstadt erlebten Sie waren Zeugen eines Begeisterungssturmes, der wohl nirgends so groß war wie hier in Berlin. Fragen Sie die Hunderttausende, die die Straßen der Vororte Berlins säumten, ob die Hitler-Jugend oder der SA.-Mann ehrlicher in ihrer Begeisterung hätten sein können, als diese, die von dem Jubel einer ganzen Nation mitgerissen wurden. Rührend die Kinder, die mit glänzenden Augen die Läufer begrüßten. Ergreifend das Heil der HJ. und des BDM. Wie eine wogende Brandung aber rauschte hinter den wenigen offiziellen Automobilen Tausende und aber Tausende Radfahrer einher. Lützows wilde, verwegene Jagd der Radfahrer.

Mariendorf taucht auf. Enger und enger wird der freigehaltene Weg für den Fackelläufer. Schon hier stehen die Menschen zu fünf hintereinander. Freude, helle, ungetrübte Freude leuchtet aus ihren Augen. Besonders der Jugend ist diese Stunde

ein unvergeßliches Erlebnis.

Bei jedem Wechsel steht die den Fackelläufer begleitende Ehreneskorte des gleichen Sportvereins stramm, die Hände zum Gruß erhoben. Die Polizei versucht verzweifelt, der begeisterten Masse Herr zu werden, aber die Wogen schl[a]gen zu hoch.

Aus den Fenstern gegenüber dem Flugplatz und in der Belle-Alliance-Straße hängt alles voll Menschen, Fahnen und Menschen, und über allem die Freude, daß das Feuer glücklich den Weg nach Deutschland gefunden hat.

Mit jeder Straßenecke, die wir in unserem „V. B."-Wagen direkt hinter den Läufern kreuzen, nimmt das Gedränge zu. Tausende von Händen winken uns zu; besonderen Beifall erhalten die dahinter mitfahrenden Griechen, die vom Verdeck des Omnibusses ihre blau-weiße Fahne und das Hakenkreuz weithin sichtbar schwingen. Vor Rührung und überschäumendem Mitgehen mit dem Empfang der Berliner Bevölkerung rannen den Athenern die Freudentränen herunter, und wenn auch vollkommen heiser, erwiderten sie ständig die Heilrufe der Zehntausende. Vom Halleschen Tor führte der Weg durch die Wilhelmstraße. Oben über uns Girlanden von einer Straßenseite zur anderen, und die von völliger Windstille herunterhängenden Hakenkreuzfahnen bilden zu der links und rechts von unserer Fahrtstraße stehenden Jugend einen gewissen Kontrast. Es geht an unserem Verlagsgebäude, am Luftfahrtministerium vorbei. Die Leipziger Straße liegt hinter uns. Und jetzt kommt

der Staffelwechsel vor der geschmückten Reichskanzlei.

Hier ist alles schwarz. Vom Propagandaministerium bis über den Kaiserhof zur Mauerstraße steht ein einziges Meer von wogenden Köpfen.

Wir sind Unter den Linden. Nur fünf Wochen war ich weg. — Ich kenne die Reichshauptstadt nicht wieder. Ein Flaggenmeer, ein Fahnenwald, kein Mensch auf der breiten Promenade, die junge, zartgrüne Linden zieren. Aber auf den Bürgersteigen stehen sie, 20, 30, 40 Glieder tief schon seit Stunden. Endlich wird ihr Warten belohnt. **Der Läufer mit der leuchtenden Fackel erscheint. Flankiert von je fünf Leichtathleten der vielen Sportklubs, die alle auf der Berliner Strecke eingesetzt wurden. Das Tempo ist scharf,** unter vier Minuten. Schwer atmen die Läufer, aber flüssig ist ihr Schritt. Immer näher kommen wir zum Ehrenmal des Unbekannten Soldaten. Mit scharfer Linksschwenkung ziehen nun die Läufer vor das Ehrenmal.

Der Läufer mit dem olympischen Feuer senkt für eine Minute die Fackel vor dem Ehrenmal,

weiter geht der Lauf hinauf zum Lustgarten, wo auf hohem Sockel der Altar aufgebaut war. Nachdem die Flamme des Altars entzündet war, marschierten die Olympia-Kämpfer auf, stürmisch begrüßt und umjubelt von Zehntausenden, die links und rechts der Straße sich aufgestellt hatten.

Und nun ging die Fackel vom Lustgarten unter dem Jubel der ganzen Bevölkerung Berlins über den Großen Stern, Das Knie, die Heerstraße entlang hinaus zum Reichssportfeld, wo pünktlich um 16 Uhr der Führer erschien.

Empfang beim Führer

Deutschland nimmt die Ausgrabungen in Olympia wieder auf

Vor der Eröffnung der Olympischen Spiele empfing der Führer und Reichskanzler in seinem Hause heute mittag die Mitglieder des Internationalen Olympischen Komitees, an ihrer Spitze den Präsidenten desselben, Graf de Baillet-Latour, sowie die Vorstandsmitglieder des Deutschen Organisationskomitees für die XI. Olympiade Berlin 1936 unter Führung seines Präsidenten, Staatssekretär Lewald. Der Präsident des Internationalen Komitees, Graf de Baillet-Latour richtete hierbei an den Führer und Reichskanzler eine Ansprache, die in der Übersetzung wie folgt lautet:

„Herr Reichskanzler!

Das Internationale Olympische Komitee betrachtet es als eine große Auszeichnung, von Eurer Exzellenz am Tage der Eröffnung der Olympischen Spiele empfangen zu werden und so die Möglichkeit zu haben, Ihnen seine tiefe Dankbarkeit für das Interesse auszudrücken, daß Sie der Olympischen Idee bezeugt haben.

Das Stadion und die verschiedenen sportlichen Einrichtungen, die Deutschland dank der unbegrenzten Hochherzigkeit Eurer Exzellenz erbauen konnte, sind mit allen modernen Bequemlichkeiten ausgestattet und erinnern in ihrer Pracht an das Kolosseum in Rom und die Kampfstätten in Olympia.

Das Dorf, in dem die Jugend von 53 Nationen beherbergt wird, ist in einer Art geschaffen, die gleichzeitig die Behaglichkeit eines Heimes mit den Vorzügen eines Klubs vereint.

Sie, Herr Reichskanzler, haben, überzeugt von dem glücklichen Einfluß, den diese Spiele ausüben, um zwischen den Völkern der Erde den Geist des Verständnisses und der Eintracht zu erwecken, nichts unterlassen, um die Anstrengungen des Organisationskomitees zu unterstützen, dessen Präsident unser lieber Kollege Lewald ist.

Die Vorbereitungen hierfür liegen weit zurück; denn Deutschland betreibt seit langem nach einem methodischen Plan

die Organisation der Leibesübungen,

die nunmehr zu einem festen Bau zusammengefügt sind. Besonders in den letzten drei Jahren haben sie den größten Aufschwung genommen unter der Führung des Deutschen Olympischen Komitees mit seinem Präsidenten Herrn von Tschammer und Osten, den ich zu seiner großen Aktivität beglückwünsche, ebenso wie ich Deutschland zu dem Erfolg beglückwünsche, den es in der körperlichen Erziehung erreicht hat.

Die verschiedenen Städte besitzen Stadien, Sportfelder und Schwimmbecken, wofür die Reichshochschule für Leibesübungen in Berlin seit zehn Jahren eine große Zahl ausgebildeter Lehrer stellt. Diese Musteranstalt ist in dankbarer Anerkennung ihrer glänzenden Vorführungen bei den IX. Olympischen Spielen in Amsterdam mit dem olympischen Pokal von 1929 ausgezeichnet worden.

Und zur selben Zeit, als diese Lehrer sich mit der körperlichen Ertüchtigung ihrer Schüler befaßten, bemühten sich die Jünger Olympias, in die Herzen der Jugend die olympische Idee einzupflanzen. Jahre sind vergangen; heute sind nicht nur die Sportsleute von ihr durchdrungen, sondern sogar das ganze Volk. Der Empfang, den dieses Volk seinen Gästen erwiesen hat, beweist, daß ein- und derselbe Gedanke die sportliche Gemeinschaft der Völker unter dem Zeichen der Fahne mit den fünf Ringen vereint.

Ich bin sicher, daß die gewaltige Anstrengung, die Deutschland zugunsten der Olympischen Spiele gemacht hat und die in der Organisation dieser Wettkämpfe so edel zum Ausdruck kommt, ein unvergängliches Zeugnis des Beitrages sein wird, den Deutschland für die Kultur der Menschheit geleistet hat. Alle diejenigen, die in sich die heilige Flamme fühlen, die von Olympia nach Berlin getragen wurde, hegen auch Ihnen, Herr Reichskanzler, gegenüber die tiefste Dankbarkeit dafür, daß Sie nicht nur die Vergangenheit mit der Gegenwart verbunden, sondern daß Sie auch zur Förderung der Olympischen Idee in der Zukunft beigetragen haben.

Antwort des Führers

Der Führer und Reichskanzler antwortete ihm mit folgenden Worten:

Verehrter Herr Präsident, meine Herren vom Internationalen Olympischen Komitee und vom Organisationskomitee!

Es ist mir eine Freude, Sie am Tage der Eröffnung der Olympischen Spiele persönlich und im Namen des deutschen Volkes willkommen zu heißen und Ihnen, verehrter Herr Präsident, für die freundlichen Worte, die Sie an mich richteten, danken zu können.

Mein Dank gilt dem Internationalen Olympischen Komitee dafür, daß es die Feier der XI. Olympiade neuer Zeitrechnung in die Hauptstadt des Deutschen Reiches gelegt und Deutschland dadurch Gelegenheit gegeben hat, einen Beitrag zum ewigen Gedenken der Olympischen Spiele zu leisten. Deutschland hat sich gern und freudig der Aufgabe unterzogen, die diesjährigen Wettkämpfe vorzubereiten in einer Form, die der großen Idee und den Traditionen der Olympischen Spiele gerecht zu werden versucht, und es hofft, damit zur Stärkung des völkerverbindenden Ideals beizutragen, das diesen Kampfspielen zugrundeliegt.

Ihnen, meine Herren des Deutschen Organisationskomitees, danke ich für die hingebende und sorgfältige Arbeit, die Sie in der Vorbereitung der Spiele geleistet haben. Der Erfolg wird, so hoffe ich zuversichtlich, Ihre Mühen lohnen.

Die Grundgedanken, die in den Olympischen Spielen erneut vor die Weltöffentlichkeit treten, sind ältesten Ursprungs. Sie gehen aus von jener Kultstätte, wo mehr als ein Jahrtausend lang die Spiele als Ausdruck religiösen Empfindens und als Zeugen des Kraftbewußtseins des griechischen Volkes gefeiert wurden. Diese ehrwürdige Stätte ist in den Jahren 1875/81 gemäß den damals mit der griechischen Regierung abgeschlossenen Verträgen durch deutsche Gelehrte ausgegraben worden; dadurch erhielt die Welt ein genaueres Bild vom Kampfplatz dieses nationalen Heiligtums der Hellenen sowie von der Art und der Durchführung der Spiele. Die Ausgrabung wurde damals nicht ganz zu Ende geführt.

Ich habe mich nun entschlossen, zur bleibenden Erinnerung an die Feier der XI. Olympiade 1936 zu Berlin die im Jahre 1875 begonnenen Ausgrabungen der olympischen Fest- und Sportstätten wieder aufzunehmen und zu Ende zu führen. Ich danke der Königlich griechischen Regierung, daß sie ihre freudige Zustimmung zu diesem Werk erklärt hat.

Es wird dadurch eine geweihte Stätte alter Kultur der heutigen Menschheit zurückgegeben werden.

Ich hoffe, daß dies mithilft, für alle Zeiten die Erinnerung wach zu halten an die Feier der Olympischen Spiele des Jahres 1936. Daß diese glücklich gelingen, ist mein und unser aller aufrichtigster Wunsch!

Hierauf begrüßte der Führer und Reichskanzler die einzelnen Herren des Internationalen Olympischen Komitees sowie des Organisationskomitees.

Im Anschluß an den feierlichen Empfang der Mitglieder des Internationalen Olympischen Komitees und des Organisationskomitees gab der Führer und Reichskanzler zu Ehren des Olympischen Komitees ein Frühstück, an dem sämtliche Reichsminister, Reichsstatthalter und die Chefs der Länderregierungen sowie eine Anzahl anderer Ehrengäste teilnahmen.

Ein Meer des Jubels

Während des Empfanges beim Führer wächst die Menschenmenge auf dem Wilhelmsplatz immer weiter an. Die ganze Wilhelmstraße entlang bis Unter den Linden sind die Männer der 3. SS.-Motorstandarte zum Spalier angetreten. Erwartungsfroh, aber nicht ungeduldig steht die Menge. Jeder weiß, daß die Abfahrt des Führers und der Mitglieder des Internationalen Olympia-Komitees und der Ehrengäste für 15 Uhr festgesetzt ist.

Motorgedröhn in der Luft verkündet das Nahen unseres stolzen Luftschiffes „Hindenburg" an. Laute Heilrufe brausen ihm entgegen, als er majestätisch den Wilhelmsplatz kreuzt.

Der feierliche Empfang beim Führer ist beendet. Die Gäste verlassen das Palais, als einer der ersten der Stellvertreter des Führers, Rudolf Heß. Jeder einzelne wird von der Menschenmenge begeistert begrüßt. Vor allem die Mitglieder des Olympischen Komitees, die immer und immer wieder danken. Die Freude über die eben erlebte Stunde steht noch allen auf den Gesichtern, teilt sich der wartenden Menge mit und pflanzt sich fort, die beiden Menschenmauern entlang, die rechts und links der via triumphalis eine Mauer bilden, die von Erwartung, von Freude, von Jubel gebaut ist.

*

Wenige Minuten vor 15 Uhr fährt im ersten Wagen der Stellvertreter des Führers, **Reichsminister Rudolf Heß,** stürmisch umjubelt, die Wilhelmstraße hinauf. Und nun folgt in rascher Folge Wagen auf Wagen mit den Spitzen der Partei und des Staates. Dr. Ley, Reichsjustizminister Dr. Gürtner, Reichswirtschaftsminister Dr Schacht, Staatssekretär und Reichsarbeitsführer Hierl, Reichsleiter Rosenberg, Reichsjugendführer Baldur von Schirach, Reichsminister Rust, der Reichsschatzmeister der NSDAP. Schwarz, Korpsführer Hühnlein. Aus dem Portal der Reichskanzlei tritt dann Dr. Goebbels. Und jubelnd grüßen die Berliner „ihren Doktor", der von Reichsleiter Amann begleitet ist. Dem Reichsaußenminister Freiherr von Neurath folgt dann eine Beiwagenmaschine, flankiert von zwei Krafträdern des NSKK. mit dem Stander des Internationalen Olympischen Komitees. In Schmuck ihrer goldenen Olympia-Ketten fahren die Mitglieder des Komitees ab, während wieder die Spitze des „Hindenburg" über den Dächern auftaucht. Den Schluß dieser Wagenkolonne bildet das Auto, in dem der Präsident des Internationalen Komitees, Graf Baillet-Latour, mit dem Präsidenten des Deutschen Olympischen Organisationskomitees, Exz. Dr. Lewald, Platz genommen hat. Die Heilrufe pflanzen sich wellengleich mit den fahrenden Wagen fort.

Und dann — nach kurzer Pause — verläßt der Wagen Adolf Hitlers die Toreinfahrt.

Tosender Jubel braust ihm entgegen, hell wirbeln die Trommeln, und jeder der Tausende sucht einen Blick des Führers zu erhaschen, der im Wagen steht und lachenden Gesichts nach allen Seiten grüßt. In seinem Wagen haben neben Obergruppenführer Brückner Brigadeführer Schaub und Hauptmann Wiedemann, die Adjutanten der Wehrmacht, beim Führer, Oberstleutnant Hoßbach, Korvettenkapitän v. Puttkammer und Hauptmann Mantius Platz genommen.

Die Straße, auf der der Führer fährt, gibt ein Bild, wie es selten und nur einzig so großartig erlebt worden ist. Der Himmel hat sich bezogen, der Blick nach rückwärts zeigt den wuchtigen Bau des Berliner Rathausturmes, hell von dem graublauen Himmel, die Standarten längs den Straßen aufgerichtet sind. Der helle Schmuck der Gebäude und die frische Farbe des Grüns sind von jenem Zusammenklang der Farben, der die Erwartung steigert und die Herzen froher macht. Als sich kurz nach 3 Uhr die lange Wagenkolonne der Gäste in Bewegung setzt, löst sich die Spannung, die langgehemmte Erwartung macht sich Luft in jubelnden Zurufen.

Voran die Spitze der Kolonne durch das Brandenburger Tor. Majestätisch wölbt sich das farbenfrohe Band der Straße vor uns, majestätisch ist dieser ganze Tag, den wir erleben. Überall, wo der Führer erscheint, kennt Begeisterung keine Grenzen. Wir sahen Menschen, die auf ihren Leitern mühsam das Gleichgewicht wahrend, winkten und jubelten, wir sahen Männer, die immer und immer wieder ihre Kinder hochhoben. Fenster an Fenster war besetzt, die ganze 10 Kilometer lange Strecke vom Wilhelmsplatz bis zum Reichssportfeld war ein Meer des Jubels, dessen Brandung immer wieder zu dem einen Ruf anschwoll: der Führer, der Führer.

Amerikanische Turnerinnen am Barren mit ungleichen Holmen

As part of the opening ceremonies the words of the Olympic oath were displayed on the stadium scoreboard where the results of the events would be announced. BA

The fireworks show the night of the opening ceremonies. NA, GRIO

1936
OLYMPICS

Track and Field

Track and Field Championships

Men

The United States continued its forty-year dominance of the Olympic Track and Field Championships at Berlin by registering seven track victories and five field championships, including the decathlon. In retaining its proud record as the foremost nation in men's track and field athletics, the America team of sixty-six men scored a total of 203 points. The final standing of the first ten nations would be as follows if points had been awarded on the basis of ten for first, and five, four, three, two, one for the next five places respectively:

1. United States, 203
2. Finland, 80¼
3. Germany, 69¾
4. Japan, $51\frac{13}{22}$
5. Great Britain, $43\frac{1}{11}$
6. Canada, $22\frac{1}{11}$
7. Italy, $20\frac{13}{22}$
8. Sweden, $18\frac{1}{11}$
9. Holland, 12
10. New Zealand, 10

The competitions at Berlin were extremely keen with 893 athletes from 42 nations entered. This is three times the number that entered the games at Los Angeles, necessitating many tiring preliminary heats.

Olympic records were equalled or bettered in sixteen of the twenty-three events on the program.

Women

Germany established itself as the foremost nation of the world in Women's Athletics when it scored 51½ points to 22⅓ points for the United States. Poland, Italy and Hungary all finished ahead of Great Britain and Canada, nations formerly very strong in the realm of Women's Athletics.

The German women gained at least one medal in every event but one, the single exception occurred in the final of the 400-meter relay when Dorffeldt dropped the baton on the last change.

Olympic records were bettered in five of the six events comprising the women's program which was inaugurated at the Amsterdam Games in 1928. The existing world record was bettered in the 100-meter run, discus throw, 400-meter relay and equalled in the 80-meter hurdles event. The only event that failed to produce a new record was the running high jump in which three women managed to clear 5 ft. 3 in. to tie for first place. In the jump-off, Csak of Hungary cleared 5 ft. 3¾ in. to take the Olympic title.

Helen Stephens, an 18-year-old, was the outstanding performer in this division of the games. Her Olympic and world record of 11.5 seconds bettered by more than half a second the time in which T. E. Burke won the Olympic 100-meter championship for men in the 1896 games at Athens. She was mainly responsible for America's victory in the 400-meter relay in which the German team suffered the misfortune of dropping the baton on the last leg while enjoying a 10-yard lead.

Lawson Robertson was the head coach of the 1924, 1928, 1932 and 1936 Olympic track teams and an Olympian in his own right.

He was born in Scotland in 1883, but soon came to the United States. In 1904 he won the AAU 100-yard race as a member of the Irish-American Athletic Club. He became its coach in 1909 and remained with the club until 1916. At that time he was hired as a track coach at the University of Pennsylvania and remained at the school until 1947.

In the 1904 Olympics he won a bronze in the standing high jump and in the 1906 Intercalated Games in Athens he won silver in the standing high jump and bronze in the standing long jump.

Except for service in World War I, he stayed at Penn his entire career. He was also assistant track coach at the 1912 and 1920 Olympics. His string of Olympic coaching years may never be broken.

Robertson died in 1951.

Dean Cromwell and the University of Southern California Track Stars

The University of Southern California has dominated the NCAA Men's Track and Field Championships since 1926, when coach Dean Cromwell brought the first trophy to the school.

Cromwell, who was the assistant track and field coach for the 1936 American team, started his career at USC in 1909. When he ended his career in 1948, he led the school to 12 NCAA championships, including 34 NCAA individual champions. He was selected as the head coach of the U.S. Olympic team in 1948.

From 1935–43, USC experienced a streak of unequalled track and field success. Nicknamed the "Maker of Champions," his trackmen at the Berlin games scored enough points (37½) to have finished among the top five in the world.

USC's 1936 competitors included Frank Wykoff, 100 meters and sprint relay; Foy Draper, sprint relay; Hal Smallwood, 400 meters; Al Fitch, 1,600-meter relay; Roy Staley, high hurdles; Bill Graber, pole vault; Earle Meadows, pole vault; Bill Sefton, pole vault; Delos Thurber, high jump; Ken Carpenter, discus; and Louis Zamperini, 5,000 meters.

Cromwell's influence extended far beyond the USC campus to the corners of the world. He personally tutored champions in every Olympic Games from 1912 to 1948. The dean of USC's track and field teams for 39 years died in 1962.

The Track and Field Coaches and Managers

Brutus Hamilton was an assistant coach for the track and field team. He was a former Olympian, winning silver in the 1920 decathlon. He also competed in the pentathlon in 1920 and 1924 but won no medals. He was the track coach at the University of California Berkeley from 1932 to 1965, winning six NCAA championships.

In 1950 he was voted Missouri's Greatest Amateur Athlete, as he was a native of the state and graduate of the University of Missouri. He died in 1970 at age 70.

The other assistant coach for the 1936 Olympics was Earle C. Hayes of Indiana University.

William J. Bingham of Cambridge was named manager with T. Nelson Metcalf of Chicago, Alfred R. Masters of Palo Alto and Edwin E. Schaefer of Buffalo as assistant managers.

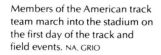

Members of the American track team march into the stadium on the first day of the track and field events. NA, GRIO

Jesse Owens

The 1936 Berlin Olympics has often been referred to as the Jesse Owens Olympics. Certainly no one else has been more associated with the events in Berlin.

Born in Alabama in 1913, Owens was the second youngest of 11 children of a sharecropper. The family moved to Cleveland, Ohio, when Owens was nine. His track career started at East Tech High School and flourished at Ohio State University where he won several AAU and NCAA championships.

His greatest achievement before the 1936 Olympics came in Ann Arbor, Michigan, on May 25, 1935, when in one hour he set five world records and equalled another. He tied the 100-yard dash record in 9.4 seconds. Ten minutes later he set a long jump record at 26′8¼″. Ten minutes later he set the 220-yard record at 20.3 seconds and fifteen minutes later he ran 22.6 seconds for the 220-yard hurdles. He also set records in the 200-meters and 200-yard low hurdles.

After this feat he would be the dominant runner in world track meets leading up to the Berlin games.

At Berlin he lived up to expectations and captured four gold medals. He won the 100 meters and 200 meters races, setting a new world record of 20.7 around a turn. He also set an Olympic record in winning the long jump and ran a leg of the 4×100-meter relay in which his team set a world record. He and his other black teammates made a mockery of the Nazis' Aryan supremacy theory. The Germans termed the black athletes "America's Black Auxiliaries."

After the Olympics Owens appeared in some post-game races in Europe but left early to return to the United States to exploit his fame by reaping some monetary benefit for himself. As a consequence the AAU barred him from future competition as an amateur athlete.

He was named the Associated Press' athlete of the year, the first track star and second black (Joe Lewis was the first) to be so honored. He beat out baseball greats Carl Hubbell, Joe DeMaggio, Dizzy Dean, boxer Joe Lewis and track stars Glenn Morris and Forrest "Spec" Towns. However Owens was bypassed in both 1935 and 1936 for the prestigious Sullivan Award given to the best amateur athlete in the United States.

At age 23, with the Olympics behind him, he turned professional but financial rewards eluded him and he experienced racial discrimination, prevalent at the time. He tried many ventures and even went back to Ohio State, but failed to obtain a degree. All the hype from being a famous athlete soon evaporated and the many big-money schemes he was approached with never materi-

Owens worked at Ohio State cleaning tables and operating an elevator in order to pay his college expenses. In 1935 he got a job running errands in the Ohio State Senate. "Tippy" Dye is the other page boy shown. OSU

Ohio State track coach Larry Snyder is shown with his greatest star, Jesse Owens. Snyder was himself a former track star at Ohio State. He accompanied Owens to Berlin and was the head coach for the United States track team at the 1960 Rome Olympics. OSU

alized. He even worked for Alf Landon's presidential campaign against Franklin D. Roosevelt.

In January 1942 he became director of a national fitness program for blacks in the Office of Civilian Defense and in April 1943 he became an assistant personnel director for black workers at the Ford Motor Company.

During World War II he raced 100-meter dash gold medalist Helen Stephens several times at baseball games and once even raced against horses in Cuba. He ran his last race in September 1950 at Milwaukee, hitting 9.7 seconds in the 100-yard dash.

In the late 1940s he was on the road with the Harlem Globetrotters, who at that time played baseball not basketball. He also started a wholesale athletic business in Detroit, but it failed. In 1949 he moved to Chicago to do public relations work for a clothing company. He also worked for the Illinois State Athletic Commission.

Eventually his PR firm prospered and Owens became an adept public speaker. He became a member of the U.S. Olympic Committee and was awarded the Presidential Medal of Freedom in 1976.

Owens' granddaughter Gina Hemphill carried the Olympic torch into Los Angeles stadium for the 1984 Olympics. It was at those games that Carl Lewis won four gold medals in Owens' events, surpassing all his records. At the 1988 Olympics in Seoul Lewis won three gold medals and took a silver in the 200-meter dash, thus missing by a few hundredths of a second the opportunity to repeat Owens' achievement a second time.

Owens' long jump record lasted 25 years and his last record fell in 1975, 40 years after he set the indoor 60-meter dash record at 6.6 seconds in Madison Square Garden.

Owens, a heavy cigarette smoker, died of lung cancer on March 31, 1980, at Tucson, Arizona. His wife, Ruth, still resides there.

The Jesse Owens Memorial Foundation, Inc., was established by a group of friends and family members following his death. The foundation was started as an Illinois not-for-profit corporation in April 1980 to provide a special conduit through which Jesse Owens' many friends around the world may perpetuate his memory and spirit, encourage individual excellence, assist underprivileged youth and foster national and international sports competition.

Owens' widow, Ruth Solomon Owens, serves as chairwoman of the foundation's board of directors.

Owens at the start of the 200-meter dash in which he took a gold medal.

The winners of the 100-meter dash. Jesse Owens took first, Ralph Metcalfe took second and M. B. Osendarp of Holland took third. NA, HH-242-HD-0171a-1

Sportswriter Grantland Rice said of Owens' record-breaking broad jump, "He seemed to be jumping clear out of Germany."
OSU

Luz Long of Germany jumped 25'9-27/32" for second place in the long jump. Owens jumped 26'5-5/16".

Jesse Owens, right, and a teammate read congratulatory letters.
NA, HH 242-HD-0174a-3

The Owens Snub

A myth has grown through the years that Hitler, who had no love whatsoever for blacks or for that matter any non-Ayran, refused to meet Owens after his 100-meter win. Actually Hitler had been congratulating winners of several events on August 2, but left at dark with threatening rain. Thus he was not on hand to meet the two winners of the high jump—both black Americans. The IOC officials suggested to Hitler that he congratulate all winners or none at all. He decided to meet the German victors in private only, not publicly. Thus when Owens won the 100 meters on August 3, Hitler did not meet him nor any other winners after that.

Owens was actually snubbed by the president of his own country. Roosevelt did not send him congratulations or even invite him to Washington, D.C.

Owens got accolades for his outstanding athletic achievements wherever he went. His unusual hat perhaps was given to him or traded by one of his fellow athletes in the Olympic village.
NA, HH 242-HD-219-7M

Owens signs autographs at the Olympic Village. He is displaying his three gold medals and the oak trees awarded gold medal winners. This photo was apparently taken before August 9 when he won his fourth gold medal on a leg of the 4×100-meter relay team. NA, HH 242-HD-219

After Berlin, Owens would never go unrecognized again. Here he responds to eager English schoolboys in London, just before returning to the United States. OSU

Jesse Owens and Mack Robinson, at the Olympic Village, celebrate their one-two finish in the 200-meter dash. NA, HH-242-HD-174a3

Smartly dressed in the only suit he owned at the time, Owens boarded a train for his hometown of Cleveland and an enthusiastic welcome. OSU

Columbus, Ohio, gave Owens a victory parade after his return from Europe. He shares the car with OSU track coach Larry Snyder. OSU

Basking in the glow of Olympic fame, Ruth and Jesse Owens attended the 1936 Ohio State University homecoming football game as the honored guests of the president of the university, Dr. George W. Rightmire. Owens' smart new outfit came from the $10,000 he received to stump for presidential hopeful Alf Landon. OSU

Owens returned to Ohio State University in 1940-41 in a futile attempt to earn his college degree. To pay his tuition, he assisted track coach Larry Snyder. OSU

1936: Golden Moment of Triumph

The Saturday Evening Post, January/February 1976

Editor's Note: In the Olympic Games of 1936, held in Berlin, a superb American athlete by the name of Jesse Owens won four gold medals. He won his first two medals with astonishing performances in the 100- and 200-meter sprints, setting new records in both. His leap in the broad jump won him a third medal, once again for a record, 26 feet 5⁵⁄₁₆ inches. And finally Jesse ran in the 400-meter relay to help set another world record and to win a fourth gold medal for the United States. As a mere boy in junior high school in Cleveland, Jesse had run the hundred yards in ten seconds flat, a phenomenal feat. That was the beginning of fame for a youngster born in 1913 on a tenant farm in northern Alabama, one of seven children who worked with their parents in the cotton fields. This splendid man who was a great-grandson of slaves, who was called by Dr. Paul [Joseph] Goebbels, the Nazi propagandist leader, a "black American auxiliary," has made everyone in America proud of his lifetime contributions as a citizen. Goebbels had to eat those words that day in '36 as Jesse swept the field time after time, and in due time was selected by sportswriters' polls as the world's "top track performer since 1900."

Jesse's fame has not dimmed through the years, as he has continued to represent the character of American athletic competition as an inspiration to youngsters, and an image of integrity which has never wavered since the days of his track triumphs. Arthur Daley once commented that "Owens was so matchless in his sheer grace and speed that his like may never be seen again." Today, Jesse Owens is scarcely a pound heavier than in his running years. Trim, erect, square-shouldered, he walks on those marvelous legs, still, like some relaxed panther ready to burst into galvanizing energy at a moment's notice. His own story of his Olympic victories tells you much about the kind of man he is.

SINCE I WAS thirteen years old, it was my dream that I might someday participate in the Olympics. It all came about simply because our junior high school coach, Charles Riley, who happened to develop quite a lot of good runners for this country, brought to our school, Fairmount Junior High School in Cleveland, Ohio, a man who at that time was known as the "World's Fastest Human Being," Charles Paddock, the great United States sprinter famous for his leaping lunge at the finish of every race.

Charlie Paddock had just returned from the 1920 Olympics in Amsterdam, Holland and he was a very nice man who settled down and just told us kids all about it. When Charlie Paddock was through talking to us, the coach came down to where I had been sitting in the front row in an end seat in the auditorium and he whispered in my ear that since there were a lot of youngsters who might want to get Charlie Paddock's autograph, perhaps I could take the problem in charge and help them line up. I did this and as a reward after the last of my schoolmates got the great man's autograph, I was invited into the coach's office to meet the famous runner. I can remember facing this great athlete as he sat on the coach's desk with one leg hanging down, and he and the coach seemed to be in such deep conversation that I was afraid I was interrupting them. But they didn't seem to mind my standing around and the great Paddock shook my hand as he left. Afterward the coach asked me, "Well, what do you think about him?" And I said, "Well, gee, coach, I sure would like to be known as the 'World's Fastest Human Being' someday." So, then, Charles Riley told me something I have never forgotten. "Everybody should have a dream," he said. "Every man must remember that dreams are high and that you must climb a ladder to reach them. Each rung of that ladder has a meaning of its own as you climb. The first rung of that ladder, of course, goes back to one important point—just how dedicated are you? How much of what you have are you willing to give to the dream? And the next rung of the ladder is your determination to train yourself to reach the dream at the top. And the third rung of that ladder is the self-discipline that you must display in order to accomplish all this. The fourth rung, which is one of the most important rungs in that ladder to your dream, is the kind of attitude you have in going about all this. By this I mean, are you capable of giving every moment that you possibly can to making this dream come true and of throwing your whole heart and soul into the effort?"

I remembered that moment nine years later when I stood at the starting line of the 100-meter race in the Olympic Stadium in Berlin, waiting to run against the finest competitors that the world had to offer. I looked down that field to the finish 109 yards and 2 feet away and then began to think in terms of what it had taken for me to get there, the number of people who had counseled and coached me; and the people who believed in me—the community from which I had come and the school which I attended. And as I looked down at the uniform of the country that I represented and realized that after all I was just a man like any other man, I felt suddenly as if my legs could not carry even the weight of my body. My stomach said that it wasn't there. My mouth was dry as cotton; the palms of my hands wet with perspiration. And as we stood there, unnoticed—unnoticed because a German boy had won an Olympic victory in another part of the stadium, and the crowd was giving him an ovation that was due an Olympic champion—this was the sight that I saw within that wonderful arena. As my eyes wandered across the field, I noticed the green grass—the red track with the white line. A hundred-and-odd thousand people crowded into the stands. And as my eyes looked upward, I noticed the flags of every nation represented there at the Olympic Games underneath that German blue sky. Now, my attention was diverted from that beautiful picture, because the whistle had been blown and we were to assemble around the starter to receive our final instructions for this historic event. After our instructions had been given every man went to his mark and adjusted hands and feet. Every muscle in his body was strained. And suddenly the gun went off. The athletes ran neck and neck for some yards, but our Ralph Metcalfe of Marquette University led the field at the fifty-yard mark. From then, the seventy to the ninety, Ralph and I ran neck and neck. And then for some unknown reason I cannot yet fathom, I beat Ralph, who was such a magnificent runner.

The greatest moment of all, of course, was when we knelt and received the Wreath of Victory and standing there facing the stands we could hear the strains of the "Star Spangled Banner" rise into the air and the Stars and Stripes was hoisted to the skies. It was then that I realized the immensity of my ambition of nine years to become a member of Uncle Sam's Olympic Team and to emerge as a victor in the Olympic Games. Yes, this was the moment I had worked for all those years. And let me say that as you stand there and watch your flag rise above all others because of your own efforts and you can say to yourself today, "I am an Olympic champion, there cannot be a greater thrill."

But we have to remember that more than victory itself, the Olympic Games teach us a sportsmanship that transcends all prejudices and national and racial lines. That year was a very difficult year because Hitler had declared the dominance of the German Aryan race and we had the impudence to come over and prove him wrong in so many cases. But there was one incident that happened in those Olympic Games which I shall never forget and which represents to me an example of how friendship and sportsmanship can transcend all obstacles when given the opportunity. The broad jump was an event that I was supposed to win with some ease because in the past I had failed only once to win first place in every track meet in which I had participated in my entire athletic career. But on this day something was going wrong. I couldn't imagine what was happening to spoil my jumping technique, but I had jumped only 23 feet 6 inches as a qualification effort and apparently was about to be eliminated. But there happened to be a young German broad jumper, Luz Long, the greatest of them all in his own country, who was watching as I took my qualifying jumps. I had already fouled twice and it looked as though I might not even be able to survive the competition. But he came over and remeasured my steps, remeasured my takeoff mark, and he laid out my sweatshirt right next to the takeoff board as a marker to help my jump. Thanks to his suggestions and confidence in me, I was able to produce a leap which qualified and opened up the pathway to ultimate victory. Luz Long jumped 25 feet $9^{27}/_{32}$ inches for a new Olympic record. I managed 26 feet $5^{5}/_{16}$ inches and so won. Luz was second; but in my book of sportsmanship he ranks first.

You can imagine how touched I was at such sportsmanship. My friendship with Luz Long, which commenced so brightly on the field of competition, continued after the Games. We became great friends and we corresponded regularly. But during World War II, sometime during the invasion of Poland, the last living traces of Luz Long were obliterated in the holocaust.

In 1951 I returned to Germany and among a delegation which came to visit me at the hotel where I was staying, there were a woman and a boy who came up and introduced themselves to me. This boy was the son of my lost friend, Luz Long, and his name was Kai. Luz Long had been only twenty-two at the time of the Olympics and as the preparation for World War II rushed across Germany, it transpired that this little boy had seen his father only three times in his life. And so I began to correspond with Kai, and then we developed our own friendship that arose from the father's noble and self-sacrificing sportsmanship and generosity. Kai Long and I continue to correspond and whenever I hear from Luz's son, my mind goes back to that afternoon in the Olympic Stadium when an athlete sacrificed his fame and victory for the sake of pure sportsmanship. And then I know that the Olympic ideal is something that should be cherished and never forgotten.

In 1960 Owens crowned his daughter Marlene as Homecoming Queen at the halftime ceremonies of Ohio State University's homecoming game. Marlene is to the left and Owens' wife, Ruth, is to the right. OSU

Having failed to acquire a baccalaureate degree, Owens was awarded an honorary Doctorate of Athletic Arts degree from Ohio State University in 1972. OSU

Still going strong at age 65, Owens continued to laud the virtues of athletics, the Olympic Games and the American way of life. He is shown here in 1978 puffing on a pipe in order to cut down on cigarettes (he had smoked a pack daily for years). He died less than two years later of lung cancer. OSU

JAMES CLEVELAND
(JESSE) OWENS
1913 - 1980

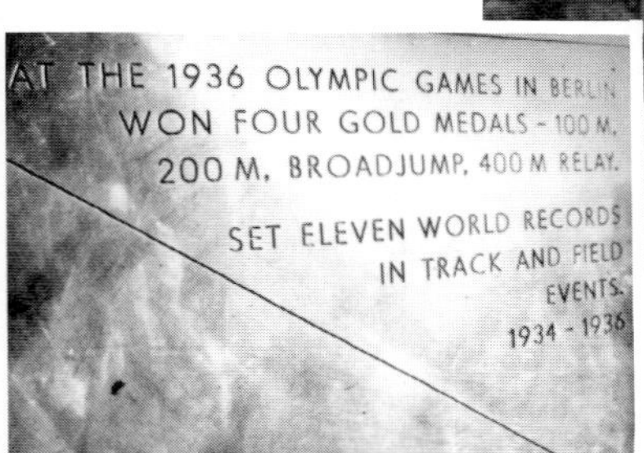
AT THE 1936 OLYMPIC GAMES IN BERLIN
WON FOUR GOLD MEDALS - 100 M.
200 M. BROADJUMP. 400 M RELAY.
SET ELEVEN WORLD RECORDS
IN TRACK AND FIELD
EVENTS
1934 - 1936

The Jesse Owens Plaza is located just north of the Ohio State University football stadium on Woody Hayes Drive. KEVIN FITZSIMMONS PHOTO

Cornelius Johnson was an 18-year-old high school student at the 1932 Olympics. He tied for first place in the high jump, but ended up in fourth place after the jump-off. At the 1936 trials he tied with Dave Albritton when both set a world record of 6', 9-3/4". Johnson took gold at Berlin with a jump of 6'8". He won or shared the AAU title five times. Johnson died young at age 33.

David Albritton, one of America's greatest high jumpers, was born in Alabama in 1913. His athletic career lasted from 1936 to 1951. He was second to Cornelius Johnson at Berlin, but won many AAU and NCAA championships representing Ohio State University. His best indoor jump was 6'8" in 1948 when he was 34 years old. He later went into politics in Ohio.

Kenneth Carpenter and **Gordon Dunn** finished first and second respectively in the discus throw at Berlin. Carpenter was born in 1913 and attended the University of Southern California. He won the NCAA and IC4A discus in 1935. At Berlin he overtook Gordon Dunn and Giorgio Oberwerger to win gold and in a later meet in Prague came within one inch of the world record.

Gordon Dunn was born in 1912 and attended Stanford University. In 1934 he won the NCAA and IC4A titles. He competed for the Olympic Club of San Francisco in 1936. He died in 1964.

Glenn Cunningham, the "Iron Man of Kansas," was born in Kansas in 1909. His leg was badly burned in a 1917 fire in which his brother died. Nevertheless, he developed into the major American mile runner of the 1930s. He won the NCAA 1,500-meter race in 1932 and took a fourth in the 1932 Olympics. In 1934 he set a world record in the mile at 4:06.7 and took a silver in the 1,500-meter race in Berlin. Two weeks later in Stockholm he set a world record in the 800-meter race at 1:49.7. He ran his fastest 1,500 in 1940 at 3:48.0. Cunningham obtained degrees from several universities and spent his life working with needy and abused children.

Earle Meadows setting a new Olympic record of 14'3¼".

John Woodruff was the outstanding American middle-distance runner. He won gold in the 800-meter race with the slowest Olympic time since 1920. He was supreme in collegiate competition at the University of Pittsburgh in the 440 and 880. He was a career army officer.

Archie Williams was a virtual unknown in track when he set a new world record in the 400 meters in the NCAA championships. At Berlin he won the gold by inches over Britain's Godfrey Brown. Williams was a graduate of the University of California, Berkeley, and was a school teacher in Marin County, California, for years. BA

Kitei Son won the gold medal in the marathon with a time of two hours, 29 minutes and 19.2 seconds. Son was a Korean but had to compete under the Japanese flag since Korea had been annexed by Japan in 1910. He was an ardent nationalist who deeply resented the country he represented. In 1986 the IOC officially changed the Olympic record, as a tribute to Son, to his Korean name, Sohn Kee-chung, and the gold medal was reallocated from Japan to Korea. Two years later at the Seoul Olympics Kee-chung carried the Olympic flame into the stadium in the opening ceremony.

Foy Draper was born in Texas in 1913 and attended high school in Los Angeles. He ran a 9.6 second 100-yard dash in high school and later ran track for the University of Southern California. He was also a champion runner in the 220-yard dash and ran the third leg of the 4×100-meter relay at Berlin, giving him his gold medal. He was killed in action in North Africa in 1943.

Ralph Metcalfe was one of the great track stars of the 1930s. He was born in 1910 in Atlanta, Georgia, and attended Marquette University in Milwaukee, Wisconsin, where he equalled the world record for the 100-meter dash eight times.

In 1932 he became the first runner to break 20 seconds in the 220-yard dash, but it was wind-assisted. At the 1932 Los Angeles games he just missed gold in the 200-meter dash when it was discovered that his lane was two meters longer than it should have been. He did win silver in the 100-meter dash.

Between the two Olympics of the 1930s he won many AAU and NCAA spring races. At Berlin he took a silver for the second time in the 100 meters and a gold as a leg of the 4×100-meter relay.

Metcalfe lived in Chicago most of his life, serving for a time on the city council. In 1970 he was elected to the U.S. House of Representatives from the 1st District of Illinois where he served until his death in 1978. He was also a member of the USOC board of directors for many years.

Forrest "Spec" Towns participated in both football and track in high school in Georgia and won a track scholarship to the University of Georgia. He trained to be a hurdler in college and equalled the world record in the 110-meter hurdles in 1936.

At Berlin he won gold in the event and at a post-Olympic race in Oslo he set an unbelievable world record that lasted for 11 years. His fast time may be attributed to the fact he was upset that he had to race in Europe after the Olympics instead of going home to join the University of Georgia football team. He won AAU and NCAA races from 1936 through 1938.

Earle Meadows was one of the greatest bamboo pole vaulters in history. He was born in 1913 in Mississippi. He was another star athlete from the University of Southern California who tied for the 1935 AAU title and for the NCAA title in 1935 and 1936. He constantly battled his USC teammate Bill Sefton for the title and in 1937 they both vaulted 14′11″, just short of history's first 15-foot vault.

Meadows had a real duel with the Japanese vaulters at Berlin, lasting into the night. He finally took gold with a new Olympic record. He went on to glory and set an indoor world record in 1941. In 1948 he narrowly missed qualifying for the Olympics and so wasn't able to defend his gold medal at the London games.

Matthew "Mack" Robinson, came from an athletic family. His brother Jackie was the first black to play major league baseball joining the Brooklyn Dodgers in 1947.

Robinson was born in California in 1914. He attended Pasadena Junior College and later the University of Oregon. At Berlin he won a silver in the 200-meter race and in 1938 won the AAU 200-meter race and in 1938 won the AAU 200-meter race and the NCAA 220-yard race. He was a star in the sprints and the long jump.

He still lives in the Los Angeles area.

Glenn Morris. LC

Glenn Morris was born in Colorado in 1912. He graduated from Colorado State University in 1934. In April 1936 Morris broke the U.S. record in his first-ever decathlon competition at the Kansas Relays. At Berlin he took gold and set a world record. After the Olympics Morris was a radio announcer, had a brief career in the movies as Tarzan and played pro football in 1940. He was seriously wounded during World War II and led a rather rough life afterwards. Morris died in 1974.

Glenn Hardin was born in Mississippi in 1910. He was one of America's greatest hurdlers ever. He took silver in the 1932 400-meter hurdles and gold in 1936. His 1934 400-meter record stood for 19 years. He retired from competition after the Berlin games. His son Billy competed in the hurdles in the 1964 Olympics. Hardin died in 1975.

A new timing device was instituted for the games. A starting pistol was hooked up to a camera on the scaffold. This allowed very accurate results. NA, GRIO

Left to right: Cornelius Johnson, high jump; Jesse Owens, 100 meters, 200 meters and long jump; and Glenn Hardin, 400-meter hurdles, receive congratulations from their teammates at the Olympic village as the first three Americans to win gold medals. Back row, left to right: Marty Glickman, 4x100-meter relay; Gene Venzke, 1,500 meters; Albert J. Mangin, 5,000-meter walk; Foy Draper, 4x100-meter relay and Forrest G. Towns, 110-meter hurdles. AP

Jesse Owens winning the 100-meter dash. Ralph Metcalfe of the U.S. was second and M. B. Osendarp of Holland was third.

Four of the fastest sprinters in the world. From left: Frank Wykoff, USA; Paul Hänni, Switzerland; Ralph Metcalfe, USA; Jesse Owens, USA. BA

American decathlon champions. From left: Robert Clark, second; Glenn Morris, first; Jack Park, third.

The final heat of the 1,500-meter run. From left: Eric Ny, Sweden; Jack Lovelock, New Zealand; Glenn Cunningham, U.S.; Luigi Beccali, Italy; Phil Edwards, Canada; J. F. Cornes, Great Britain; Miklos Szabo, Hungary; Gene Venzke, U.S. Lovelock won the race and set a new world and Olympic record. Cunningham was second and Beccali third.

Members of the 4x400-meter relay team who came in second, just behind Great Britain. NA, HH-242-HD-0315

Members of the 4x100-meter relay set a new Olympic and world record of 39.8 seconds. Italy won the silver medal and Germany the bronze. From left: Jesse Owens, Ralph Metcalfe, Foy Draper and Frank Wykoff. Wykoff participated in the 1928, 1932 and 1936 relay teams, each winning the gold medal and establishing new world records. NA, HH 242-HD-276

Marty Glickman and Sam Stoller

There are few stories of the 1936 Olympics to match that of these two track stars. Marty Glickman was born in New York City in 1917. He was an all-around athlete in high school and at Syracuse University. He played professional football and basketball for one year in 1939. He also competed in all the major national and international track meets, both indoor and outdoor from 1935 to 1939. He was the captain of the Syracuse University track team from 1938–39.

Glickman was in the trials at Randall's Island in New York for a place on the 1936 Olympic track team. Jesse Owens, Ralph Metcalfe, Mack Robinson, Frank Wyckoff, Foy Draper and Sam Stoller, along with Glickman, competed in the 100-meter dash. Supposedly, the top three finishers would run the race in Berlin, the others would make up the 4×100-meter relay team. Glickman and Stoller made the relay team.

"Wyckoff, Draper of U.S.C., Sam and I," Glickman related, "had been passing the baton for the two weeks we had been in the Olympic Village. Sam was leadoff, I ran backstretch, Foy ran the turn and Frank ran the anchor leg.

"The morning of the day we were to run, Lawson Robertson, the head track coach, and Dean Cromwell, the assistant coach, called a meeting and told us that Sam and I, the only Jews on the track team, were being replaced by Owens and Metcalfe. The coaches said they heard a strong rumor that the Germans were hiding their best sprinters and saving them to upset the American team. We were stunned."

Owens protested but was told to "do as you're told." Glickman protested also and stated, "Sam and I are the only two Jews on the team. There's bound to be a lot of criticism back home."

And there was a huge controversy for a while. The Americans won the race, the Germans placed third.

In the history of the games no American track and field contestant failed to compete unless he was ill or injured, except for Glickman and Stoller. There have been many questions as to exactly why the two men were replaced. Glickman further states, "I believe that Avery Brundage told Robertson and Cromwell to drop us from the relay team to save Hitler further embarrassment by having two Jews stand on the winning podium before 120,000 Germans and the world's news media. The only way we could have lost that race is if we had dropped the baton."

Glickman and Stoller watched the race from the stands that day.

(The author has learned that a reported note from Hitler to Brundage exists stating that if the Jews were not removed from the team he would shut down the games. It is supposed to be in the collection of Brundage's secretary, but this could not be confirmed at press time.)

Glickman went on to a distinguished career in sports broadcasting in his native New York. He was the New York Giants broadcaster for 23 years, 22 years with the Brooklyn Dodgers and New York Yankees, 21 consecutive years of calling the New York Knicks on radio and 15 years as a director and consultant with HBO. He even invented the basketball term "swish." He also has worked with a lot of young broadcasters, including Marv Albert and Sugar Ray Leonard.

During World War II he was in the U.S. Marines in the Pacific. A list of all his sports involvements would fill several pages. In 1992 he was inducted into the Sportscasters Hall of Fame.

Glickman and his wife, Margie, now live in New York City.

Sam Stoller was from Cincinnati, Ohio, and attended the University of Michigan. After World War II he had a long career in films and the broadcasting business. He died in the late 1980s.

Glickman, left, and Stoller training on board the S.S. *Manhattan*. MARTY GLICKMAN COLLECTION

OLYMPIA AUSWEIS
№ 10487
Gültig bis 1. Oktober 1936
XI. Olympiade Berlin 1936
Martin Glickman
MARTIN I. GLICKMAN
AUG. 14-1917 Bronx-N.York
2313-62nd Street
Brooklyn N.Y. United States of Am
ORGANISATIONSKOMITEE FÜR DIE XI. OLYMPIADE BERLIN 1936 E.V.
Dr. Diem

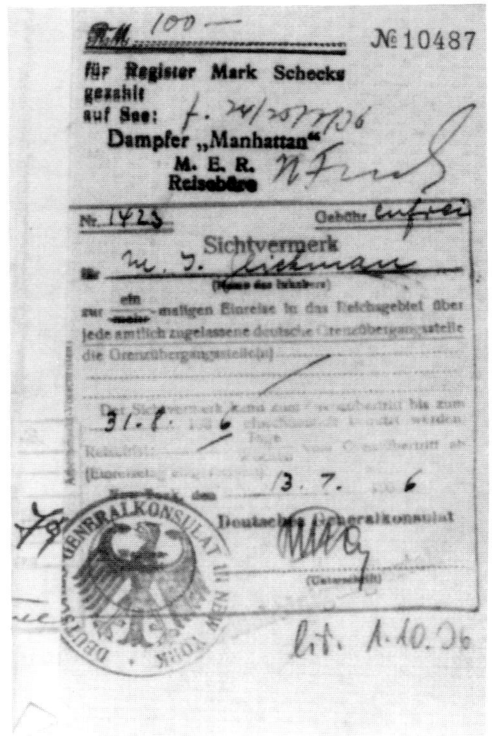

RM 100 —
№ 10487
für Register Mark Schecks gezahlt auf See: f. 24/2077/36
Dampfer „Manhattan"
M. E. R. Reisebüro
Nr. 1423
Sichtvermerk
für M. I. Glickman
Deutsches Generalkonsulat
lit. 1.10.36

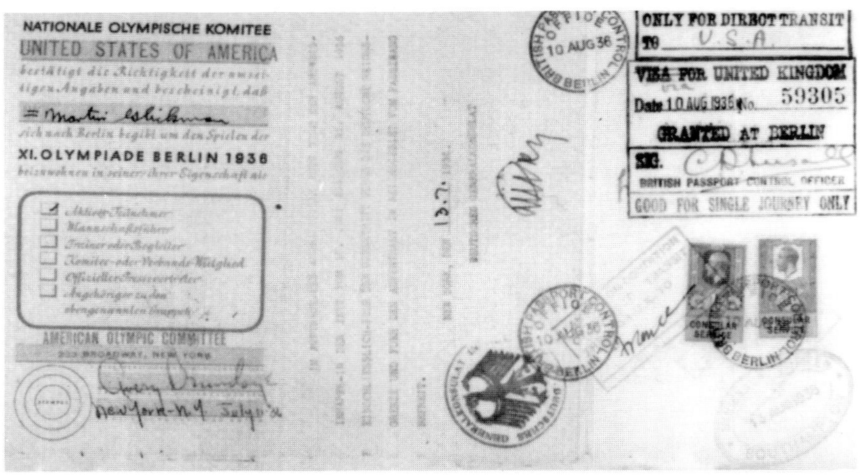

NATIONALE OLYMPISCHE KOMITEE
UNITED STATES OF AMERICA
bestätigt die Richtigkeit der umseitigen Angaben und bescheinigt, daß
Martin Glickman
sich nach Berlin begibt um den Spielen der
XI. OLYMPIADE BERLIN 1936
beizuwohnen in seiner/ihrer Eigenschaft als
AMERICAN OLYMPIC COMMITTEE
New York-N.Y. July 10 '36
ONLY FOR DIRECT TRANSIT TO U.S.A.
VISA FOR UNITED KINGDOM
Date 10 AUG 1936 No. 59305
GRANTED AT BERLIN
BRITISH PASSPORT CONTROL OFFICER
GOOD FOR SINGLE JOURNEY ONLY

A special German passport was issued to each American team member.
MARTY GLICKMAN COLLECTION

Track team members on board the S.S. *Manhattan*.
MARTY GLICKMAN COLLECTION

Glickman and Stoller sat in the stands while their teammates ran the relay. MARTY GLICKMAN COLLECTION

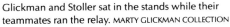

Marty Glickman in his New York apartment, 1995.

Glickman Charges Politics; 2 Jews Cut from Relay Team

BERLIN, Aug. 8. (AP)—Charging that politics influenced revision of the American sprint relay team line-up, Marty Glickman, New York Jewish boy who was left off the quartet with another Jew, Sam Stoller of Cincinnati, today fired a blast aimed at the American Olympic coaching staff.

While sitting in the press box viewing the United States' record-equalling victory in the trials, Glickman, a sophomore at Syracuse university, said:

"The heats failed to show the necessity for shaking up the lineup after Stoller and myself long practiced the stick-work. We did not know until this morning's conference with Head Coach Robertson just who would run. It looks like politics to us."

Asked to elaborate on his charge, Glickman said tersely:

"Cromwell's influence looking out for Southern Californians."

He referred to Dean Cromwell, a member of Robertson's staff and track coach at the University of Southern California. Both Foy Draper and Frank Wykoff, who ran today, are his former pupils.

Stoller, who was 21 years old today, did not appear at the stadium leading Glickman to say:

"A fine present for Sam, wasn't it?"

"Any American combination might have run 40 seconds flat this afternoon," he continued, "since there was no pressure involved. I am willing to admit the team picked, at its fastest, probably can break 40 for a new record but this talk about the Germans and the Dutch being so tough looks like a false alarm on the basis of today's trials."

The Associated Press learned that Stoller had been told he would run and was the most surprised man on the sprint squad when informed he had been displaced by Draper.

One of the great 1,500-meter races in Olympic history pitted six of the seven top finishers from 1932. Glenn Cunningham from Elkhart, Kansas, held the record for the mile race. Jack Lovelock, a medical student from New Zealand, beat Cunningham at Princeton University in 1935 in "The Mile of the Century" race. Luigi Beccali of Italy won the gold in 1932. Phil Edwards of Canada won bronze in 1932, but finished fourth in Berlin. It was an exciting race from start to finish with Lovelock beating Cunningham by four yards and setting a new world record of 3:47.8. Lovelock was thrown from a horse in 1940 and suffered complications of dizziness and double vision. Nine years later, while living in New York City, he became dizzy in a subway station, fell onto the tracks and was killed by an oncoming train.

Jesse Owens passes the baton to Ralph Metcalfe (right) after the first leg of the 4x100-meter relay. Runners for the Canadian team, which came in fifth, are on the left. Italy was second, Germany was third and Holland sixth.

The American women's track and field team. Standing: manager Fred Steers, Martha Worst, Annette Rogers, Kathlyn Kelly, Gertrude Wilhelmsen, Louise Stokes, Betty Robinson, coach Dee Boeckmann. Kneeling: Evelyn Ferrara, Helen Stephens, Harriet Bland, Alice Arden. Sitting: Tidye Pickett, Simone Schaller, Josephine Warren, Olive Hasenjus, Betty Burch. Missing from the photo are chaperon Katherine Dunnette and Anne O'Brien.
ALICE ARDEN COLLECTION

Coach "Dee" Boeckmann

Dolores "Dee" Boeckmann, the first woman to coach an Olympic team, grew up with the Olympics. She was born in 1904 in St. Louis, Missouri, the year and site of the third Olympics. She was a member of the first U.S. women's track and field team, which competed in the 1928 Olympic games.

She was designated to coach the 1936 women's team, which won two of the six events. She also had to work with German managers to feed the team and to work with her team on techniques and strategies for the track and field events.

During military operations in World War II, Korea and Vietnam she coached and ran recreational programs in Iceland, India, China, Japan and the Pacific. She was the first woman appointed to chair an AAU committee and she coached the first Japanese women's team for the Asian Games on the Pearl Islands.

She died in St. Louis in 1989.

Harriet Bland was born in St. Louis, Missouri, in 1915. She was a member of the St. Louis AC team that won the AAU relay in 1935. At Berlin she ran the first leg of the 4 × 100-meter relay team that won the gold medal. She attended Mary Institute and later became Mrs. William Green. She is deceased.

Helen Stephens: The "Fulton Flash"

The U.S. Olympic Women's track team has been blessed with many world-class athletes since women's track was introduced into the Olympics in 1928. Perhaps the greatest of them all, but who unfortunately has been pushed into obscurity, was Helen Stephens of the 1936 Olympics.

Stephens, who would be known as the "Fulton Flash" and the "Missouri Flash," grew up on a farm in Callaway County, Missouri, near the town of Fulton in the central part of the state. Even as a small child she was fast and could beat any boy who would race her home from school.

As a 15-year-old high school freshman, she was discovered by Coach Burton W. Moore. He had clocked her at 5.8 seconds in the 50-yard dash, a time that equaled the existing women's record. Another time in a physical education class, Stephens equaled the women's record in the standing broad jump.

Coach Moore took Helen under his wing and trained her for eventual international competition. In 1935, the world's fastest woman trackster was a Polish girl with the difficult to pronounce name of Stanislawa Walasiewicz (nicknamed Stella Walsh by sportscasters).

Walsh owned most of the world's women's track records at the time, but in a 50-meter dash final at the National AAU meet in St. Louis she was beaten by the "Fulton Flash." Stephens went on in that meet to set new world records in the 200-meter dash, the standing broad jump and first place in the shot put.

The 1936 Olympics would prove to be Helen's greatest triumph. She could enter only three events, according to Olympic rules. Two of her best events, the shot put and standing broad jump were not even Olympic events. Instead she qualified for the discus, the 100-meter dash and was a member of the 4×100-meter relay team.

She finished a distant 10th in the discus, as this was not really a strong event for her. In a preliminary heat of the 100-meter dash, she set a new world's record of 11.4 seconds, but the time was disallowed because of a wind factor. However, she went on to set the world's record in the final heat at 11.5 seconds, beating Stella Walsh by two one-hundredths of a second. This record would stand until it was broken by Wilma Rudolph in 1960.

Hitler met Stephens after the race in his private box. She later stated: "Hitler comes in and gives me the Nazi salute. I gave him a good old Missouri handshake. He took my hand, put his arm around me, pinched me, and invited me to spend a weekend with him."

Helen Stephens after her victory in the 100 meters. BA

The women's 4×100-meter relay team, which consisted of Harriet Bland, Annette Rogers, Elizabeth Robinson and anchor Helen Stephens, beat the German team in the final run. The German anchor, Ilse Dorffeldt, dropped the baton on the final exchange, allowing the American team to win (it is speculative as to whether the Americans would have won anyway).

After the Olympics, Helen remained an amateur for two years with the intention of competing in the 1940 Tokyo Olympics. But, being bored with a lack of good female competition, she joined the House of David basketball team, giving half-time demonstrations of her shot put and running abilities. She also became a basketball and softball player and participated as a fencer, swimmer and bowler. She even ran a series of exhibition races against Jesse Owens.

For 25 years, she worked as a librarian in St. Louis for the Defense Mapping Agency Aerospace Center and then retired to Fulton where she helped coach at her alma mater, William Woods College.

Even as a senior citizen, she won seven medals at the 1980 Senior Olympics and eight medals at the 1981 meet.

Stephens never married and died on Jan. 16, 1995.

The world's two fastest humans, Helen Stephens and Jesse Owens.

Despite her world record, Helen Stephens is being scolded by her coach, Dee Boeckmann. BA

Helen Stephens meets Hitler after winning the 100-meter run.
NA, HH 242-HD-0148

The Women's 4x100-Meter Relay

Just as the men's relay team won its race, the women ran away with their race, but only by accident.

The German team of Emmy Albus, Kathe Krauss, Marie Dollinger and Ilse Dorffeldt were the team to beat and had set a new world record of 46.4 seconds in the first round.

The American team consisted of Harriet Bland, Annette Rogers, Elizabeth Robinson and Helen Stephens.

In the finals, the German team was on its way to victory and possibly a new world record when Dollinger passed the baton to Dorffeldt, who dropped it. The team was disqualified and the Americans took first place, the British, second, and the Canadians, third.

The Germans were heartbroken and Hitler called them to his private box to console them.

Twenty-four years later, Marie Dollinger sat in the stands at the 1960 Rome Olympics and watched her daughter, Brunhilde Hendrix, run the third leg of the same relay on the German team. They won the silver medal, three one-hundredths of a second behind the Americans.

The winning American 4x100-meter relay team. From left: Annette Rogers, Helen Stephens, Harriet Bland, and Betty Robinson. NA, HH 242-HD-277-2

In 1986 the four members of the 4x100-meter relay team met for a 50th anniversary reunion. Clockwise from bottom left: Harriet Bland, Annette Rogers, Helen Stephens, Betty Robinson and Miss Bland's attendant, Jo Warren. ANNETTE KELLY COLLECTION

Annette Rogers Kelly was the first American woman to win back-to-back gold medals at the Olympics. Mrs. Kelly now makes her home in Niles, Illinois, a suburb of Chicago. She was a member of the 1932 and 1936, 4 × 100-meter relay teams, teams that won gold in both Olympics.

Annette was born in 1913 in Chicago and excelled at the high jump when she was just 12 years old. At 16, she qualified for the 1932 Olympics in the high jump, 100-meter dash and 4 × 100-meter relay team. She placed fourth in the high jump at Los Angeles and won her first 4 × 100-relay team gold medal.

In 1933 she won the AAU 100-yard run and was a member of the 4 × 100-relay team of the Illinois Women's Athletic Club, breaking the world's record for the anchor leg in 1932 at 49.4 seconds.

At the Olympic trials in Providence, Rhode Island, for the 1936 games she was the only member of the 1932 relay team to make the 1936 team. She also qualified again for the high jump and 100-meter dash. She came in fourth place in the high jump and fifth in the 100-meter dash.

But it was in the relay that she and her teammates excelled once again, winning the 4 × 100-meter relay, thus her back-to-back gold medals in the same event in successive Olympics.

Annette hung up her track shoes after the Olympics. While at Northwestern University, she was offered a playground job with the Chicago Board of Education. Since this was during the Depression, she needed the job. Unfortunately, at this time, if you worked in any sports-related field you were no longer considered an amateur and thus no longer eligible for the Olympics.

As it turned out it wouldn't have made any difference as there were no Olympics for the next 12 years because World War II prevented games in 1940 and 1944.

She spent 32 years with the Chicago school system, teaching physical education. In 1938 she married Peter Kelly and they have lived in Niles since 1954, raising three children.

Annette Rogers Kelly has been inducted into the Chicago Sports Hall of Fame, the Northwestern University Hall of Fame and the U.S. Track and Field Hall of Fame. Her record of two medals stood until the 1980 Olympics in Moscow.

Annette Rogers won the high jump in the final Olympic trials at Providence, Rhode Island, on July 4, 1936. She jumped 5′2½″. ANNETTE KELLY COLLECTION

The 4x100-meter relay team on the winners' podium. From left: Bland, Rogers, Robinson, Stephens. ANNETTE KELLY COLLECTION

Pete and Annette Rogers Kelly at their home in Niles, Illinois, 1994. ANNETTE KELLY COLLECTION

Betty "Babe" Robinson was born in 1911. As a 16-year-old from the playgrounds of Chicago she participated in the 1928 Olympics. She trained with the boys' track squad because her high school had no girls' team. She was "discovered" when a teacher saw her running to catch a train. Shocked that she made it, he asked if he could clock her the next day. The results were astonishing and, in Amsterdam, in 1928, she captured the first gold medal ever awarded in the women's 100-meter race. She also won a silver medal in the 4×100-meter relay.

After the 1928 Olympics she set a world record for 100 yards and in 1929 set another world record in the 50-yard dash. In March 1931, she set world records for 60 and 70 yards.

Unfortunately she was severely injured in a plane crash in 1931, was in a coma for seven weeks, and was out of competition for three and one-half years. In 1936 she made the women's 4×100-meter relay team and won her second gold medal. She still could not fully bend her leg at the knee, so had to start from a crouch position.

After her retirement she continued to participate in sports as an official AAU timekeeper. She was the first woman ever awarded a varsity "N" by Northwestern University. She lives with her husband in the Denver area.

Mr. or Ms. Stella Walsh?

There is quite a story about one of the world's greatest female athletes. Stanislawa Walasiewicz was born in Poland in 1911 and settled in the United States with her parents shortly thereafter. Since her name was difficult for Americans to pronounce, she grew up as Stella Walsh.

On May 30, 1930, she broke the 11-second barrier for the 100 yard dash—the first woman to do so. It was expected that she would compete in the 1932 Olympic Games for the United States and win one or more gold medals.

At this time however, no Olympic competitor could make a living in either recreation or physical education and be eligible for the American team. Walsh was not an American citizen in 1932 and one day before she was to take out naturalization papers, she rejected it, accepted a job with the Polish government in New York and announced that because the Americans would not let her work or furnish any financial help, she would compete for her native country of Poland.

At Los Angeles, she beat Hilde Strike of Canada in the 100-meter race by a half-yard and equaled the world's record of 11.9 seconds.

In 1936 she lost to Helen Stephens in the 100-meter race by two one-hundredths of a second. A Polish journalist in Berlin accused Walsh of being a man but the German officials issued a statement that a sex test was given and she was a female.

This is not the end of the story, however.

On Dec. 4, 1980, Walsh unfortunately got caught in a robbery attempt shootout in a discount store parking lot in Cleveland, Ohio. She was shot to death. An autopsy showed that she did have male sexual organs.

So this "woman" who won 41 A.A.U. titles, set 11 world records and gained two Olympic medals was not quite a woman at all!

Alice Arden, like many of the Olympic participants, was an all-around athlete. While Arden made the U.S. team in the high jump, her best track and field event was the long jump, which was not an Olympic sport in 1936. She did not win a medal in Berlin. She also excelled in basketball at Baldwin High School on New York's Long Island, and was voted the outstanding athlete among both boys and girls on Long Island while she was still in high school.

Arden's one claim to fame was in 1933 at the Chicago World's Fair when she broke the great Babe Didrikson's American high jump record. Arden's record stood unmatched for more than 20 years.

Following her trip to the Olympics, she played basketball with a travelling team. In one game she jumped center against a strapping young man named Russell V. Hodge. They were later married and had a son named Russell A. "Rusty" Hodge. Rusty would compete in the 1964 Tokyo Olympics in the decathlon, placing ninth. In 1966 he would set a world decathlon record. He now lives and works in the Tacoma, Washington, area. Alice and Rusty are the only mother-son Olympians in U.S. Olympic history.

The Hodges had their own business in New York and live near the village of Roscoe.

Alice Arden Hodge and her husband, Russell. ALICE HODGE COLLECTION

Alice Arden Hodge and her son, Rusty. ALICE HODGE COLLECTION

Alice Arden with friends before the Olympics. ALICE HODGE COLLECTION

Members of the women's track and field team "hamming it up" at their quarters in Berlin. From left: Harriet Bland, Simone Schaller, Gertrude Wilhelmsen, Tidye Pickett (at the piano), Annette Rogers, Helen Stephens. ALICE HODGE COLLECTION

A COMPLETE NEWSPAPER For ALL the Family

FORT DODGE MESSENGER and Chronicle

UNIVERSAL IN ITS FIELD

HOME EDITION

M. & C. NO. 29 | TUESDAY EVENING, AUGUST 4, 1936 | 12 PAGES | PER COPY FIVE CENTS

U. S. PILES UP OLYMPIC WINS

TRACK STARS TAKE FINALS IN 3 EVENTS

Jesse Owens Betters the Record for Broad Jump

BERLIN, Aug. 4. (AP)—Team point totals in Olympic track and field competition after today's events: (Points on unofficial 10-5-4-3-2 basis).

Men's track and field: United States 83; Germany 38½; Finland 30¼; Japan 9½; Canada 9; Italy 8; Sweden 5; Holland 4; Philippines 4; Poland 3; Great Britain 2; Brazil 2; Argentina 1; Greece 1.

Women's track and field: Germany 38; Poland 14; United States 12; Japan 7; Austria 3; Sweden 1.

By ALAN GOULD.
Associated Press Sports Editor.

BERLIN, Aug. 4. (AP)—Topped off by Jesse Owens' record smashing broad jump victory for his second title of the 11th Olympiad, Americans swept all three men's track and field finals, and broke even in two women's events today. It was one of the biggest days the United States ever has enjoyed in Olympic competition.

The tan thunderbolt from Ohio State bettered the Olympic broad jump record five times, winning the championship with a leap of 26 feet, 5 21-64 inches, after twice bettering the Olympic 200 meter record of 21.2 seconds with successive performances in 21.1 seconds, pacing 11 others, including Mack Robinson of Pasadena, Cal., and Bobby Packard of Rockford, Ill., into the semifinals.

The triumphs of Glenn Hardin of Greenwood, Miss., in the 400-meter hurdles and lanky Johnny Woodruff, University of Pittsburgh Negro freshman, in the 800-meter run, combined with Owens' second gold medal performance boosted the United States point total to 83, assuring retention of the team championship after only three days of competition before crowds aggregating 300,000.

BERLIN, Aug. 4. (AP)—The question whether Jesse Owens bettered Ed Hamm's Olympic broad jump record in his first leap this afternoon was definitely settled in the Negro's favor.

Owens cleared 7.74 meters, 25 feet, 4 47-64 inches. Hamm's record, made at Amsterdam in 1928, is listed in most record books as 25 feet, 4¾ inches, 1-64th of an inch more than Owens. Investigation revealed, however, that Hamm's jump actually was 7.73 meters which correctly translated into feet and inches is 25 feet, 4 11-64 inches.

Helen Stephens of Fulton, Mo., meanwhile, recaptured the women's 100-meter sprint crown for America, beating the listed world record of 11.8 seconds for the third time in two days and dethroning Stella Walsh of Poland. Miss Stephens' winning time was 11.5 seconds.

Woodruff, 21-year-old star, won the hard way. The Negro was boxed badly twice, tripped once and ran most of the last lap on the outside, collaring Canada's Phil Edwards at the head of the stretch and then fighting off a closing challenge by Mario Lanzi of Italy. The American beat the Italian by slightly less than two meters with Edwards fading in the last twenty meters. Woodruff's time was 1:52.9.

Hardin, holder of the world and Olympic records of 50.6 and 52 seconds, respectively, won the gold medal in 52.4 seconds. Johnny Loaring of Canada was second; Miguel White of the Philippines, third, and Joe Patterson, of Oklahoma City, fourth.

Summaries

Summaries in Olympic track and field competition today:

200-meter first trials (first three in each heat qualify for quarter-finals).

First heat—Won by Beveren, Holland, 21.4 seconds; second Beswick, Argentina, 22.1; third, Taniguchi, Japan, 22.2; fourth Almeida, Brazil; fifth, Salcedo, Philippines.

Second heat—Won by Osendarp, Holland, 21.7; second, Schein, Germany, 22.0; third, Pennington, Great Britain, 22.1; fourth, Yazawa, Japan; fifth, Dondelinger, France.

Third heat—Won by Jesse Owens, United States, 21.1 (betters Olympic mark of 21.2 made by Eddie Tolan, United States, in 1932); second, Orr, Canada, 21.6; third, Neckermann, Germany, 21.8; fourth, Sweeney, England; fifth, Guzman, Philippines.

Fourth heat—Won by Humber, Canada, 22.1; second, Gyenes, Hungary, 22.1; third, Kinner, Austria, 22.4; fourth, Bronner, France; fifth, Chen, China.

Fifth heat—Won by Haenni, Switzerland, 21.9; second, Frangoudis, Greece, 22.1; third, Sir, Hungary, 22.2; fourth, Dannaher, South Africa; fifth, Poh, China.

Sixth heat—Won by Theunissen, South Africa, 21.7; second,

Track Stars—
(Continued on Page 2)

Fort Dodge Man Named President Of Iowa Moose

First Place Given to Robert E. Estlund—After Heated Contest Fort Dodge Chosen Location for 1937 Meeting.

Robert E. Estlund of this city was named president of the Iowa association of the Loyal Order of Moose and Fort Dodge was awarded the 1937 convention of the lodge at the close of the annual conclave in Iowa City last weekend.

More than 1,500 delegates attended the Iowa City convention, the association's 23rd annual meeting. The Women of the Moose held their annual conference in connection with the sessions.

Mr. Estlund succeeds Charles Bowers, Des Moines attorney, as state president. Lawrence Dawson of Waterloo was named first vice president; Ed Zea of Mason City, second vice president; Louis Lang of Muscatine, third vice president; Leo E. Kohl of Iowa City, George Dustin of Des Moines and William Wachter of Sioux City, trustees, and E. U. Meyer, Davenport, secretary-treasurer.

Wins Over Sioux City.

Fort Dodge was awarded next year's convention in a spirited contest with Sioux City.

The Iowa City conference was one of the most successful in the history of the Iowa order, Mr. Estlund said on his return this morning.

The order has enrolled more than 1,600 new members in the state this year, bringing the Iowa membership to 12,000. In the country at large, more than 64,000 persons have become affiliated with the Moose organization during the past year.

Plans were launched at the convention for a vigorous membership drive during the coming 12 months.

Local Delegates.

The Fort Dodge delegation to the convention included Senior Past Dictator Henry G. Mueller, Junior Past Dictator Paul E. McConville, Dictator Robert C. Lents, Leroy Maly and Mr. Estlund, who is secretary of the local lodge.

Features of the [illegible] concerts by the Des Moines [illegible] band, which received top honors in the recent national convention in Chicago and an exhibition by the Davenport drill team, also a first place winner at the national meeting.

Sunday was one of the feature days of the convention, according to the Fort Dodge delegates.

In the afternoon, the country home of the Iowa City lodge was dedicated at Lake Macbride state park. In the evening, a farewell banquet was held at the Iowa Memorial Union with more than 500 in attendance. Speakers included Judge J. Willis Pierson of Mooseheart, Ill., regional director; T. J. Parker, dictator of the Iowa City lodge; Joe Lillie of Des Moines, member of the supreme forum; Mayor Thomas E. Martin of Iowa City and Mrs. George Seydel, conference leader.

Named on Committee.

Mr. Estlund with Fred Kroeger of Burlington and Louis Lang of Muscatine was delegated to investigate the possibility of establishing a state Moose bulletin.

The Fort Dodgers were extremely happy to have won the 1937 convention for their home town. The Moose conclave will be one of the biggest conventions to be held in the city next year. The dates will be set later but will be about the same as this year, Mr. Estlund said.

WAR STARTED IN WESTERN EUROPE 22 YEARS AGO

NEW YORK, Aug. 4. (AP)—It was 22 years ago today that western Europe felt the first sharp conflict of the World war.

On Aug. 4, 1914, marching German troops crossed the Belgian border and began a [illegible] advance toward Paris.

REPORT KARPIS LEAVES STORY OF KIDNAPING

ST. PAUL, Aug. 4, (AP)—The Dispatch today said a written statement purporting to be Alvin Karpis' own story of the kidnaping of William Hamm Jr., St. Paul brewery owner, is in existence and is being sought by the United States department of justice.

Continuing, the Dispatch said: "Copies are reported held by Lewis L. Anderson, attorney, who has been engaged by Thomas A. Brown in connection with possible charges against him growing out of the testimony in the recent Hamm kidnaping trial. Brown, head of the automobile theft department, is under suspension and is a former chief of police.

"Copies and possibly the original are reported to have been submitted to defense attorneys for John P. Peifer, who was convicted of the Hamm kidnaping plot at the trial and who committed suicide. A. M. Cary, one of the attorneys, declined today to [illegible] naping.

"The statement relates what purports to be the 'inside' details of the kidnaping."

GENERALLY FAIR OVER IOWA TODAY

DES MOINES, Ia., Aug. 4. (AP)—The weatherman forecast generally fair weather for Iowa tonight and tomorrow, but he also predicted that temperatures probably will hold below 90, both today and tomorrow.

Meager showers fell at scattered points throughout the state last night and thin clouds continued drifting over much of the state this morning.

Des Moines and Dubuque measured .06 of an inch. Council Bluffs and Davenport reported traces of rain early today.

Lamoni and Waterloo reported the top temperature yesterday, 96, and Inwood, the low, 54.

ROOSEVELT SAYS DROUGHT TRIP IS NON-POLITICAL

HYDE PARK, N. Y., Aug. 4. (AP)—President Roosevelt said today his forthcoming inspection trip through some of the drought-stricken states would not be political.

He made this statement in answer to a question and then followed the unusual procedure of letting news men quote him thus:

"It is a great dis-service to the proper administration of any government to link up human misery with partisan politics."

He discussed the drought and held what he called the usual monthly conference on finances with a group of officials from Washington. In the party were Secretary Morgenthau, Daniel Bell, acting budget director; Aubrey Williams, deputy WPA administrator; Corrington Gill, assistant administrator, and Rexford G. Tugwell, under secretary of agriculture, and resettlement administrator.

IOWA DEMOCRATS WANT ROOSEVELT TO VISIT STATE

DES MOINES, Aug. 4. (AP)—E. H. Birmingham, democratic state chairman, said today Iowa democratic leaders are seeking to induce President Roosevelt to visit Iowa when he makes an inspection tour of the drought area, probably next week.

Birmingham said he would talk by telephone some time today with James A. Farley, democratic national chairman, concerning an Iowa visit by the president.

MURRAY ASKS PLAN TO MAKE SURE OF SEED CORN SUPPLY

DES MOINES, Ia., Aug. 4. (AP)—Ray Murray, Iowa agriculture secretary, said today he has written Henry Wallace, federal agriculture secretary, urging adoption of a federal seed corn program to stave off what he said was apt to be a drastic shortage of seed corn next spring.

Murray said he suggested that the government provide for a federal purchase program as done during the 1934 drought, or a federal seed corn loan plan which would enable farmers with seed corn to [illegible] until the spring.

Under [illegible] program, the [illegible] bought seed corn and [illegible] for resale to farmers [illegible] price plus a storage [illegible]

WASHINGTON, Aug. 4. (AP)—The AAA said today the department of agriculture's drought committee planned to buy 2,000,000 bushels of seed grains to assure a supply for farmers in the drought stricken areas.

The grain, it was explained, would be sold to farmers who lack seed at cost plus carrying charges. It was estimated $10,000,000 would be needed to finance the purchases.

STATE HUNTS GANG LOOTING CREAMERIES

Two More Robberies Spur Search for Thieves

DES MOINES, Aug. 4, (AP)—North Iowa officers, reinforced by two state agents, spurred their search today for a gang of butter thieves after robberies at Oran, in Fayette county, and Dumont, in Butler county [illegible] operated by [illegible] and 1,000 pounds from the Oran creamery.

Both creameries are on highway No. 10, but are more than 50 miles apart.

Glen Schmidt, investigation bureau chief, said indications "point to the same gang which has raided a score of north Iowa creameries, although it's possible the gang had two crews operating last night."

At both points, however, Schmidt said, tracks left by the robbers' truck were identical.

Harvey Mighell was arrested at Audubon last week for investigation in connection with the butter robberies. He later was released on bond. The state bureau said four other men were under suspicion.

Schmidt said Agents William Zelinsky and Al Haight, who are trying to trail down the robbery gang, believe the looters sell their stolen butter through an illicit creamery "probably located in Omaha or that vicinity."

FARM RELIEF COMMITTEES ARE URGED

Kraschel Suggests Township Advisers on Drought Aid

DES MOINES, Aug. 4, (AP)—Lieutenant Governor Nels G. Kraschel telegraphed Governor Clyde L. Herring in Washington, D. C., today suggesting that Iowa drought stricken farmers "be requested to select drought advisory committees."

"To insure a sympathetic understanding and a practical administration of the drought relief program," Kraschel wired, "I suggest that the farmers of each drought township be requested to select from their number a committee of three to be known as the township drought advisory committee.

"If they are recognized by federal, state and county agencies offering assistance to drought stricken farmers, these committees will not only insure a just distribution of the benefits offered, but will be capable of perfecting practical plans for conserving the limited feed supply and a workable plan for preventing the slaughter of breeding stock.

"Thousands of pigs are going to market that should be retained for fattening.

"Iowa also is faced with loss of breeding stock which it cannot afford to lose.

"Only practical farmer committees can cope with this problem."

Herring now is in Washington arranging the drought relief setup for Iowa with federal officials.

A group of Woodbury county farmers late yesterday took steps toward organization of farmers to assist in developing and administering the drought relief program.

Meeting at Sioux City they passed resolutions, which included [illegible]

WASHINGTON, Aug. 4, (AP)—Iowa's drought relief program will get underway next week, Governor Clyde L. Herring said here today.

Governor Herring's announcement followed conferences with federal officials, during which the Iowa chief executive outlined a request for $2,250,000.

Although the precise amount of money available for drought relief was not revealed, it was announced that the funds would come from the resettlement administration to be used as loans for the purchase of livestock feed and as outright grants to stricken farmers.

"The funds are strictly for relief and therefore will be administered through county relief administrations already set up," Herring said.

Ralph Kittenger, state relief administrator, who with L. S. Hill, Iowa works progress administrator, and Professor George Keller, assistant to Hill, accompanied Governor Herring to Washington, will be in charge of the state organization to administer relief. [illegible] showed 25,000 loans for livestock and feed grants, and [illegible] loans to farm families were [illegible]. There are 215,000 farm families in the state. [illegible] the total number of farm[illegible] who were expected to receive aid is 35,000.

Feed loans will be about $100 each, and cash relief about $20 a month to each family, Herring said.

DES MOINES (AP)—The William Gordon, Inc., a Des Moines concern organized to manufacture [illegible] filed articles of incorporation with the secretary of state. [illegible] Thompson of Muscatine is [illegible] president of the company and [illegible] Thompson of Muscatine, secretary.

THE WEATHER

[illegible] Generally fair tonight and Wednesday. Cooler in south and [illegible] portions tonight.

[illegible]

In Nearby States

[illegible]: Cloudy, occasional rain in south, cooler in north and central portions tonight; Wednesday partly cloudy to cloudy, rain in extreme south.

[illegible]: Cloudy, occasional rain in south and central portions, cooler in north and central portions tonight; Wednesday partly cloudy.

Minnesota: Partly cloudy to cloudy tonight and Wednesday; warmer in north portion tonight and in north and central portions Wednesday.

South Dakota: Mostly cloudy tonight and Wednesday; warmer in north portion Wednesday.

Nebraska: Partly cloudy tonight and Wednesday; cooler in south-east portion tonight.

Naval Building Race Will Start January 1

From the capitals of the large nations comes news of plans to increase naval strength. The following article gives a clear picture of the situation.

By DEWITT MAC KENZIE.
Associated Press Staff Writer.

NEW YORK, Aug. 4, (AP)—The great naval building contest among the major powers has been definitely set to get under way in earnest on Jan. 1—the earliest possible date allowed by treaty.

Britain has just taken the initiative with the announcement that on New Year's day she will lay the keels of two battleships, the biggest and most expensive of all sea-going fighting machines.

This will be a few hours after the expiration of the naval pact which precluded such construction. It is a decade since England built one of those floating forts.

For the first time in some 15 years the United States will embark, it is reliably indicated, on a similar program to keep abreast of Britain.

Japan, the other member of the Big Three, promptly signaled that she would build not two but four of these vast implements of death. This is in line with Nippon's demand for parity with America and England and her notification of withdrawal from the naval treaty because she could not obtain equality.

France, Italy and Germany already are building battleships, and Russia is embarking on naval expansion.

The expenditure will be heavy, since each battleship may cost something like $50,000,000. But they are only one item in the contest.

This year's program alone, if equally distributed, would cost nearly $4 for each person in America, $6 in England and $6 in France. Italy has a low mark of $3—not overlooking her huge and continuing military expenditure in the Ethiopian [illegible].

Naval [illegible]

The latest [illegible] estimates for the year 1936 [illegible] they may have been [illegible] have since [illegible]:

United States, [illegible]; Britain, [illegible]; France, [illegible]; Italy, [illegible]; Germany, not announced; Russia (for military defense), [illegible]; Japan (for [illegible] defense), [illegible].

The battleships of the United States, Britain and Japan are comparatively old. The West Virginia, typical of this class of ship, is America's latest and was completed 13 years ago. England's best are the Nelson and the Rodney, completed in 1927.

Germany has the newest battleships, the Admiral Scheer, completed in 1934, and the Deutschland, in 1933. They are of only 10,000 tons each, but it has been claimed they are the most formidable fighting ships afloat.

Germany is building three more battleships. France has three under construction and Italy two.

Tonnage Strength.

The comparative tonnage strength of the five great powers, as the building competition gets into full swing, follows:

	British C'wealth	United States	Japan	France	Italy
Capital ships	474,750	455,400	272,070	163,933	86,532
Cruisers	351,266	220,275	213,185	202,239	174,894
Aircraft carriers	115,350	92,000	99,420	22,146	
Destroyers	199,244	247,190	124,122	[illegible]	91,488
Submarines **	51	84	37	[illegible]	[illegible]

**Total number

Real Estate Taxes Up Nearly 15 Per Cent Here Despite Refund

Substantial Boost in City Assessment and Raise in School Taxes Account for Part of Increase—State Income Tax and Sales Tax Are Additional.

In spite of the state's three point tax program, so-called property tax relief measure, and a refund of $161,815.96 announced yesterday for Webster county by the state tax board, town and rural tax bills of this county range as much as 15 per cent higher than they were a year ago, courthouse tax records show.

This increase of course takes no measure of the additional money the property owner has paid in state income and sales taxes to relieve his home or farm of property taxes.

The state, with this year's refund of approximately 4 mills, has succeeded in wiping out its own levy against real estate, but has eliminated only nine-tenths of one mill of the balance of taxes. In other words, the state tax board collected $3.10 for every $1,000 of assessed property value and now has turned around to refund $4.00.

This year's refund, although three times as great a cash amount is not as large as the one returned to the Webster county taxpayer last year.

Return Greater Last Year

In 1935, no state levy was collected, but the state board refunded approximately $1.38 cents for every $1,000 of assessed property valuation. This year, the amount returned per $1,000 of valuation exceeds the state's levy by 90 cents. On this basis, the taxpayer's return in 1935 was greater by 48 cents than it is this year.

Even with the state refund, Fort Dodge property owners this year are paying exactly 14.70 per cent greater taxes than they did in 1935. The state has eliminated through its refund a part of the local increase. The remainder is accounted for by a substantial boost in city assessments and a small raise in school taxes.

The county board of supervisors made a slight reduction in its [illegible] property taxes in most tax districts.

Tax Comparison

To obtain a tax comparison on Fort Dodge property for the past few years, an actual piece of property was taken and its tax record followed through four years.

In 1933, the last tax collected before the first state refund, this property was assessed at $2,800 and paid a tax of $100.10. In 1934, the evaluation was cut 20 per cent, but the tax bill dropped very slightly. The following table shows the increase in taxes.

	Evaluation	Tax	Refund	Net Tax
1933	$2,800	$100.10	None	$100.10
1934	2,240	98.98	$2.46	96.52
1935	2,240	99.74	3.10	96.64
1936	2,240	116.34	8.96*	107.38

* Estimated.

On a Farm

A corresponding increase was found in tracing the tax records of an 80-acre farm over the same period. Of course, the percentage of increase varies because no two rural townships levy the same tax millage. A Johnson township farm was selected, however, because its total millage most closely approaches the average for Webster county rural districts.

	Valuation	Tax	Refund	Net Tax
1933	$5,346	$100.72	$....	$100.72
1934	4,322	102.04	4.77	97.27
1935	4,322	102.62	6.00	96.62
1936	4,322	128.14	17.32	110.82

Here the percentage of increase is 14.20 per cent.

The state tax refund will be credited on the tax books. When the taxpayer pays the last half of his taxes, which are due Sept. 1 and delinquent Oct. 1, the amount of the refund will be deducted. If the taxpayer paid all his taxes last spring, a refund check will be mailed to him from the offices of County Treasurer Verne E. Hale.

The deduction will be made on both real and personal property, not, of course, on moneys or credits or special assessments.

For every $100 of taxes paid this year by a Fort Dodge property owner, the refund will amount to $7.70. The rural districts will receive an average refund per $100 taxes paid of $13.83. In Webster county towns other than Fort Dodge, the average refund will amount to $10.42.

The following table shows how much each type of taxing district paid to the state for every $100 of tax assessment, and how much the state will refund. The Fort Dodge state tax refund is an actual figure based on the state's estimated 4 mill return. The refund for rural districts and towns in the county outside Fort Dodge is an average, and the actual refund will vary according to whether the district's total tax millage is greater or smaller than the average listed here.

	Total Millage	Tax bill of	Paid to state	Returned by state	Actual difference
Fort Dodge	51.94	$100	$5.97	$7.70	$1.73
Rural districts	29.361*	100	10.49	13.83	3.14
Other towns	38.407*	100	8.07	10.42	2.33

*Average.

A Fort Dodger or Webster county farmer or townsman, interested in determining the increase in his state taxes since the inauguration of the three point tax program, can make a fair estimate by deducting the amount of the state's refund from the money he has paid this year in state sales and income taxes.

LATE BULLETINS

WASHINGTON, Aug. 4. (AP)—The American Federation of Labor's executive council today considered what action—if any — to take against John L. Lewis, president of the United Mine Workers, and his colleagues charged with "insurrection" against the organization.

TOPEKA, Kans., Aug. 4. (AP)—An armored railroad car, reported reliably to be carrying Alvin Karpis, confessed kidnaper, and 19 other prisoners to Alcatraz federal prison, in San Francisco bay, passed through Topeka today, attached to a regular Union Pacific passenger train.

ST. PAUL, Aug. 4. (AP)—A request the investigation of Walter Liggett's assassination in Minneapolis last December be continued, was sent to the state attorney general today by Mrs. Liggett.

DETROIT, Aug. 4. (AP)—Charles T. McCutcheon, the bacteriologist approached by a high-ranking Black Legion officer in an abortive plot to infect Jews with typhoid fever by contaminating milk, today was dismissed by Dr. Henry F. Vaughn, city health commissioner.

COVERS A BET BY COUGHLIN

PROVIDENCE, R. I., Aug. 4. (AP)—[illegible] story today that Frederick L. Jenckes, former head of the Manville-Jenckes company, has publicly guaranteed to cover the bet offered at East Providence last Sunday by the Rev. Charles E. Coughlin, who declared in a speech that he would wager $25,000 at 3 to 2 that Rep. Lemke, union party candidate for president, would lead Landon in the November election.

Mr. Jenckes said that he had wired Father Coughlin he was prepared to place $16,666.66 in escrow in a Providence bank and that his counsel had advised him that the bank could accept the $25,000 end, likewise.

DETROIT, Aug. 4, (AP)—At the office of the Rev. Charles E. Coughlin it was indicated today that the priest had not yet seen the telegram sent him by Frederick L. Jenckes of Providence, R. I., who wired acceptance of Father Coughlin's offer to bet $25,000 at 3 to 2 that Representative William Lemke will poll more votes in the national election than Governor Alf M. Landon.

Until Father Coughlin has seen the telegram and considered it there will be no statement from the priest, his assistants indicated.

Father Coughlin offered to make the wager in a speech last Sunday at East Providence, R. I. In his wire Jenckes said he was ready to put his $16,666.66 in escrow and asked the priest to acknowledge his acceptance.

SETTLE FARM DEBT CASES

WASHINGTON, Aug. 4, (AP)—The resettlement administration announced today that 1,373 distressed farm debt cases in Iowa have been adjusted through efforts of the voluntary farm debt adjustment committees.

The committees began work last September and the report showed a reduction in Iowa of $2,934,151. The original indebtedness in the cases was $10,988,137 and was reduced to $8,053,986 through lowering of the rate of interest or reduction of the debt.

The average reduction per case was $2,137, bringing the average debt remaining to $5,866.

DUBUQUE BREWER DIES

DUBUQUE, Ia., Aug. 4 — (AP) — Alphons L. Rhomberg, 78, president of the Dubuque Star Brewing company, died Monday night of a heart attack while playing a game of bridge.

At the table were his brother, T. E. Rhomberg; his sister, Mrs. W. E. Klauer, wife of the president of the Klauer Manufacturing company and owner of the Julien Dubuque hotel, and Mrs. Julius Mathey, a friend of the family.

Mr. Rhomberg was born in Dubuque county and was one of the city's business leaders for over half a century.

KILLED ON R. R. TRESTLE

FAIRMONT, Minn., Aug. 4 — (AP) — Struck by a train apparently while walking on the trestle, W. M. Horton, 40, a coal miner of Ottumwa, Iowa, was killed instantly last night. He was identified by a brother, 53, with whom he had been working in the harvest fields in this vicinity.

CAMPAIGNERS EYE VOTE IN THREE STATES

Primaries in Missouri, Kansas and Virginia

(By the Associated Press)

LOUISVILLE, Ky.—Senator M. M. Logan holds lead over former Governor J. C. W. Beckham in close race for democratic senatorial nomination.

ST. LOUIS—Major Lloyd C. Stark backed by Pendergast organization, contests with William Hirth, foe of Pendergast, for democratic gubernatorial nomination in today's primary. Jesse W. Barrett, James J. Barrett and Claude L. Lambert seek republican nomination.

TOPEKA, Kan.—Senator Arthur Capper bids for republican renomination in contest with Walter Neibarger and H. L. Stout. Four candidates seek the democratic nomination: Dempster O. Potts, Omar Ketchum, John H. Arnett and Robert George.

RICHMOND, Va.—Virginia's primary today is marked by lack of contests. The only democratic rivalries are over two nominations to the national house of representatives.

WASHINGTON, Aug. 4, (AP)—Political leaders watched for any possible hints of national sentiment today as voters of three states cast their ballots in primaries.

The primaries, part of a series of 11 which will be held this month, were in Missouri, Kansas and Virginia.

The Missouri voting [illegible] something of a test of [illegible] leader.

Hirth, running for the democratic nomination for governor, assailed the Pendergast group day in and day out. Opposing him for the nomination was Major Lloyd C. Stark, nurseryman who had Pendergast backing.

For the republican nomination the fight was three-cornered. Candidates were Jesse W. Barrett, former state attorney general; James J. Barrett and Claude L. Lambert.

In Kansas

In Kansas, the home state of Governor Alf M. Landon, leaders of both parties strove to get out a big vote, for psychological purposes. Candidates for governor, senator, representatives and other posts were being nominated, but in many cases there were no contests.

There was interest in the bid of Senator Arthur Capper, republican, to secure renomination over two rivals, Walter Neibarger, Tonganoxie editor, and H. L. Stout, Fort Scott business man.

Virginia, traditionally democratic, had only two contests for democratic nominations to the national house of representatives. Senator Carter Glass was not involved in the primary, having already been declared his party's nominee for senator.

Political observers watched with interest a close race in Kentucky, where a primary was held last week. With tabulation of votes nearing completion, Senator M. M. Logan held a plurality of about 3,000 over former Governor J. C. W. Beckham for the democratic senatorial nomination.

Campaigns Speed Up.

A hum of activities in the Roosevelt and Landon camps heralded the imminent beginning of the more intensive stage of the national campaigns.

After conferring with President Roosevelt at Hyde Park, democratic national committeemen indicated he had signaled full steam ahead.

"It is reported that we are prepared to conduct an aggressive campaign from now until November," said Chairman James A. Farley. "We are not losing any time. We are ready to go."

Drought problems occupied part of Mr. Roosevelt's time yesterday, as they did in the case of Gov. Landon also. Mr. Roosevelt conferred with Secretary Wallace and others and ordered a complete report on relief activities.

In a radio talk, Landon advised Kansas business men to "work out practical plans" for cooperation with farmers in avoiding the necessity of sacrificing "valuable breeding animals by sending them to market."

During the day, Mr. Landon talked over the political situation with Senators Townsend of Delaware and Steiwer of Oregon. After conferring with William Allen White, editor, at Emporia, the governor planned to drive today to Independence, his home town, to cast his ballot in the primary.

Opposing political forces continued to fire at each other.

Republican Chairman John D. M. Hamilton said in a speech at Bismarck, N. D., that Roosevelt

Campaign—
(Continued on Page 2)

1936

OLYMPICS

The Basketball Games

BASKETBALL IN THE Berlin Olympics had many twists and turns, including a forfeit because of a civil war, a ban against tall players and a championship game in the mud.

The only Olympics prior 1936 to include basketball was St. Louis in 1904—it was a demonstration sport in the 1924 and 1928 games. And the only teams competing in St. Louis were American, as the game was little known outside the U.S.

By the 1930s, many other countries had integrated the game into their sports programs and the International Olympic Committee decided to include the sport in Berlin. The Amateur Athletic Union (AAU), the YMCA and the National Collegiate Athletic Association (NCAA) had pushed this idea for years in this country and with the international sports federation.

A committee known as the Olympic Basketball Committee was formed to pick an American team, coaches, the tryout locations and to raise money. The first meeting was in Chicago on July 6, 1935. Dr. Walter E. Meanwell of the University of Wisconsin was elected chairman and J. Lyman Bingham of the AAU later was the committee's representative on the American Olympic Committee.

From the onset the committee emphasized that the final team picked would consist of amateur players only. Committee members prepared a set of rules that consisted largely of extracts from the AAU, covering the definition of amateur standing, residence, etc., with one important addition: "That no team may compete in the tryouts unless organized and playing a regular schedule of games on or before December 15."

NCAA rules for individual eligibility were followed to the letter: To be eligible for competition every man entered must be a bona fide student working for a degree; No man may compete who has represented his college in intercollegiate meets for more than three years in aggregate; Each competitor must have been a calendar year in residence at the institution he represents and he must be an undergraduate eligible for athletic competition according to the standards required by his institution and his conference.

Playoffs would have be required and there was much disagreement as to which teams would be eligible to participate. It was finally agreed that the first and second teams from the AAU National Championships in Denver; the winner of the YMCA National Championships in Peoria, Illinois, and five college teams to be selected by a system of playoffs throughout the United States would be chosen.

Financing was a never-ending problem in basketball as with other sports. All the proceeds from the college playoffs were earmarked for the Olympic fund. Many colleges indicated they would participate in the playoffs, but when it came time to sign up only a small number of schools actually played.

The country was broken up into 10 regions with tournaments in each region. The five colleges that were to represent the NCAA in the final Olympic tournament were: Temple University, University of Arkansas, DePaul University, Utah Agricultural College and the University of Washington.

The AAU tournament in Denver was won by the Globe Oil and Refining Company team of McPherson, Kansas, with the runner-up being the Universal Pictures team from Hollywood, California.

The YMCA tournament was won by a team from Denver. When this team went to New York for the championships authorities discovered that team members had played under another name in another tournament and they were disqualified. The Wilmerding, Pennsylvania, YMCA was designated the new entrant.

A national tournament was held from April 3–5, 1936, at New York City's Madison Square Garden. Unfortunately, attendance was low and expenses were greater than income. As a basis for selecting the Olympic team, it was agreed that eight players would be selected from the winning team, five from the second-place team and one at large from the remaining players in the tournament. The winning team's coach would be the team coach and the assistant coach would come from the second team. Dr. Joseph A. Reilly of the Kansas City Athletic Club was selected as team manager.

As an added attraction at the tournament, a pass-in-review before Dr. James Naismith, inventor of basketball, was included. He also addressed the crowd on the early history of the game. {*Editor's note:* Dr. Naismith was snubbed when he arrived in Berlin. No reception was given him nor did he receive passes to the games. The American team finally got him some free tickets and put together a small parade and reception. He was allowed to open the basketball competition.}

The final team was selected as follows: from Universal Pictures: Frank Lubin, Carl Shy, Dwayne Swanson, Art Mollner, Don Piper, Sam Balter and Carl Knowles (an eighth man was dropped pending an investigation of his eligibility); from Globe: Francis Johnson, Joe Fortenberry, John "Tex" Gibbons, Jack Ragland, Willard Schmidt and William Wheatley; Ralph Bishop of the University of Washington was chosen as the 13th member of the squad from the remaining teams in the tournament. James Needles of the Universal team was the head coach and Eugene Johnson of Globe, the assistant.

The Universal Film Studio was the original sponsor of the team, but withdrew its support at the last minute to protest the treatment of Jews in Germany (the studio was predominantly Jewish-operated at the time). The studio demanded its name be removed from the player's shirts, although it appears this never happened.

Without this backing, the team had to play its way across the country to earn enough to get to New York and board the S.S. *Manhattan*. In each city the team played, it earned enough to reach the next city east.

When the 14 players and coaches arrived in Berlin they immediately landed in a sea of controversy. Unbeknownst to the American officials, the three-second rule had been abolished, each team was limited to seven players at a game, all games would be played on outdoor courts and the maximum height for players would be 6′2″.

The height limit would have eliminated the tallest American players and after a strong complaint this rule was rescinded. The Americans split up their 14-man team into two squads, one featuring the six Globe players and Ralph Bishop, the other featuring the seven Universal players. Each unit would play one game and then sit out the next.

In the opening round, the Americans were supposed to play Spain but due to the civil war raging in that country, the Spanish team never showed up. Thus the United Stated won by forfeit 2–0.

The European champion team was Estonia, the Americans' next opponent. Estonia was defeated by the Universal team 52–28.

The Americans received a bye in the third round and the Globe unit handily defeated the Philippines, 56–23. Before this game the Globe team had to improvise uniforms as theirs were stolen from their lockers the night before.

In the semi-finals, the Universal unit defeated Mexico, 25–10. The final game pitted two North American teams—the United States and Canada. All games were played on old clay tennis courts and because it had rained the day before the final game, the courts were soaked. At the end of the half, the Americans led 15–4. The final score at the end of the rain-soaked game saw America victorious, 19–8.

Joe Fortenberry, the American center, scored as many points as the entire Canadian team. Because the Globe team won the final game, its players were the only members of the American team allowed to receive the gold medals at the official ceremony.

In the consolation game, Mexico defeated Poland for third place.

It is interesting to note that the average age of the American players was mid-twenties, and Jack Ragland was a ripe old 50. Of the 14 players, three are still alive as of late 1995—Sam Batter, Francis Johnson and Frank Lubin.

After a 32-year lapse, basketball won a permanent place in the 1968 Olympics with 22 nations participating, the largest number of team competitors on the program. The United States would win every Olympic championship (in 1980 the U.S. boycotted the Olympics) until 1988 when the Soviet Union came in first and Yugoslavia, second.

1936 USA MEN'S OLYMPIC GAMES ROSTER

NAME	POS	HGT	WGT	AGE	AFFILIATION/SCHOOL	HOMETOWN
Sam Balter	G	5-10	150	26	Universal Pictures (UCLA)	Los Angeles, CA
Ralph Bishop	F	6-3	185	20	University of Washington	New York, NY
Joe Fortenberry	C	6-9	175	25	Globe Oilers (Wichita State)	Chesterfield, MO
John Gibbons	G	6-1	175	28	Globe Oilers (Southwestern)	La Habra, CA
Francis Johnson	G	5-11	175	25	Globe Oilers (Wichita State)	Chesterfield, MO
Carl Knowles	F	6-2	165	26	Universal Pictures (UCLA)	Los Angeles, CA
Frank Lubin	F	6-7	250	26	Universal Pictures (UCLA)	Glendale, CA
Art Mollner	G	6-0	160	23	Universal Pictures (L.A. J. C.)	Westlake Village, CA
Don Piper	G	5-11	160	25	Universal Pictures (UCLA)	Peoria, IL
Jack Ragland	G	6-0	175	50	Globe Oilers (Wichita State)	Tucson, AZ
Willard Schmidt	C	6-10	190	26	Globe Oilers (Creighton)	Stanton, NE
Carl Shy	G	6-0	170	27	Universal Pictures (UCLA)	Hollywood, CA
Dwayne Swanson	F	6-2	175	22	Universal Pictures (USC)	El Toro, CA
William Wheatley	F	6-2	175	27	Globe Oilers (Kansas Wesleyan)	El Cerrito, CA

HEAD COACH: James Needles, Universal Pictures (CA)
ASSISTANT COACH: Eugene Johnson, Globe Oilers (KS)
MANAGER: Joseph Reilly, Kansas City Athletic Club (MO)
ATHLETIC TRAINER: Eddie Zanzaai, Princeton University (NJ)

RESULTS *of* OLYMPIC BASKETBALL

First Round	Second Round	Third Round	Fourth Round	Semi-final Round	Final Round
Esthonia 34 France 29	U. S. A. 52 Esthonia 28	Philippines 39 Esthonia 22	U. S. A. 56 Philippines 23	U. S. A. 25 Mexico 10	U. S. A. 19 Canada 8
Chile 30 Turkey 16	Chile 23 Brazil 18	Italy 27 Chile 19	Mexico 34 Italy 17	Canada 42 Poland 15	
Switzerland 25 Germany 18	Philippines 32 Mexico 30	Japan 28 Mexico 22	Peru defaulted to Poland.		
Hungary defaulted to Czechoslovakia	Japan 43 Poland 31	Canada 27 Switzerland 9	Canada 43 Uruguay 21		
Italy 44 Poland 28	Uruguay 36 Egypt 23	Uruguay 28 Czechoslovakia 19			
Peru 35 Egypt 22	Peru 29 China 21	Poland 33 Brazil 25			
Mexico 32 Belgium 9	Italy 58 Germany 16				
Latvia 20 Uruguay 17	Czechoslovakia 25 Switzerland 12				
Canada 24 Brazil 17	Canada 34 Latvia 23				
Japan 35 China 19					
Byes into second round: U. S. A., Philippines.		Byes into fourth round: U. S. A., Peru.		**Match for Third Place** Mexico 26 Poland 12	

Consolation Round Contested by the above losers	Consolation Round Contested by the above losers		
Egypt 33 Turkey 23	Mexico 32 Egypt 10		The above losers contested together for the fifth and sixth places in the final ranking as follows:
China 45 France 38	Brazil 32 China 14		Peru defaulted to Uruguay.
Uruguay 17 Belgium 10	Czechoslovakia 20 Germany 9		Philippines 32 Italy 14
	Poland 28 Latvia 23		**Fifth and Sixth Place Winners**
Byes: Germany, Poland, Brazil.	Bye: Esthonia.		Philippines 33 Uruguay 23
The above winners and the teams with byes are included in the draw for the Second Round	The above winners and the team with a bye are included in the draw for the Third Round		

FINAL RANKING

1—U. S. A.
2—Canada.
3—Mexico.
4—Poland.
5—Philippines.
6—Uruguay.

THE MEDAL WINNING TEAMS

First Place: U. S. A.—Johnson, Fortenberry, Ragland, Knowles, Wheatley, Bishop, Swanson.

Second Place: Canada—Stewart, A. Chapman, Wiseman, Allison, C. Chapman, Aitchison, Peden.

Third Place: Mexico—C. Morca, Moreno, Spilsbury, Leija, Robert, Cordero, H. Morca.

A third round game between Estonia and the Philippines. The Philippines won 39 to 22.
NA, HH 242-HD-370-1

Second-round game between the Philippines and Mexico. The Philippines won 32-30.

As a keepsake of their stay at the Olympic village the American basketball team, which won the gold medal, poses for a photograph. Their steward and two German soldiers also pose. BA

In a consolation game Poland beat Latvia 28 to 33.

Sam Balter was a member of the gold-medal United States basketball team, one of five current or former UCLA players named to the 1936 team. He was captain of the UCLA basketball team and an All-American in 1929. He coached and taught at El Segundo High School from 1931–35 and played for Universal Pictures' AAU team in 1936.

His major fame came as a broadcaster for three decades. He was the first coast-to-coast Mutual Network Sportscaster in the history of radio, broadcasting from KHJ, Los Angeles, and WFIL, Philadelphia in 1938. Balter was also play-by-play commentator for the Cincinnati Reds in 1942; the "Voice of the UCLA Bruins" for both football and basketball, 1945–52; UCLA and USC televised games play-by-play commentator, 1950–52; KLAC Radio, Los Angeles, sports director, 1946–62; Voice of the Hollywood Stars and the Los Angeles Angels baseball teams, 1946–50; play-by-play commentator for the first college football game ever televised in Southern California, USC versus Utah, 1950; pool broadcaster (radio) covering the birth of the United Nations in San Francisco in 1945; ABC Radio, West Coast Sports Director, 1962–65; plus commentator on many other radio programs through the years. He appeared in several movies: "Babe Ruth Story," "Fear Strikes Out," "The Jackie Robinson Story" and "Champion." He also appeared in the television series "Ben Casey," "Untouchables," "Superman," "Climax" and "My Three Sons."

Balter has been voted into the UCLA Athletic Hall of Fame; Los Angeles City Schools Hall of Fame; National Basketball Hall of Fame; was named Top Sportscaster of the Era by the *Los Angeles Times* in 1974; the Nation's #1 Sportscaster by *Variety* in 1953; received the St. Louis Sporting News Award, Best Commentator in the West, and was named to the International Jewish Hall of Fame and the Southern California Sports Broadcaster Association Annual Awards Hall of Fame as "Man of the Year" in 1993.

Sam and his wife, Mildred, live in Los Angeles, California.

Frank Lubin was perhaps the greatest basketball player of his time, which was before the advent of professional basketball. Lubin was born in 1910 in Los Angeles and played for UCLA. After graduating in 1931 he went on to play in AAU competition until he was 54 years old. He was on the Universal Studios team in Berlin and was captain of the team. He also played on the 20th Century Fox team when it won the 1941 national championship. He was an AAU All-American 10 times and coached the Lithuanian national team to the 1939 European championship.

Lubin has been inducted into the Helms Basketball Hall of Fame. Most of his working life was spent in Hollywood as a grip. His nickname was "Frankenstein" and although he never played the part he was a stand-in and stunt man for the role. He now lives in the Los Angeles area.

Francis Johnson was one of several players on the 1936 team who played for Wichita University. He was an all-around athlete at the school in football, basketball and track. He played for the Globe Oilers in 1936 and played an additional three years in the AAU, winning the 1938 national championship. He worked for the John Deere Company and was a well-known horse breeder.

American and Mexican basketball teams on the victory stand receiving first and third prizes.

1936
OLYMPICS

Swimming and Diving

AMERICAN SWIMMERS AND divers won the team championship in men's swimming and diving events to displace Japan, which won the 1932 Olympics. Jack Medica in the 400-meter freestyle, Adolph Kiefer in the 100-meter backstroke, Richard Degener in the springboard diving and Marshall Wayne in the platform diving were the American winners.

Peter Fick of the New York Athletic Club, world's record holder for the 100-meter freestyle, was a disappointing sixth in the event. Jack Medica took a second in the 1,500-meter freestyle, Albert Van de Weghe took a second in the 100-meter backstroke and the American team of Ralph Flanagan, John Macionis, Paul Wolfe and Jack Medica took second in the 800-meter relay. Marshall Wayne was second and Al Greene third in springboard diving and Elbert Root was second in high diving.

The American women's team also won the team championship, but only by the slimmest of margins over Holland, and only because of the team's predominance in diving.

Rita Mastenbroek of Holland was a one-woman swim team, winning the gold medal in the 100-meter and 400-meter freestyle and 400-meter relay and silver in the 100-meter backstroke.

Lenore Wingard of the American team was third in the 400-meter freestyle and Alice Bridges was third in the 100-meter backstroke. For the first time since American women competed in the 400-meter relay in 1920, the team of Katherine Rawls, Bernice Lapp, Mavis Freeman and Olive McKean came in third behind Holland and Germany.

In springboard diving it was a clean sweep for the Americans: Marjorie Gestring, first; Katherine Rawls, second; and Dorothy Poynton-Hill, third. In high diving, Hill was first and Velma Dunn, second.

The American water polo team was made up of members of the Los Angeles Athletic Club with alternates from various clubs around the country. Hungary, the defending champion, narrowly beat Germany for first place. The American team managed to win only one game, against Uruguay, in the first round.

Three Olympic divers. From left: Käte Köhler, Germany, and Americans Velma Dunn and Dorothy Poynton-Hill.

Eleanor Holm was one of the most interesting members of the American team. A veteran of the 1928 and 1932 Olympics, she was born in 1913 in Brooklyn, New York, a daughter of a fireman. She taught herself to swim but later was coached by Lou Handley, maker of Olympic champions. Handley developed Holm into the star backstroker of the New York Women's Swimming Association.

At the 1928 Amsterdam Olympics she competed as a 14-year-old, but won no medals. By 1932 she was the national champion in both the backstroke and individual medley and won a gold medal in the backstroke and as a member of the relay team.

In 1930 she briefly worked for Florenz Ziegfield.

By 1936 she held six world records in the backstroke; her 100- and 200-yard backstroke records lasted for 16 years. All totaled she had won 29 national championships by the time she made the 1936 Olympic team and was expected to win another gold medal.

She was still only 23 but was already married to Art Jarrett. "I had been around. I was no baby," she stated. "Hell, I married Art Jarrett after the '32 Games. He was the star at the Coconut Grove, and I went to work singing for his band. I used to take a mike and get up in front of the band in a white bathing suit and a white cowboy hat and high heels. I'd sing "I'm an Old Cowhand." Warner Brothers had signed me as an actress—not a swimmer, an actress. Anyway, here I'd been working in nightclubs when I made the team in 1936. Actually, I quit the band a month before the trials to go into training for the Olympics."

On the S.S. *Manhattan* she spent a lot of time in the first-class section with her writer friends, such as Charles MacArthur and Ben Hecht. Team members were supposed to stay in compartments below decks, four to a room.

One night she had been partying in first class when, as she recalled, "This chaperon came up to me and told me it was time to go to bed. God, it was about nine o'clock, and who wanted to go down in that damn basement to sleep anyway? So I said to her, 'Oh, is it really bedtime? Did *you* make the Olympic team or did I?' I had a few glasses of champagne. So she went to Brundage and complained that I was setting a bad example for the team, and they got together and told me the next morning that I was fired. I was heartbroken."

After several attempts at reconciliation, she was officially banned from the games by the American Olympic Committee. She did attend the games as a spectator and became a favorite of the U.S. newspaper crowd and the Nazi hierarchy. "I was listed as a correspondent for INS or someone, but I never wrote a word," she recalled. "Paul Gallico wrote everything under my name. I was asked to the Nazis' big receptions, and, of course, Brundage and all the big shots would be there too, trying to ignore me! . . . Göring was fun . . . lots of chuckling. And so did the little one with the clubfoot (Josef Goebbels). Hitler asked to see me, and through his interpreter he said if I'd been on the German team, they'd have kept me on the team and then punished me after the Olympics—if I had *lost*! Hitler asked me himself if I got drunk—he seemed very interested—and I said no."

After she returned home she got more offers than if she had won a gold medal. In 1937 she turned professional and starred in Billy Rose's Aquacade at the Great Lakes Exposition in Cleveland and at the 1939 and 1940 New York World's Fair. She ended up marrying the flamboyant Billy Rose, who had divorced his wife, Fanny Brice.

In 1938 Holm made her only motion picture, *Tarzan's Revenge* with fellow Olympic athlete Glenn Morris. After she married Rose in 1939 she retired to run their household in Mount Kisco, New York. *Time* magazine put her on the cover of its Aug. 21, 1939, issue, only 11 days before World War II began.

Billy Rose was a very difficult man to live with and Holm finally divorced him in 1951. Because of alimony payments she did not remarry until Rose died in 1966. At that time she married Tom Whalen and they now make their home in North Miami, Florida.

Eleanor Holm Whalen is a true Olympic star and a most interesting lady.

Eleanor Holm and an escort at the Olympic Stadium.
NA, HH 242-HO-0529-1

A much-publicized photo of Eleanor Holm.

Eleanor Holm in her Olympic outfit. ISHF

Olympians Glenn Morris and Eleanor Holm played in the 1938 movie *Tarzan's Revenge*. It was directed by D. Ross Lederman and also starred George Barbier, C. Henry Gordon, Hedda Hopper and George Meeker. Morris cavorted capably in this adventure about an evil African ruler who covets Holm. No other Tarzan film had the main character off screen for such long periods of time.

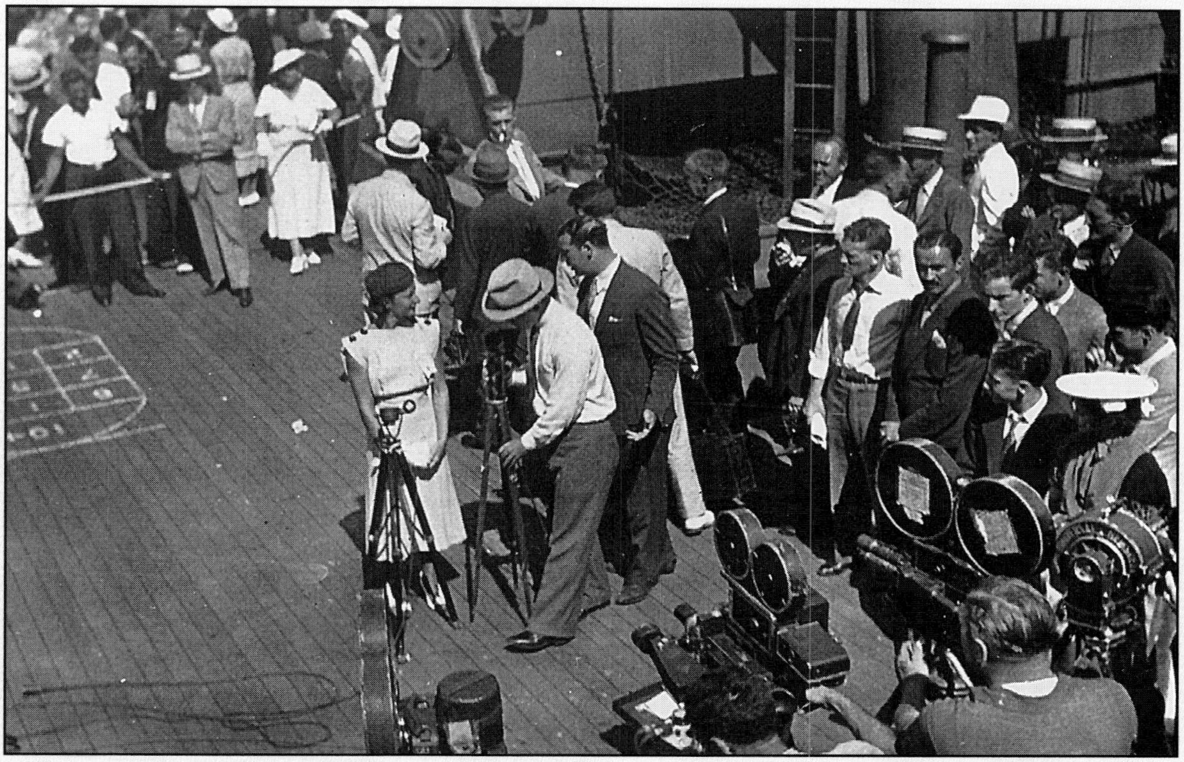

A news conference was held on board the *S.S. Manhattan* for Eleanor Holm after she was barred from participating in the Olympic games. NBHF

Eleanor Holm made the cover of *Time* magazine on Aug. 21, 1939, for her performance at the New York World's Fair. Just 11 days later World War II would begin.

The winning women's 400-meter relay teams marching to the victory stand. Germany, second, Holland, first, and the United States, third. Holland set a new Olympic record.

Members of the women's swimming team. From left: Mavis Freeman, Iris Cummings, Olive McKean and Velma Dunn.
NA, HH-242-HD-457-4

American divers, from left: Katherine Rawls, Velma Dunn, Dorothy Poynton-Hill and Marjorie Gestring. BA

Marjorie Gestring roomed with her mother and carried a good-luck teddy bear to the pool while on board the S.S. *Manhattan*. This was because she was, at 13 years old, the youngest member of the American women's diving team and by the end of the 1936 Olympics, the youngest gold medalist in Olympic history.

At the finals of the springboard diving event Gestring beat the favorite, Katherine Rawls of Florida, by 1.02 points. Another American, Dorothy Poynton-Hill, came in third.

At the 1932 Olympics, Marjorie, a native of Los Angeles, was inspired by Georgia Coleman, the U.S. springboard champion. Fred Cady, the great diving coach took Marjorie under his wing and coached her through the '36 Olympics and national indoor and outdoor springboard titles in 1937 and 1938 and the national platform title in 1939.

Gestring would have been at her top form for the 1940 Olympics had they been held. She attended Stanford University during World War II and was seriously injured in an exhibition dive that affected her back for the rest of her life.

She tried out for the 1948 Olympics, still only 25 years old, but missed the team by only one point. She held several positions in the public relations field after retiring from competitive diving and moved to Hawaii after her marriage. After raising three children, early widowhood brought her back to California where she again married and settled in Newport Beach. She died in 1995.

Jeanette Campbell of Argentina took second in the 100-meter freestyle race.

Marjorie Gestring.
LEFT: LC, RIGHT: NA, HH 242-HD-0393-1

Dorothy Poynton-Hill was America's premier woman diver of the late 1920s and 1930s. Just after her thirteenth birthday she placed third in springboard diving at the 1928 Olympics, the youngest American Olympic medalist in history.

She won successive gold medals in high diving at the 1932 and 1936 Olympics, plus a bronze medal in springboard diving in Berlin. In addition she won seven AAU titles.

After her retirement from competition, she taught aquatics at her "Dorothy Poynton Aquatic Club" in Los Angeles.

Dorothy Poynton-Hill and Peter Fick. BA

Dorothy Poynton-Hill in one of her spectacular dives. LC

Big Jack and Little Margie Annex Unguarded Gold Medals Left Around Olympic Pool

Japanese Menace Is Humbled by Medica. Blond Angel Outdives Florida Mermaid, Katherine Rawls.

Berlin, Aug. 12.—(AP)—A pair of last ditch battlers from the Golden West, Big Jack Medica of Seattle and little Margie Gestring of Los Angeles took all the gold medals left unguarded around the Olympic swimming stadium today.

Medica scored a sensational victory over the Japanese menace in the 400-meter free style championship, passing Shumpei Uto 20 meters from home to win by one length of his long arms in Olympic record-making time of 4:44.5.

Thirteen-year-old Margie dived like a blond angel to beat out her teammate, Katherine Rawls, in the springboard event after the Florida mite had appeared to have the title in her grasp.

With Miss Rawls second and Mrs. Dorothy Poynton Hill, Los Angeles, third, America swept the top places in the second diving event in as many days, duplicating the blanket finish by Dick Begener, Marshall Wayne and Al Greene in the men's springboard event.

At the end of the fifth struggle in the Olympic tank America held three gold medals, Japan two; Hungary and Holland, one each. Furthermore the men held a two-point lead over Japan in the fight for team honors, 38 to 36, while the girls led Holland, 20 to 17 1-2.

What made Medica's and Margie's triumphs all the more noteworthy was the magnificent manner in which each had responded under pressure. Neither was suposed to win, but nobody could have told it when they saw defeat staring them in the eye.

Medica, who had only barely recovered from a chest cold, trailed the fleeting little Uto a full length when they turned into the final 100 meters. Probably no one among the 20,000 in the stadium except Medica thought he had any hope of overtaking the Tokyo terror.

But when they hit the final turn, 50 meters from home, the Washington star had reduced the deficit to half a length and gained still more with his powerful deep-water kick off the wall.

WEDNESDAY'S HERO.

By United Press.

Jack Medica of Seattle, whose powerful stroking upset the favored Japanese swimmers and gave the United States an unexpected first place in the 400-meter free style swim.

Medica, apparently refusing to show his true form in training or the preliminary eliminations, not only won the event but cracked two Olympic marks as well.

His time of 4 minutes, 44.5 seconds, broke the record of 4:48.4 set by Buster Crabbe of 1932, and the later mark of 4:45.5 made by Shumpei Uto of Japan in Monday's qualifying heat.

Katherine Rawls from Fort Lauderdale, Florida, was the most versatile swimmer on the American team. She won a silver medal in the 1932 Olympic springboard diving event and repeated it again in Berlin. She also took a bronze as a member of the 4 × 100-meter freestyle relay team and placed seventh in the 100-meter freestyle race.

She won 33 AAU titles in freestyle, breaststroke, individual medley and diving and was undefeated in the individual medley for eight years. She was the first American woman to win four national championships at a single meet at the 1937 AAU championships and repeated this in 1938.

Retiring in 1938, Katherine Rawls became in World War II one of the original 25 women to form the WASPs (Women's Airforce Service Pilots) to ferry combat planes from factories to airfields around the United States. Rawls died in 1982.

An unusual photo, possibly a demonstration before the start of the swimming events. NA; HH 242-HD-0524

GEORGE SHERRY PHOTO

John Higgins made the 1936 Olympic swim team as a high school student and placed fourth in the 200-meter breaststroke. He is a native of Providence, Rhode Island, and graduated of Ohio State University. In 1936 he became the first man to set a world record using the then-new butterfly armstroke and breaststroke frog kick. At one time he held 10 world records and 21 American records. He was the swim coach at the U.S. Naval Academy for more than 20 years. He is a member of the International Swimming Hall of Fame.

Jack C. Medica was one of America's greatest swimmers in the 1930s. He was a high school senior in Seattle when he went to the 1932 Olympics as a member of the 800-meter relay team.

He reached his peak as a swimmer during his four years at the University of Washington. He swam in the 50-yard, 100-yard and 200-yard freestyle events and won all of them.

Medica won at least four or five AAU crowns each year from 1933 through 1936, but his most unusual trophy was a University of Michigan varsity letter. He never went to Michigan but he took enough points away from Yale and Iowa for Michigan to win the national title. Coach Matt Mann said, "He doesn't have a team at Washington and he sure swam well for Michigan so I sent him a letter sweater."

He held 11 world records for the 200-meter, 400-meter, 500-meter and 800-meter freestyle; for the 220-meter, 300-meter, 440-meter and the 1,000-yard freestyle and freestyle records for both the half-mile and the mile.

At the Berlin Olympics he was the gold-medal winner at 400 meters and silver-medal winner in the 1,500-meter race and competed in the 800-meter relays.

After the Olympics he competed around the world but retired in 1939 to become assistant swim coach at Columbia University. He was the freshman coach at the University of Pennsylvania from 1940 to 1943 and varsity coach from 1943 to 1958. He was also a full professor in physical education at the school until retiring in 1976. He died in 1985 at age 71.

Jack Medica winning the 400-meter race. LC

Jack C. Medica, gold medal winner in the 400 meters, flanked by the second and third place Japanese team members. ISHF

Adolph "Sonny" Kiefer was the greatest backstroke swimmer of the 1930s and perhaps the greatest of any decade. He was born in Chicago in 1918 and swam for the University of Texas. In 1935 he broke 11 American and world backstroke records in five weeks. Swimming for the Lake Shore Athletic Club in Chicago he made the 1936 Olympic team and won a gold in the 100-meter backstroke with a new Olympic record of one minute and 05.9 seconds.

He set 17 world records between 1935 and 1944, none broken until 1950. In addition he won a total of 18 AAU titles.

During World War II he was put in charge of swimming instruction for the entire U.S. Navy. He ended his competitive career in 1946. He later formed his own company involved in the manufacture of swimming pool accessories and swim-related items. He now lives in the Chicago area.

Adolph Kiefer in front of the Olympic bell at the Olympic stadium before it was hoisted into position. ISHF

Adolf Kiefer. ISHF

Adolf Kiefer wins the 100-meter backstroke.

Albert Van de Weghe won a silver medal in the 100-meter backstroke in Berlin. He swam for the Newark, New Jersey, Athletic Club and set world records in the 100- and 200-meter backstrokes. At Princeton University he won three NCAA titles and several AAU titles. He was a chemical engineer for Dupont for 35 years.

Ralph Flanagan won a silver medal in the 4 × 2000-meter freestyle relay. He swam for the Miami, Florida, Athletic Club and the Miami Biltmore Aquatic Club. He participated in the 1932 Olympics, but did not win a medal. Although Flanagan was in the finals of the 400- and 1,500-meter freestyles in 1936, he did not place. In all, he won 20 AAU titles and set 26 American and two world records. He worked for the American Red Cross and as a safety director in Los Angeles for many years. He died in 1988.

John Macionis was born in Philadelphia in 1916. At Central High School he set a school record in the 220-yard freestyle, which stood for years. He also held many national and international interscholastic swimming titles in the 1930s. In 1935 he won the Senior National AAU 440-yard freestyle while at Yale University.

He made the Olympic team in the 400-meter freestyle and the 4 × 200-meter relay where his team won a silver medal. After arriving in Berlin he developed an ear infection and so wasn't able to practice. This gave him an opportunity to see all the track events and some social displays. One evening while attending the opera, he was seated in a parquet box, courtesy of local Berliners, when everyone but him stood up and yelled out, "Sig Heil, Sig Heil." All of a sudden he was yanked up by two Brownshirts. When he asked those around him about this treatment he was told, "Everybody stands for Der Führer."

In 1937 and 1938 he won the NCAA 1500-meter freestyle and set several world records. After graduating from Yale he went to work for Campbell Soup Company and during World War II served with the U.S. Coast Guard. He worked in dairy sales until retiring in 1981.

Macionis has never stopped swimming. For the past 14 years he has won in his age group the International Hall of Fame Ocean Mile Swim, as well a being the oldest contestant for the past three years. Macionis has been inducted into several swimming halls of fame, including the International Swimming Hall of Fame. He and his wife, May, have been married for 54 years and divide their time between Elkins Park, Pennsylvania, and Ft. Lauderdale, Florida.

Peter Fick held the world record for the 100-meter freestyle from 1934-1944. At Berlin, however, Fick managed only a sixth place finish in the event.

John Macionis in 1936.
JOHN MACIONIS PHOTO

Olympic men's diving team. Left to right: Dick Degener, University of Michigan; Elbert Root, Detroit, Michigan; Marshall Wayne, Miami, Florida; Al Greene, Lake Shore Athletic Club, Chicago, Illinois. Photo taken at the final tryout site, Rocky Point Pool, Warwick, Rhode Island, August 1936. ISHF

Dick Degener was a diving champion at Detroit's Central High School, the Detroit Athletic Club and the University of Michigan before winning the gold medal in the three-meter springboard diving event in Berlin.

He began his athletic career at age 10, when his father, one of Henry Ford's first employees, paid $10 for his son to take diving lessons. By the time he was 21, a prominent swimming official declared the name Dick Degener to be synonymous with diving grace and perfection.

Degener won a bronze medal at the 1932 Olympics as well as many AAU, Big Ten and NCAA indoor and outdoor diving championships.

He gave up competitive diving after the 1936 Olympics but dived for Billy Rose's Aquacade for a while. He spent his working career as a clothing salesman and manufacturer's representative. He died in Grand Rapids, Michigan, in 1985 at age 83.

Marshall Wayne was a double winner in Berlin, taking gold in high diving and a silver in springboard diving. He was a member of the Biltmore Athletic Club in Miami and was the AAU outdoor platform diving champion in 1934 and 1936. After the Olympics he joined, along with Dick Degener, Billy Rose's Aquacade for shows at the Cleveland, New York and San Francisco World's Fairs.

During World War II Wayne joined the U.S. Army Air Forces and flew with the 8th Air Force in Europe. He had to bail out over Italy and tore the ligaments in his left knee. For the next 27 years he flew for Pan American World Airways and made a few commercials. He relates how he made one commercial for Camel cigarettes, but is now ashamed of it. He lives in Hendersonville, North Carolina.

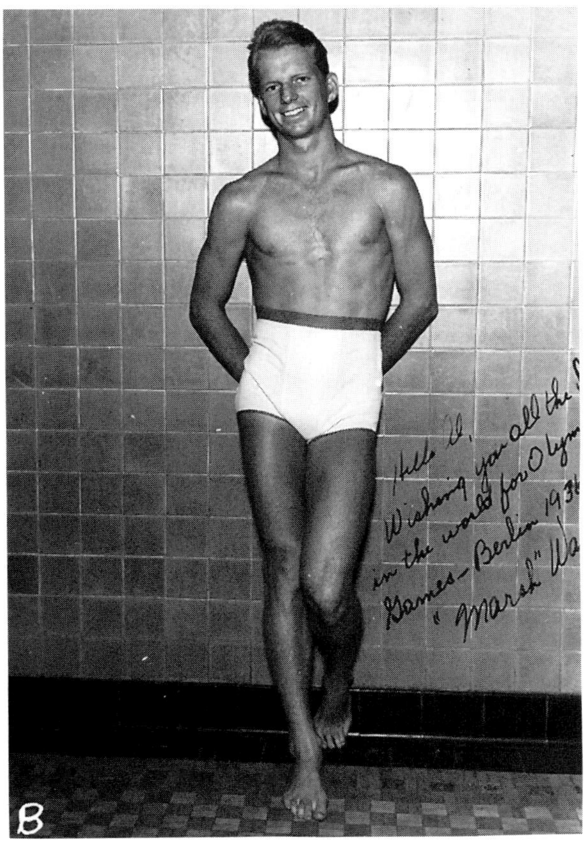

Marshall Wayne in 1936 and in 1993. MARSHALL WAYNE PHOTOS

The platform and high diving boards.

1936
OLYMPICS

Water Sports

Canoe Championships

Canoeing was added to the Olympic program for the first time. Demonstration events were held at Paris in 1924.

Canoeists from Austria were very successful taking three first, three seconds, one third and two fourths. The canoeists from Germany competed with almost equal success winning two championships, three seconds, two thirds and two fourths. The United States finished in sixth place in the team rankings with one third, one fourth and three fifths.

The canoeing events were held at Grünau and over courses of 1,000 meters and 10,000 meters (about 6¼ miles).

Ernest Riedel of Teaneck, New Jersey, made the best showing of the American canoeists finishing third in the 10,000-meter single kayak and fourth in the 1,000-meter single kayak. Joseph Hasenfus and Walter Hasenfus of Needham, Massachusetts, paired to finish fifth in the Canadian double event at 10,000 meters. Joseph Hasenfus was fifth in the Canadian single event at 1,000 meters while Clarence R. McNutt and Robert Graf, both of Philadelphia, Pennsylvania, were fifth in the Canadian double over the 1,000 meter course.

The traditional regatta course was situated to the east of Berlin in the lake district of Grünau. Forty thousand spectators could follow the rowing races on a straight 2,000-meter course.

Rowing Championships

The German oarsmen completely dominated the rowing events, winning five of the seven races on the program. The great victory scored by the Washington University crew in the eight-oared event and by Great Britain in the double sculls, were the only two events not won by the Germans. The United States finished third with 16 points. Germany was first with 59 points and Great Britain second with 18 points. In spite of the heavy rain, which fell a good deal of the time during the Olympic Regatta at Grünau, a capacity crowd turned out for each of the three days of racing.

The winning Four-Oared Shell Without Coxswain team from Germany gives the Nazi salute. BA

The winning German Star Class yacht "Wannsee" manned by Dr. Peter Bischoff.

After a hard race, the United States (top) won the eight-oared championship, defeating Italy and Germany by less than one second.

Ernest Riedel, one of America's greatest kayakers, won the only medal in the sport for the U.S. team. His bronze in the 10,000-meter kayak singles was only one of dozens of medals and championships Riedel won between 1923 and 1947. At 47 years old he also participated in the 1948 Olympics.

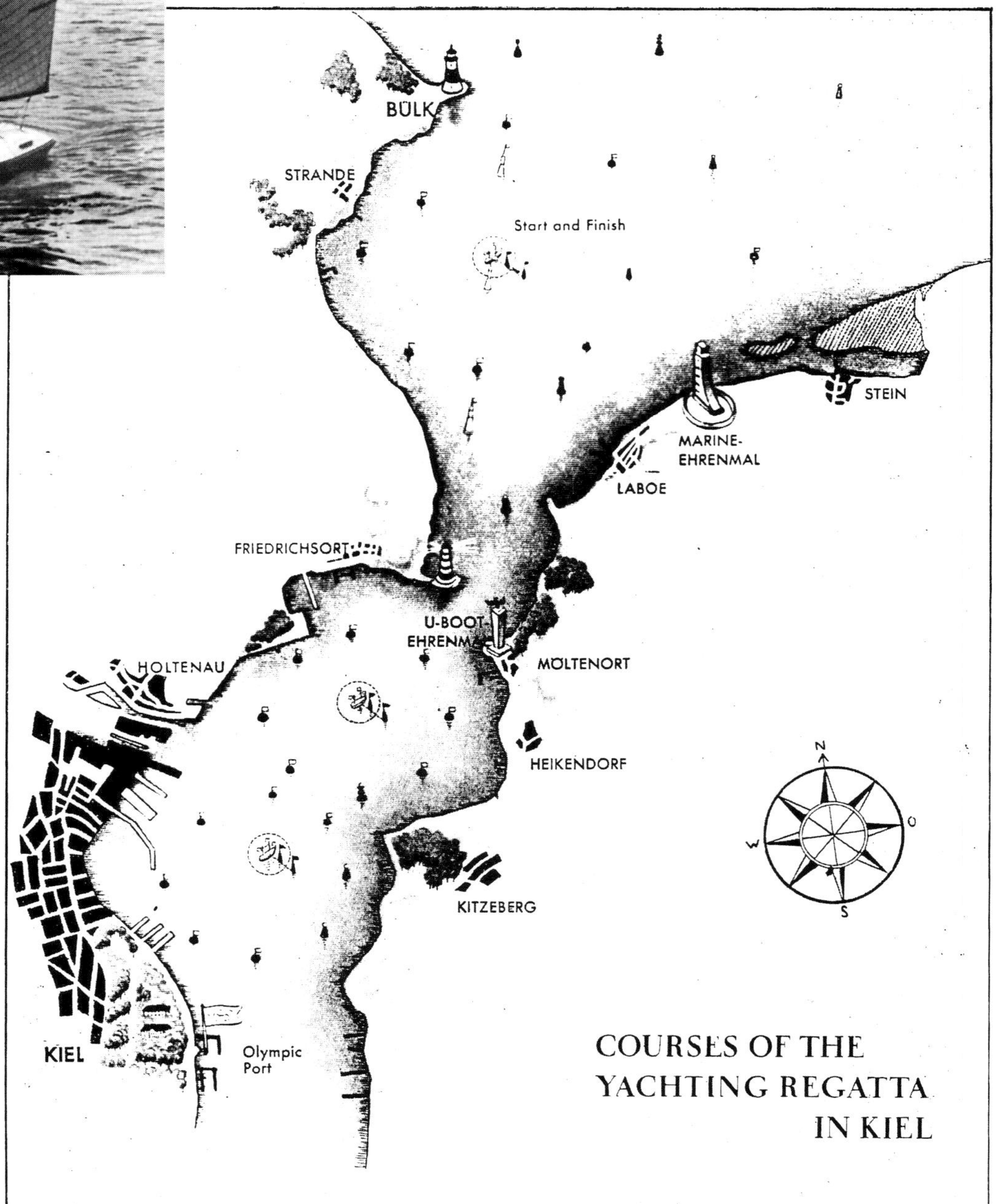

COURSES OF THE YACHTING REGATTA IN KIEL

1936
OLYMPICS

Gymnastics

Gymnastic Championships

Men

Germany's oldest tradition in competitive athletics was brilliantly sustained in the Olympic gymnastic championships. Germany won five Olympic titles including the individual men's all-around and the coveted team championship. The United States finished tenth among the fourteen countries represented by teams of eight men each.

Germany's outstanding gymnasts were Karl A. M. Schwarzmann and Konrad Frey. Schwarzmann placed in the following events: 1st—all-around individual competition, 1st—long horse, 3rd—parallel bars, 3rd—horizontal bar, 4th—flying rings. Konrad Frey also placed in five events: 1st—side horse, 1st—parallel bars, 2nd—horizontal bar, 3rd—all-around individual competition, tied for 3rd—free exercises.

The gymnastics competition took place at the Reichssportfeld in the Dietrich Eckart Stadium. This was the first time in Olympic history that the gymnastic events were held outside the Olympic stadium. Canvas shelter was provided in case of rain and ample space was available for several events to be conducted simultaneously. 25,000 enthusiastic spectators attested to the interest in this sport and the eminence of Germany as a gymnastic nation. Switzerland, Finland, Czechoslovakia and Italy finished behing Germany in that order.

All-around Individual Competition

1. Karl A. M. Schwarzmann, Germany, 113.100 points
2. Eugen Mack, Switzerland, 112.334 points
3. Konrad Frey, Germany, 111.532 points
4. Alois Hudec, Czechoslovakia, 111.119 points
5. Michael Reusch, Switzerland,
   and Martti Uosikinnen, Finland, 110.700 points

48. Frank Cumiskey, United States, 99.001 points
63. Frederick H. Meyer, United States, 94.500 points
78. Chester W. Phillips, United States, 90.733 points
82. Arthur Pitt, United States, 89.066 points
83. Frank O. Haubold, United States, 88.133 points
85. Alfred A. Jochim, United States, 86.867 points
90. Kenneth Griffin, United States, 83.801 points

All-around Team Competition

1. Germany, 657.430 points
2. Switzerland, 654.802 points
3. Finland, 638.468 points
4. Czechoslovakia, 625.863 points
5. Italy, 615.133 points
6. Yugoslavia, 598.598 points
7. Hungary, 591.930 points
8. France, 578.266 points
9. Japan, 568.171 points
10. United States, 551.301 points
11. Austria, 545.433 points
12. Luxembourg, 516.500 points
13. Bulgaria, 452.331 points
14. Romania, 363.465 points

Women

The first Olympic gymnastics competition for women, taking up the entire third day, gave the United States a fifth placing among eight nations with teams of eight women each. The events were parallel bars, balancing beam, side horse vault, one compulsory and optional exercise each, and two optional team drills—one free hand and one with hand apparatus.

Germany was hard pushed by Czechoslovakia and Hungary to finish ahead of them in that order.

1. Germany, 506.50 points
2. Czechoslovakia, 503.60 points
3. Hungary, 499.00 points
4. Yugoslavia, 485.60 points
5. United States, 471.30 points
6. Poland, 470.30 points
7. Italy, 442.30 points
8. Great Britain, 408.30 points

Anita Bärwirth of the champion German women's gymnastic team.

Fred Meyer, the ranking gymnast in the United States in 1935, also spent 47 years working on the floor of the New York Stock Exchange. He was there on Black Tuesday, Oct. 8, 1929, when the market crashed. As a 22 year old Meyer made the 1932 Olympic team and, along with his six team members, won a silver medal in the team competition. Italy took the gold. In 1936 the team did not place, in part, because as Meyer states: "There were no planes back then. We had to go over by ocean liner, and with the boat reeling from side to side, we couldn't train."

Along with his work at the stock exchange he taught gymnastics at night and judged competitions on weekends. He taught for 18 years before retiring in 1959. He judged his last competition in 1978.

Meyer is in the Gymnastics Hall of Fame and the Cumiskey Hall of Fame, named for Frank Cumiskey, a colleague from the 1932 and 1936 U.S. gymnastic teams.

Fred and his wife, Bertha, now make their home in Burke, Virginia.

A large crowd is on hand to watch some of the gymnastic competitions at the Dietrich Eckart Stadium. NA, HH-242-HD-0337

An American gymnast performs on the parallel bars. NA, HH242-HD-346-25

1936 OLYMPICS

Wrestling and Boxing

Wrestling Championships

The Olympic wrestling championships at Berlin attracted competitors from 28 countries, which resulted in the largest entry ever received.

The American team was by far the best that has ever represented the United States in the Olympic games.

Frank W. Lewis of Cushing, Oklahoma, won the welterweight championship. Ross Flood of Blackwell, Oklahoma; Francis E. Millard of North Adams, Massachusetts; and Richard L. Voliva of Bloomington, Indiana, finished second in the bantamweight, featherweight, and middleweight classes respectively. The wrestlers from Sweden finished in second place for the team championship with one victory, one second place and two third places.

Kristjan Palusalu of Estonia, in addition to winning the heavyweight championship in free-style wrestling, also won the Greco-Roman heavyweight championship. The United States did not enter a team in the Greco-Roman style of wrestling.

Deutschland Hall. The large number of wrestling entries required two rings.

Boxing Championships

The boxing competitions were held at Deutschland Hall and attracted the largest entry ever received in all classes from flyweight to heavyweight.

The boxers from Germany carried off top honors winning the flyweight and heavyweight classes, finishing second in the welterweight and light-heavyweight divisions and third in the featherweight division. The middleweight and light-heavyweight titles went to France while Argentina did particularly well winning the featherweight championship, placing second in the heavyweight division and taking third in the middleweight and light-heavyweight classes.

The boxers from the United States did not do as well as expected, Louis Lauria of Cleveland, Ohio, placed third in the flyweight class and Jack Wilson also of Cleveland, placed second in the bantamweight class. Theodore E. Kara of Cleveland was defeated in the quarter-finals by C. Catterall of South Africa. The same fate fell Andrew Scrivani of Chicago, who dropped a close decision to E. Agren of Sweden. Chester Rutecki of Chicago, failed to reach the quarter finals, being beaten by I. Mandi of Hungary. James Clark Atkinson of Jamestown, New York, drew a bye in the first round, defeated B. V. Ahlberg of Finland in the second round but was eliminated by H. Chmielewski of Poland in the quarter-finals. In the light-heavyweight division Carl Vinciquerra of Omaha, Nebraska, was eliminated in his first bout losing to M. Amin of Egypt. In the heavyweight division Arthur Oliver of Chicago drew a bye in the first round but was defeated by O. Tandberg of Sweden in his first encounter.

Frank Lewis was the Olympic welterweight champion.

Frank Lewis of Stillwater, Oklahoma, was the only member of the U.S. wrestling team to win a gold medal.

As a tall, skinny college freshman, he was "a little tired" after six years of wrestling and planned to give full attention to his studies at Oklahoma State University. But he needed a physical education credit and figured that a wrestling class would provide an easy grade. Members of the class were required to compete in the all-college intramurals and when he failed to win the championship his pride was stung. He decided to concentrate on wrestling again.

A state high school champion and four-time medalist from 100 to 155 pounds, he possessed the raw talent to be a champion. Because of his rapid growth, Lewis didn't have the stamina to wrestle the longer college matches. Because of a minor heart condition, his coach had to devise a special training routine to build stamina without putting a strain on his health.

Despite these difficulties, he established a collegiate record of 45 victories against just five defeats, winning the NCAA championship in 1935 and placing second the year before.

In 1935, he won the national freestyle title and became the first contestant to be officially recognized as outstanding wrestler of a national AAU tournament. A year later he swept undefeated through the series of Olympic trials, then defended his position against his alternate on the boat to Europe.

In the Olympic games, he scored a fall the first day, another the second day. He wrestled three times the third day, but stamina no longer was a problem and two more falls offset a narrow loss to Tur Andersson of Sweden. He won the welterweight division.

After the Olympics and college graduation Lewis entered the oil business in his native Oklahoma. He is married to the former Virginia Lee Wilson and they have four children.

Frank Lewis is an outstanding citizen of Stillwater, Oklahoma, and a Distinguished Member of the National Wrestling Hall of Fame in Stillwater.

Frank Lewis at the Wrestling Hall of Fame.

1936

OLYMPICS

Other Sports

Fencing Championships

The fencing events at Berlin were for the most part held in two large gymnasiums (Turnhälle) and in an extensive amphitheater (Kuppelsälle), accommodating in all ten strips. Bouts in épée, however, except for one day when rain forced some of the team matches indoors, were held in the open air on hard clay tennis courts where eight strips were in almost constant use.

The matches were well attended and, although most of the sessions, other than final rounds, were not as crowded as in 1932 in Los Angeles where all events were conducted in a single hall, it is probable that 1936 set an all-time record for attendance at Olympic fencing events.

Helene Meyer was a German Jew who moved to the U.S. in 1932. Under pressure Germany put her on the 1936 women's fencing team. She placed second to the Hungarian Illona Schacherer-Elek. Here she gives the Nazi salute on the winner's podium.

Weight Lifting Championships

Fifteen nations participated in the five classes of weight lifting at Deutschland Hall, August 2 to 5. The heavyweight championship was contested before a record crowd of 20,000 spectators.

Although Egypt won two classes—Mohammed Ahmed Mesbah in the lightweight division and Khadr E. Touni in the middleweight division, Germany won the heavyweight class and German lifters scored two seconds, two thirds, two fourths and one fifth.

America's one victory was gained by Anthony Terlazzo of York, Pennsylvania, who established an Olympic total of 688½ lbs. Terlazzo was pressed by the two Egyptians, Saleh Mohammed Soliman and Ibrahim H. M. Shams, but he enjoyed the unusual distinction of bettering the best efforts of all his opponents with every single lift he made. Before the Olympic tryouts, Terlazzo trained down from the lightweight class to the featherweight division.

Awards ceremony for middleweight weightlifting champions. Adolf Wagner, Germany, third; Khadr Touni, Egypt, first; Rudolf Ismayr, Germany, second.

Cycling Championships

Robert Charpentier of France won the 100-kilometer road race and was a big factor in France's triumph in the 100-kilometer team race and 4,000-meter pursuit race. France's representatives garnered three championships, two seconds and two thirds. The cycling events were held on the specially banked wooden track in the cycling stadium. The road race started and finished on the Avus Speedway over a practically flat course.

One hundred riders started in the 100-kilometer road race and only half that number finished. The men were started in one group and on account of the narrow road, many mean spills resulted.

The track was located at the athletic field of the Berlin Sport Club in Charlottenburg near the northern entrance of the "Avus." It was 400 meters long and 6.3 meters wide.

The winning 2,000-meter tandem race, Ernst Ihbe and Charly Lorenz, of Germany.

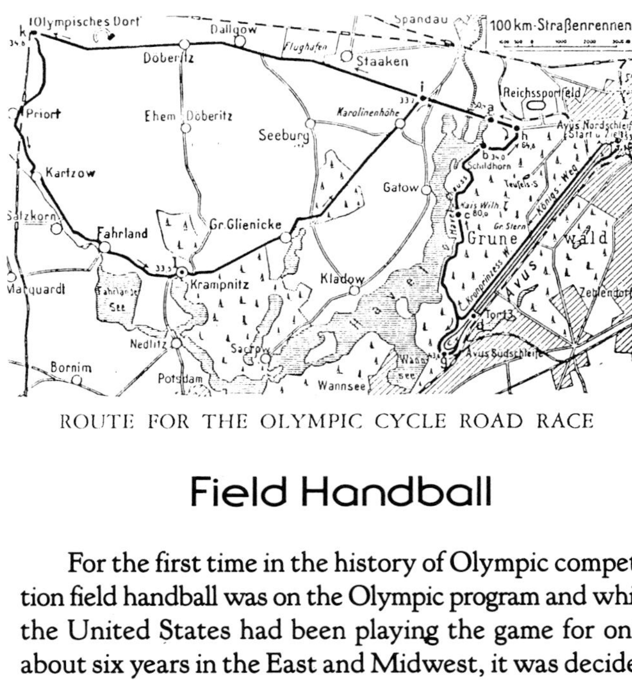

ROUTE FOR THE OLYMPIC CYCLE ROAD RACE

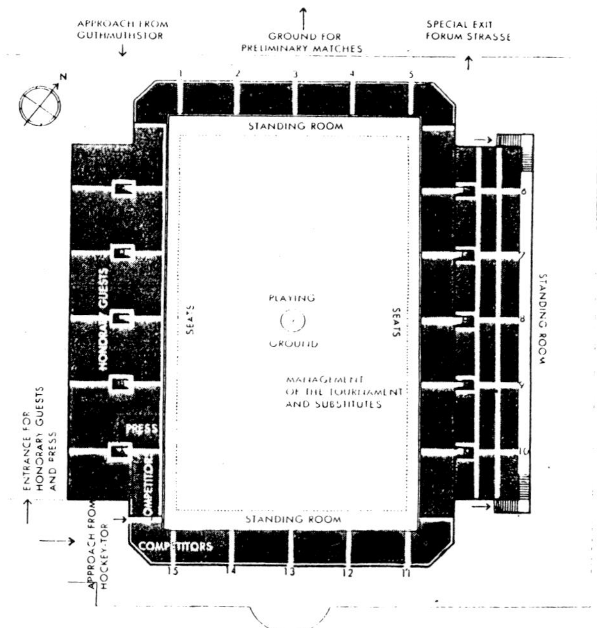

The field hockey stadium.

Field Handball

For the first time in the history of Olympic competition field handball was on the Olympic program and while the United States had been playing the game for only about six years in the East and Midwest, it was decided to take a team to Germany to give the men a chance at international competition. After the Eastern AAU District Championships had been decided two teams of 12 men each were selected of the best and most promising players and they played against picked Eastern District teams. From these two teams the Olympic team of fourteen men was selected and sent abroad with player-coach Willy Renz from Philadelphia.

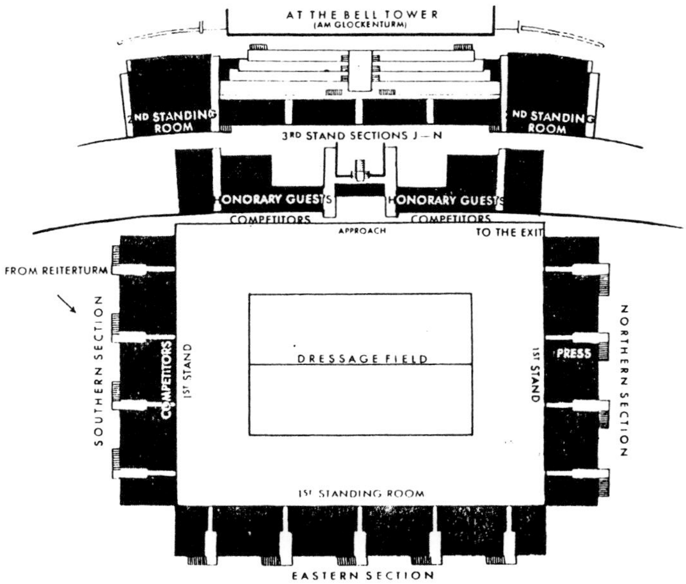

The equestrian grounds at the Reichssportfeld. Cross-country riding took place in Döberitz and jumping in the Olympic Stadium.

A groom of the Mexican polo team in an unusual pose.

Earl Thomson won a silver medal in the three-day event, which was the only medal won by the American team in the equestrian events at Berlin. At 36 Thomson was the oldest equestrian participant to win a medal and is co-holder of the most medals won by an American Olympic equestrian.

During World War II he was chief of staff of the 10th Mountain Division, the famed ski troops. He retired in 1954 as a full colonel.

Polo Championship

The United States Polo Association decided that the United States would not be represented. Five nations were entered, Argentina, Mexico, Great Britain, Hungary and Germany. It was agreed that the tournament should be played in two sections—Great Britain, Argentina and Mexico to play each other in the top bracket and Germany and Hungary in the lower half. It was further stipulated that the losers of the top half and the winners of the lower half should play for third place. This set-up was chosen because the Argentine team totalled a handicap of about 27 goals, Mexico 16 to 18 goals, Great Britain 26 goals, Hungary 6 to 8 goals and Germany 3 to 4 goals. The Organizing Committee desired to make a favorable presentation of this sport. The games were contested on the splendid 30-acre tract known as the "Maifeld." In the final Argentina defeated Great Britain 11 goals to 0.

Soccer Championship

Italy scored over Austria to take the Olympic championship 2 goals to 1 after two 15-minute overtime periods. Norway downed Poland 3 to 2 for third place.

The United States, although it had a very strong team, had the misfortune to draw Italy in the first round and was eliminated 1 goal to 0 after a scoreless first half. This game was vigorously contested and two American players, George Nemchik and William Fiedler, were injured. Italy continued to the finals by eliminating Japan 8 to 0 and Norway 2 to 1 in a closely contested game.

Field Hockey Championship

Field Hockey had been played by American men for only about ten years, and in view of the fact that it required a high degree of skill as well as speed and endurance the team did not finish among the winners at the Olympics. In the United States the game was first taken up by former college athletes and because there was no time to develop younger players with a degree of proficiency equal to that of the pioneers, the 1936 Olympic team consisted of pretty much the same players as did the 1932 team and the average age was not much under thirty.

Charles Leonard won a silver in the Modern Pentathlon, which closely follows skills used in the military for centuries—running, swimming, riding, shooting and fencing. Leonard was a graduate of West Point and was a runner, a swimmer and an expert marksman. At Berlin he was the first competitor in Olympic history to make a perfect score in shooting. He retired from the U.S. Army as a major general in 1967 after teaching at West Point.

Modern Pentathlon Championship

America's three representatives in the modern pentathlon taken as a team, were the most successful, with Germany second and Sweden third. The modern pentathlon event is an all-around competition comprising the 5,000-meter cross-country ride on horses drawn by lots; fencing with épée, pistol shooting, 300-meter swim and 4,000-meter cross-country race.

The competition took place over a period of four days, riding being held on the first day, shooting and fencing on the second, swimming on the third and cross-country on the fourth.

This event was introduced by Baron Pierre de Coubertin, who was desirous of interesting military leaders of all countries in a competition that would appeal especially to soldiers. The final ranking is obtained by adding together the number of first places earned by each of the competitors. In a case where two competitors have similar rankings, the one with the best placing in any one event is given precedence.

The event was won by Lt. Gotthardt Handrick of Germany, who finished ahead of Lt. Charles F. Leonard of St. Petersburg, Florida. Lt. Leonard got off to a poor start in the riding, finishing fifteenth in a field of forty-two. He was tenth in the fencing, where his teammate Lt. Frederick Weber finished first. He was most adept at the pistol shooting. The targets were disappearing silhouettes at 25-meter range and each competitor fired 20 shots. Lt. Leonard was credited with a perfect score—200 out of a possible 200, followed by Lt. Weber with 194. He was sixth in the swimming, covering 300 meters in 4 minutes, 40.9 seconds. He was ranked seventh in the 4,000-meter cross-country run in 14 minutes, 15.8 seconds.

Lt. Alfred D. Starbird finished in seventh place, followed by Lt. Frederick Weber in ninth place. The former competitor completed his entire competition, including the gruelling 4,000-meter cross-country race, with a broken bone in his foot.

Rifle Shooting Championship

The United States was not represented in the Miniature Rifle competition at 50 meters. The National Rifle Association favored non-participation, claiming that the program was totally inadequate.

The winner was Willy Rogeberg of Norway. He shot a perfect score, firing 30 shots (15 series of two) and landed every one in the bull's eye to finish with 300 points, a new Olympic record. Second place was taken by Dr. Ralf Berzseny of Hungary, third by Wladyslaw Karas of Poland.

Pistol Shooting Championship

Torsten Ullman of Sweden won the target pistol event at 50 meters and finished third in the automatic pistol competition at 25 meters. In the 50-meter pistol event there were 50 competitors from 20 countries and in the automatic pistol shooting there were 60 competitors from 23 nations. The shooting events were held at Wannsee and the competition was very keen.

1936
OLYMPICS

Demonstration Sports

BASEBALL HAS ALWAYS been a true American sport. It started in the United States and has become the Great American Pastime. Today it is played throughout North and South America and in Japan but only in a very limited way in the rest of the world.

In 1936 it was even less popular in the world but because of its tremendous popularity in the U.S., it was made a demonstration sport at Berlin.

Tryouts for the two teams, made up entirely of American players, were held in the spring of 1936 at Stanford University in Palo Alto, California, Western Michigan College in Kalamazoo and in Baltimore, Maryland. Twenty-one players were selected and three coaches were named—Harry Wolter from Stanford, Leslie Mann, who played for the Boston Braves, and Judson Hyames of Western Michigan College.

The team was part of the large American contingent that went over on the S.S. *Manhattan*. At the Olympic Village, they were put up in a house named Brandenburg, named after the city of the same name.

On August 12, the largest crowd to ever watch a baseball game, more than 100,000, turned out at night in the Olympic stadium. The two teams, one named "World Champions," and the other "Olympics," played before a somewhat bewildered crowd, which thought there was not enough action to call this a real game. (Europeans, of course, are used to the fast-moving game of soccer.)

The final score was 6 to 5, but the winner didn't really matter. Thus ended the tenure of the sport in the Olympics for decades to come.

Baseball team members on board the S.S. *Manhattan* on the way to Germany.
NBHF HERBERT SHAW PHOTO

The American demonstration baseball team. Standing from left: Norman Livermore, Curtis Meyers, Ron Hibbard, William Sayles, Carson Thompson, Thomas Downey, coach Judson Hyamer, Dinty Dennis, umpire Tiny Parker, Clarence Keegan, Gordon W. Mellatrat, Henry Wagnon, Fred Herringer, Emmett W. Fore. Kneeling from left: Herman W. Goldberg, Leslie McNeece, Earnest Eddowes, Dow Wilson, Paul Amen, manager Leslie Mann, coach Harry Walter, Grover Galvin, Charles Simons, Richard Hanna, Ralf Carlsten, Herbert Shaw.
NBHF CARSON THOMPSON PHOTO

Herbert Shaw and famous comedian Joe E. Brown at the Olympic Village. Brown would also be a world traveler with the USO during World War II.
NBHF HERBERT SHAW PHOTO

Herman Goldberg, the one player of the Jewish faith on the baseball demonstration team said he encountered little discrimination in the 1936 games, although it's well known that religion played a part in these Olympics.

Goldberg was born in 1915 in Brooklyn, New York. He grew up in an orthodox home with his father operating a hardware store and his mother working in education. His education was typical but he did have a keen interest in athletics, especially baseball.

He played amateur youth baseball in Brooklyn, semi-pro ball in Queens and Long Island, and was on high school teams and the Brooklyn College team from 1931 to 1935. He also played minor league ball for the Rome Colonels of New York and the Paducah Indians of Kentucky.

When baseball was selected as a demonstration sport in Berlin, Goldberg tried out for the team in Baltimore, Maryland. He was one of the 21 players selected and was the catcher for the World Amateurs team that played the U.S.A. Olympics.

He remembers his arrival in Germany as told to editor Peter Levine in his Baseball History 3, "An Annual of Original Baseball Research."

"In the first place, when we arrived in the Olympic Village, we were assigned to different houses. The baseball team stayed at a house called Brandenburg, which housed 28 people. In the Olympic Village—*Olympischen Dorf*—instead of housing the athletes in college dormitories or in huge, high-rise apartments which could be turned into low-cost public housing after the games, Germany taxed every city fifty percent of the cost of erecting smaller buildings that would hold twenty to forty athletes. The city of Brandenburg put up fifty percent of the cost of our house, and Hitler's *Reichstag*, or parliament, put up the other fifty percent. The buildings were called by the donor city's name, and the mayor of Brandenburg came to visit us one day.

"I was curious about a door in the hallway of our home which did not open into a hall closet. I opened it and saw a big chain across the staircase. I looked around; I shouted, "Anybody down there?" No answer. I dropped the chain and I walked down to the basement. I saw a cavernous cement floor with nothing on it. There were enormous overhead garage doors, almost the size of half a tennis court—huge doors and huge ramps leading to the doors. Then the *Hausmann* and the *Hausfrau*, the couple in charge of the building, making the beds and cleaning up the rooms, saw that the chain was down and they both shouted at me, "Get out of there!" I came upstairs. Later I found out that the *panzer*, or tank, units were going to move into this house and several others after the Olympics, and the oversized basement was where big tanks were going to be stored. The floors were about a foot deep of concrete; they were very solid. As soon as the American athletes and other athletes left the Olympic Village, it became the military academy of Germany."

Because of his Olympic play he was signed by the Detroit Tigers, but wound up playing for a minor league team. After one season he went back to school for his master's degree in education of the deaf.

Goldberg spent his working career in education and eventually became an assistant secretary of education in the U.S. Department of Education.

In 1960 he went to Bologna, Italy, as a Fullbright professor and he took baseball with him. He helped set up a semi-pro baseball league throughout the country.

Goldberg has been a success in every aspect of his life. He and his wife, Harriette, now live in Bethesda, Maryland.

Catcher Herman R. Goldberg and International League umpire and Olympic umpire George L. "Tiny" Parker.
NBHF HERMAN GOLDBERG PHOTO

A member of the American baseball team practices before the exhibition game. LC

Action at the Olympic demonstration baseball game on August 13. Herbert Shaw of the Olympishesmeisters is at bat. Norman Livermore of the Weltmeisters is the catcher and George Parker is the umpire. NBHF HERBERT SHAW PHOTO

Gliding

As the host country Germany was allowed to demonstrate gliding—a national sport that was unfamiliar to the rest of the participating countries.

The modern sport of gliding originated in Germany so the country invited a number of foreign gliding groups to the games to introduce the sport to the athletes and visitors from around the world.

According to Wolfgang Späte, one of Germany's top pre-war glider pilots and Luftwaffe pilots during World War II, the assembled gliders met at Staaken Aerodome and flew over Berlin for several days. There was also an airshow at Berlin-Tempelhof Airfield.

Little did the world know that Germany's gliding efforts were partially a mask to train pilots for the Luftwaffe, which was to rain terror across Europe and the British Isles starting in September 1939.

Ernst Udet of the reconstituted German Luftwaffe (Air Force) stands with a biplane (top) and glider (right). Both are marked with the five-ring Olympic logo. Udet performed in Berlin and also for the winter games. He was the top-ranking surviving ace of World War I, with 62 kills, and shot himself in November 1941 when he realized that Nazi Germany would lose the air war in World War II. NA, HH

This photo appeared in a German magazine at the time of the Olympics. The caption read: "Through the air like an eagle. The first memorable attempts by glider flight pioneer Otto Lilienthal have given rise to a science, a bold sport for the youth, and fulfillment of mankind's dream: Gliding. Germany was the trail blazer in this sport. Now, the slender gleaming bodies of giant birds with wide-spread wings gliding over mountains and valleys are ubiquitous, and the knowledge of aerodynamics and thermics makes courageous long distance and high altitude flights possible. The beautiful art of gliding will be shown on August 4 at the Staaken air field."

Edith Frieda Reichardt Mendyka, who now resides in Los Angeles, was a German participant in the team handball competition, which was introduced at the 1936 Olympics. She had been on the all-German national team for seven years and was one of its leading scorers. She also tried out for the track and field team in the javelin, but because she placed fourth in the trials failed to qualify.

Edith married John Mendyka in Berlin on Aug. 18, 1939. It took more than a year before she could get her visa and passage to America to meet her husband in Los Angeles, because Germany had considered her too good an athlete to let go.

She continued her sports career, founding a team handball league in the Los Angeles area. She also competed in track and field until she was 82 and still competes on occasion. She has held more than 30 world records in a number of events.

Her husband, John, played rugby and was on the all-German national team that toured Europe. He was also a track athlete specializing in the 110-meter hurdles. John left Germany in 1929 but returned in 1936, still a German citizen, to try out for the Olympic team in the hammer throw. Placing fourth in the trials, he did not qualify for the team.

The Mendyka family are all athletes. Karen, born in 1942, was the junior javelin champion in 1960 and placed second in the senior nationals that year. She tried out for the 1960 Olympics, but did not make it. In 1961 she was second in the nationals in the javelin and toured Europe with the American track and field team. In 1962 she won the national women's javelin championship. She was a track coach at Northwestern University for many years.

Karen married Bob Huff (now deceased) and their children were also champion athletes. Michael played baseball in college and has finished 11 years in professional baseball and tried out for the 1988 Olympic team. Malia played soccer, baseball, basketball, water skied and snow skied. In college she played rugby and captained the Dartmouth water ski team. Matt played baseball in college and one year of professional baseball with the Texas Rangers. He tried out for the 1996 Olympics in team handball.

John Mendyka in 1936. KAREN HUFF COLLECTION

Edith Mendyka, center, playing team handball. KAREN HUFF COLLECTION

Edith Mendyka at the master's track meet, age 83. KAREN HUFF COLLECTION

1936

OLYMPICS

The Closing Ceremonies

This report, with minor editing, was taken from the *American Olympic Committee Report, 1936, Games of the XIth Olympiad Berlin, Germany, IVth Olympic Winter Games, Garmisch-Partenkirchen, Germany.*

ON THE AFTERNOON of August 16, a crowd of more than 110,000 people once again filled every seat in the huge stadium, drawn by the attraction of the equestrian "Prix des Nations" (jumping event) and, last, but not least, the closing ceremony of the games. Enthralled, they witnessed the superb, rhythmic grace of horse and rider in the dressage competition and were thrilled as the world's finest military horsemen guided their spirited mounts over the sportiest course ever offered for Olympic competition. Darkness started to fall as the last competitor finished and the victory ceremonies concluded. No one rose to go. The audience silently awaited the ceremony which would bring to an end the Games of the XIth Olympiad.

The Olympic band broke the silence of the huge multitude with a stirring march reminiscent of the parade of nations on the opening day. From the tunnel on the west end of the stadium emerged the bearer of the banner of Greece leading all of the other nations into the stadium in alphabetical order. At the closing ceremony only those carrying the banners and flags of their respective countries appeared. They marched down the straightaway and came to a stop in front of the Tribune of Honor. By this time darkness had completely fallen and down in the shadow, the President of the International Olympic Committee—Count Henri de Baillet-Latour—was calling upon the youth of the world to assemble in four years at Tokyo, there to celebrate the Games of the XIIth Olympiad. As his words were spoken to the silent assemblage, the large Olympic flag was slowly lowered from the central mast and distant cannons roared in a farewell salute.

Count Baillet-Latour then turned the Olympic flag over to Mayor Lippert of the City of Berlin, to be held in the city hall until the 1940 Olympic Games at Tokyo.

Trumpets were sounded and a farewell song was heard while the flags and banners were carried back to the tunnel with the great five-ringed Olympic flag bringing up the rear of the procession. The Olympic torch was slowly extinguished and the spectators gradually worked their way out of the stadium. Thus the Games of the XIth Olympiad passed into history.

The organizing committee tendered a farewell dinner to the participating athletes at Deutschland Hall immediately following the ceremony.

Scenes at the closing ceremonies. Top, ribbons were attached to the lowered flag of each participating country. Bottom, five of Germany's athletes solemnly carry out the Olympic flag. TOP: NA, HH-242-0518-2

1936
OLYMPICS

Post-Olympic Competitions

This report, with minor editing, was taken from the *American Olympic Committee Report, 1936, Games of the XIth Olympiad Berlin, Germany, IVth Olympic Winter Games, Garmisch-Partenkirchen, Germany.*

AS USUAL OUR American athletes were very much in demand for appearances here and there in Europe following the Olympic Games in Berlin. International athletic laws require that invitations to foreign athletes must be extended through the respective governing bodies of the countries extending the invitation and the countries in which the athletes reside. In some instances these invitations were received in the United States a full two years before the Olympic Games were scheduled to be held. Because of the large number of invitations and the always difficult task of raising the necessary funds to defray the expenses of the American team, the American Olympic Committee for the first time in the history of America's participation in the Olympic Games or international contests, decided to levy a tax on the gross receipts of all athletic events in which members of the American Olympic team engaged, in addition to all necessary traveling and living expenses in connection with their participation in such events.

In line with this action, and to simplify the arrangements and have some central control over these post-Olympic contests, President Brundage appointed a committee on post-Olympic tours with Daniel J. Ferris as Chairman.

Our special committee decided that ten percent of the gross receipts should be the amount that each organization sponsoring international events in which American Olympic athletes participated should pay for this privilege.

The British Empire-U.S.A. dual track and field meet at London, which has been held quadrennially after each Olympic meet since 1924, was exempt from this ruling but a special arrangement was entered into whereby they remitted fifty percent of the British International Board's share of the net receipts. It was also necessary for the Committee to modify the conditions in one or two other cases in which the Chairman, acting for the Committee, felt it was more advisable to accept a flat guarantee rather than a percentage of the gate receipts. More than $8000 was paid into the American Olympic Committee treasury as a result of the post-Olympic competitions in which our athletes engaged.

For several months prior to the sailing of the American team from New York, Ferris carried on negotiations with the various governing bodies abroad with respect to our athletes competing in these international meets. It was not possible to complete all of the important details until personal conferences were held at the Olympic village in Berlin with the officers of these foreign governing bodies or their representatives.

The invitations handled by the committee included: Track and field, men—groups to nine different countries; swimmers, men and women—to seven countries; track and field, women—two countries; field handball team—several matches in Germany; baseball team—exhibition games in England; water polo team—exhibition matches in Hungary and Germany; basketball team—matches in England and France; boxing team—matches in Germany.

The success of the American track and field athletes increased the desire of foreign countries to have the outstanding stars appear in their athletic centers. All countries wanted Owens, Cunningham, Woodruff, Williams, Morris, Towns, Johnson and men of that caliber. With nine countries angling for these stars the committee's job was made all the more difficult. Ferris was interested to see as many of our athletes as possible go on one or more of these tours in order that they might have an opportunity to see something more than the Olympic village during their first, and for many perhaps their last trip, to Europe. As a result 58 of the 60 members of the American track team were invited to go on tours.

An American manager, or manager-coach, was named to accompany each group. It was his duty to see to it that the athletes were properly transported, housed, fed, and not imposed upon as regards the number and kind of events in which they would engage. Ample allowance was made by the sponsoring organizations to cover all such expenses. The various tours were tentatively arranged before the Olympic Games started. Ferris made inquiries of the outstanding athletes on our team to ascertain which tour they would prefer to take if they had their choice. Wherever possible he arranged to have them go on the trip of their selection. The managers appointed were depended upon to keep the members of their team informed of final arrangements.

Three days before the close of the track and field section of the Olympic games a chart was placed on the bulletin board in the central house in which the track and field athletes were quartered showing clearly which tour or tours each athlete was selected for and the location and date of such competition. This was a confirmation of the verbal notification which had previously been given to all athletes invited.

Probably the most important of all these post-Olympic meets was the British Empire-U.S.A. dual meet held at White City Stadium in London and attracted 90,000 spectators. First places only counted in determining the winning team and the United States scored 11 firsts to three for the British Empire.

In most of these post-Olympic meets the American athletes added to the glory that was theirs as a result of their Olympic successes.

The largest group of swimmers to participate in post-Olympic tours was the team which made a three week's tour of Poland. They took part in swimming meets or exhibitions in seven Polish cities.

Peter Fick, John Higgins, Jack Kasley, Ralph Flanagan, Jack Medica, Albert Van de Weghe, Taylor Drysdale, Arthur Lindegren, John Macionis and Elbert Root competed.

The field handball team participated in three matches in Stettin, Augsburg, and Bremen, Germany. The majority of the members of this team were German-Americans.

An invitation was received from Hungary for the American water polo team to engage in a series of pre-Olympic matches and permission was obtained from the American Olympic Swimming and Water Polo Committee to arrange for this series of games as it was felt it would give the American players much-needed experience prior to their participation in the Olympic Games. However, it was impossible to raise the necessary funds and this tour had to be abandoned. The team did engage in a post-Olympic meet at Frankfurt-on-Main where it went down to defeat before a strong German aggregation after an exciting match.

The organizations which had tendered invitations for the American basketball team to engage in exhibition matches in England and France were unable to finance the trip and this tour had to be abandoned.

Other international contests engaged in by American athletes were as follows:

The women's track and field team participated in an international track and field meet at Wuppertal, Germany. The meet in Amsterdam, Holland, for which an invitation had been received was not held.

The boxing team engaged in two matches at Bremerhaven and Hanover, Germany.

The one happening which caused the greatest upset in the committee's plans after final completion, was the withdrawal of Jesse Owens from the team which toured in Sweden. After definitely accepting the invitation to accompany the team, and completing a part of the tour, he changed his plans hurriedly and sailed for home instead of going through with the trip to Sweden, causing great disappointment in Sweden where he was extensively advertised and it was hard to explain to the track fans of Sweden his non-appearance in these meets.

1936 OLYMPICS

Welcome Home Ceremony

MOST OF THE American team boarded the S.S. *President Roosevelt* in Hamburg and arrived in New York on August 28. The track team arrived on September 2. Jesse Owens, who refused to travel with his team to Stockholm, had already returned to the United States and rejoined them in time for the official welcome parade in New York.

Owens and his wife, Ruth, rode in the first limousine as the parade traveled up Broadway to Harlem, back down Lenox Avenue, then crossed the Triborough Bridge to the Randall's Island stadium where a public reception was held.

Flamboyant Mayor Fiorello H. La Guardia presented each participant with medals and made a speech praising them as "splendid examples of American youth and American sportsmanship."

One interesting sidenote to the welcome home ceremony: In Harlem, the black section of New York, Owens and his teammates were given a rather cool reception. Apparently the citizens were interested more in boxing and baseball stars. Also, Jack Dempsey was riding beside Owens. As it turns out Dempsey had refused to fight a black boxer, so the citizens would not cheer Owens at his side.

Newspapers in New York were full of articles about the return of the American Olympic team.

By JAMES A. BURCHARD.

Perhaps the highlights of the Olympic team reception was reached at an early hour last evening when Mrs. Dorothy Poynton Hill, winner of the platform diving in Berlin, parked a bottle of soda water on the desk of the Commodore Hotel, outstared the attendant dowagers and sucked happily on half a dozen straws.

"No soda water in Berlin," said Mrs. Hill. "I had to eat ice cream. Believe me, this is a real pleasure. If I ever go abroad again I'll take a case of soft drinks with me."

* * *

Mrs. Hill was one of the most popular Olympic members as the

DOROTHY POYNTON HILL.

steamship Roosevelt nudged into a safe mooring in the twilight. Close to 300 members of the U. S. team came home. The rest are due to arrive September 3 and join in a mass parade to Randall's Island, where medals will be presented by officials representing New York City.

* * *

Due to a misunderstanding, some fifty of the athletes said they couldn't remain on deck for the medal presentation. They were broke and eager to go home. Informed, however, that all expenses would be paid during the interim, they changed their minds. So thirty New York hotels will be full of Olympians for the next few days.

A prime topic of discussion was the suspension of Mrs. Eleanor Holm Jarrett. "She got what she deserved," said Helen Stephens, the 100-meter victor. The other girls were more charitable in their views. Miss Stephens didn't feel very good anyway. She put on twenty pounds in Europe, and now bends the beam at 175. Miss Stephens expects to return to William Woods College in Missouri and work off her excess weight.

* * *

The professional urge seems to be catching. Possibly taking the cue from Jesse Owens, many of the Olympic stars have their eyes on dollars. Mrs. Hill is through as an amateur, and will enter the movies or any other paying enterprise. Alice Arden, the high-jumper, will listen to the song of silver. She's just 22 and probably the best-looking girl ever to pull on a pair of spiked shoes. Betty Robinson, member of the winning 400-meter relay team, would take a job as chaperon on the 1940 team.

* * *

There were a good many squaks on deck. Glenn Hardin, low-hurdle king, cussed the officials. So, in milder fashion, did Gene Venzke. The officials, said the boys, rode first class while the athletes were No. 3. The badge-wearers got the best of everything.

* * *

"Every athlete had to pay out about $300 of his own money," said Hardin. "Laundry bills were high and it was worth your bank roll to have a suit pressed. The officials took in about $12,000 in the British Empire games, but it didn't seem to help. I'm sort of fed up. I expect to get a screen test, so maybe I won't have to worry about hurdles from now on."

* * *

Venzke had a few complaints of his own. "There was no understanding between the athletes and officials," said Gene, the Penn ace. "The officials were wearing sweat shirts in the Olympic village, but the athletes couldn't get them. I think the officials could be cut down 80 per cent in the future. There was too much squabbling."

* * *

Much in demand was Lawson Robertson, track and field coach. "Germany won the games," said Robbie, "but we didn't have teams in piano, free-hand sketching and back-seat driving. In my opinion Jesse Owens was the best of them all. He did over 27 feet in a jump that was called foul. The A. A. U. will hate to lose him, but he can't be blamed. I was much impressed with Adolph Hitler's right hand. It reminded me of Max Schmeling.

* * *

Jack Dempsey and Stanley Howe, executive secretary to Mayor La Guardia, greeted the athletes yesterday. . . . Dempsey is throwing a banquet to the boys and girls tonight. . . . Pat Kelly,

GLENN HARDIN.

a big shot in the A. A. U., sailed on the cutter. . . . He revealed he kidded his wife recently by purchasing an eight-pound bluefish after talking of his piscatorial abilities.

* * *

The photographers kept Betty Robinson busy. . . . She's good-looking, and she staged a comeback after breaking her leg in an airplane accident in 1931. . . . Mrs. Hill never will forget how Hitler stood up and cheered a diving exhibition. . . . Joseph Raycroft had nothing to say. . . . "What is there to say?" he asked. . . . And other officials said, "Ditto." . . . While the athletes wept.

WELCOME HOME!

The American Olympic team was given a rousing reception upon its return to New York in late August. The city presented each athlete with a commemorative medal. The Mayor's Committee on Reception to Distinguished Guests arranged a week's program of entertainment that included a series of dinners, baseball and basketball games, sightseeing and broadcast programs and a parade up Broadway, culminating with a public reception at Randall's Island.

A Message from Mayor LaGuardia to the Members of the American Olympic Team returning on the President Roosevelt:

The Mayor's Committee of Welcome has made complete arrangements to provide for your comfort, entertainment and enjoyment from the hour of your arrival in New York Harbor to the grand climax of New York City's reception and welcome to all the returning Olympic athletes on Thursday, September third.

On September third, an old-fashioned ticker-tape parade up Broadway from the Battery to Harlem will give New York's millions an opportunity to express their pride and joy over the great achievements of America's participants in the 1936 Olympic Games.

At one o'clock the Mayor will provide a luncheon for the City's guests to be held at New York's new municipal stadium at Randall's Island.

Immediately after luncheon the City of New York will bestow commemorative medals not only upon each of the point winners in the 1936 Olympics but upon each of the participants.

In the presentation of these attractive medals, each bearing the name of the recipient and carrying on one side the Seal of the City of New York and on the other side the original Olympian symbol of victory, the Mayor will be assisted by world-famous old timers in the field of sport, heroes of days gone by, such as:

Jack Dempsey	Babe Ruth
Benny Leonard	Vincent Richards
Jack Curley	Johnny Dundee
Bill Robinson	Maureen Orcutt (Crews)
Paul Pilgrim	John Flanagan
Pat McDonald	Jimmy Braddock
Chick Meehan	Lou Little
"Red" Burman	Matt McGrath
Mickey Walker	Gene Tunney
Jack Johnson	Mel Sheppard
Frank Kramer	Philadelphia Jack O'Brien
Fred Spencer	Perry Charles
Gertrude Ederle	Lou Handley
Eileen Riggin	Earl Sande

Sam Langford

This presentation ceremony will be broadcast to your own home town so that your relatives and friends can listen in through arrangements made with three major networks, NBC, CBS and MBS.

In the evening you will be the guests of the Mayor's Committee at one of America's famous supper theatres, the French Casino, for a brand new show which has just opened.

During the five days intervening between your arrival here and the monster reception on September third, you will not only have a key to the heart of the City of New York, but you will be provided with rooms, meals, transportation and entertainment of every variety, during each day and evening, without any cost to yourselves.

A more detailed schedule of events and entertainment will be included in your copy of the souvenir program presented by the Mayor's Committee.

Best wishes good luck Jack Dempsey

Bill Robinson

Welcome Olympians

THE CITY OF NEW YORK

TO THE RETURNING ATHLETES:

¶ Like all Americans, regardless of race, creed or color, every New Yorker is proud and happy over the achievements of the representatives of our country in the 1936 Olympic games. ¶ You displayed clean sportsmanship, outstanding courage and a determination to win which brought credit and honor to all of us who from this side of the ocean followed your efforts and accomplishments through the press, the radio and the movies, and thus shared your triumphs with you. ¶ There is no such thing as a tangible key to the City of New York, but you have earned and we extend to every one of you a key to the heart of our community. ¶ We want your visit here to be remembered always as one of the really pleasant episodes in the great adventure which you have been and are experiencing. ¶ We wish for each of you a future that will measure up in happiness and success to all your present hopes and aspirations.

F. La Guardia

Mayor of the City of New York

Program of Entertainment

Arrangements have been made for the Olympic Athletes to be the guests of the City of New York, through the courtesy of the Hotel Men's Association. Accommodations, meals and entertainment will be free of charge. Specific assignments for hotel accommodations and meals will be made on the boat after you reach Quarantine. Everything on the program is free to members of the 1936 American Olympic Team.

Friday, August 28th

After Boat Docks, Inter-Olympic basket-ball game at the Hippodrome Theatre.

12:00 P.M. Midnight Supper at a famous New York night club.

Saturday, August 29th

Bus ride, boat ride, studio broadcast, movies, dancing, baseball. Arrangements for any or all of these events can be made at the desk of your hotel or through the Mayor's Office (Telephone COrtland 7-1000—ask for Olympic Committee).

7:00 P.M. Olympic Night at Jack Dempsey's — a gala night of entertainment at Jack Dempsey's famous restaurant.

Sunday, August 30th to and including Wednesday, September 2nd

Movies
Boat rides
Studio broadcasts
Bus rides
Dancing
Sightseeing at all the principal points of interest around New York

All through the courtesy of

The City of New York
New York Yankees
National Broadcasting System
St. George's Pool, Brooklyn
Roxy Theatre
Columbia Broadcasting System
Mutual Broadcasting System
Park Central Pool, New York
Palisades Park

Continued on following page

(Detailed hour by hour program enclosed.)

Program of Entertainment

Continued

Tuesday, September 1st

11:00 A.M. Olympic Athletes will be the guests of Former Governor Alfred E. Smith at the Empire State Building, the tallest skyscraper in the world.

Thursday, September 3rd

A.M. Old fashioned ticker tape parade up Broadway from the Battery to Harlem.

1:00 P.M. Mayor's luncheon to Olympic Athletes at New York's Municipal Stadium at Randall's Island.

Immediately after the luncheon the City of New York will bestow commemorative medals upon each of the participants in the 1936 Olympic games.

7:30 P.M. Olympic Athletes will be guests of the Mayor of New York City at one of New York's famous supper theatres, the French Casino, at which a brand new show, recently opened, will be staged.

Welcome Home Parade

New York City
September 3, 1936

Jesse Owens in the parade.
JIM OSBORNE

The welcome home parade, Alice Arden, left, and Harriet Bland, below. ALICE HODGE PHOTOS

1936
OLYMPICS

The Winter Games

THE IVTH OLYMPIC Winter Games at Garmisch-Partenkirchen, Germany, February 6 to 16, was the greatest festival of winter sports that the world has ever witnessed. Twenty-eight nations represented by more than 1,000 athletes took part in the five sports and two demonstrations comprising the program. The organizing committee was headed by Dr. Karl Ritter von Halt, assisted by Baron Peter von le Fort as Secretary.

Norway scored a total of 22 places in the various competitions with seven firsts, five seconds, three thirds, three fourths, one fifth and three sixths. Germany was second with 12 places; Sweden third with nine places; Finland fourth with 10 places; Austria fifth with nine places. The United States did not fare as well as was expected, finishing in sixth place ahead of Great Britain with ten places. The only victory scored by the United States was in the two-man bobsled (Ivan E. Brown and Alan M. Washbond).

The following tabulation shows the number of competitors and countries represented in the various sports:

	Countries	Competitors
Skiing	27	266
Skating	16	52
Ice Hockey	15	173
Bobsled	13	95
Figure Skating	17	84

Germany as host nation was represented by a team of 143 competitors. The United States' representation at the games was 90, most of the group sailing January 3 on the S.S. *Manhattan*.

The American ice hockey team and the figure skating team were housed at the Hotel Husar. The ski team, speed skating team and the bobsled team were assigned to the Post Hotel. The teams were quite comfortable considering the scarcity of accommodations and the fact that about 75,000 people were attracted each day from Munich.

The games were declared open by Chancellor Hitler in a blinding snowstorm before a capacity crowd of 15,000, which taxed the facilities of the ski stadium. The American flag was carried by Rolf Monsen, ski veteran of three Olympiads.

The closing ceremony likewise was similar to that of the summer games and was most impressive, being held in the brilliantly lighted ski stadium.

The Germans gave several banquets and entertainment, including a farewell dinner for all of the contestants at Munich. each competitor received an elaborate invitation, a ticket to the ball and a book of coupons that entitled him to a ride to Munich on a special train met by a brass band, and a dinner including a suitable souvenir. The farewell ball was a delightful affair with 2,000 in attendance.

This report, with minor editing, was taken from the *American Olympic Committee Report, 1936, Games of the XIth Olympiad Berlin, Germany, IVth Olympic Winter Games, Garmisch-Partenkirchen, Germany.*

PROGRAMME

OF THE

IVth OLYMPIC WINTER GAMES

1936

Thursday, 6th February:
11 a.m. Opening Ceremony in the Olympia Ski Stadium / 2.30 p.m. Ice hockey / 9 p.m. Ice hockey.

Friday, 7th February:
9 a.m. Ice hockey / 11 a.m. Downhill race for ladies and gentlemen / 2.30 p.m. Ice hockey / 9 p.m. Ice hockey.

Saturday, 8th February:
9 a.m. Ice hockey / 11 a.m. Ski-ing: slalom for ladies / 2 p.m. Bob-races / 2.30 p.m. Ice hockey / 9 p.m. Ice hockey.

Sunday, 9th February:
10 a.m. Ice hockey / 11 a.m. Ski-ing: slalom for men / 2 p.m. Bob-races / 2 p.m. Figure-skating (compulsory figures) / 9 p.m. Ice hockey / From 9.30 a.m. Eisschiessen display on the Riessersee.

Monday, 10th February:
9 a.m. Ski-ing: 4 × 10-km. relay race and figure-skating (compulsory figures) / From 9 a.m. Eisschiessen display on the Riessersee / Evening: Festival for competitors.

Tuesday, 11th February:
9 a.m. Figure-skating (compulsory figures) / 11 a.m. Skating race (500 metres) / 2 p.m. Bob-races / 2.30 p.m. Ice hockey on the Riessersee / 9 p.m. Ice hockey.

Wednesday, 12th February:
9 a.m. Figure-skating (compulsory figures) / 10 a.m. Skating race (5,000 metres) / 10 a.m. Ski-ing 18 Km race special and combined event / 2 p.m. Bob-races / 2.30 p.m. Ice hockey on the Riessersee / 9 p.m. Ice hockey.

Thursday, 13th February:
9 a.m. Figure-skating (compulsory figures) / 10 a.m. Speed skating (1,500 metres) / 11 a.m. Ski-jump (combined event) / 2.30 p.m. Pair-skating / 9 p.m. Ice hockey.

Friday, 14th February:
8.30 a.m. Military ski patrol race (display competition) / 9 a.m. Speed skating (10,000 metres) / 10 a.m. Ice hockey / 2.30 p.m. Figure-skating (free skating for men) / 9 p.m. Ice hockey.

Saturday, 15th February:
8 a.m. Ski-ing: 50-km. race / 10 a.m. Ice hockey / 2.30 p.m. Figure-skating (free skating for ladies) / 9 p.m. Ice hockey.

Sunday, 16th February:
11 a.m. Ski-jump, special event on the Great Olympic Jump / 2.30 p.m. Ice hockey, followed by the Closing Ceremony in the Olympia Artificial Ice Stadium.

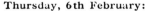

Published by the Reichsbahnzentrale für den Deutschen Reiseverkehr, Berlin, in co-operation with the Organizing Committee for the IVth Olympic Winter Games, 1936, Garmisch-Partenkirchen

K 735 100—●. Printed in Germany

IVth Olympic Winter Games

1 9 3 6

GARMISCH-PARTENKIRCHEN

6th TO 16th FEBRUARY

PRICES OF SINGLE TICKETS

The advance sale of single tickets for various events at the IVth Olympic Winter Games, 1936, will begin on the 15th July 1935. Orders for places for the following events will be accepted under the existing conditions of sale. The advance sale for all other tickets and events will not begin until the 1st January 1936.

A) Opening Ceremony

in the Olympic Ski Stadium on 6th February 1936 at 11 a.m.

Stand D, numbered seats	RM.	**10.—**
Stand B, numbered standing room	„	**8.—**
Stand C, numbered standing room	„	**5.—**

B) Ski-ing (in the Olympic Ski-ing Stadium)

1. Long-distance races

Start and finish in the Olympic Ski Stadium

4×10-km. relay race on 10th February at 9 a.m.

18-km. race, special and combined event, on 12th February at 2 p.m.

Military ski patrol race on 14th February at 8.30 a.m.

50-km race on 15th February at 8 a.m.

(The following prices are for each separate event)

Stand A, numbered seats	RM.	**5.—**
Stand D, numbered seats	„	**5.—**
Stand B, numbered standing room	„	**4.—**
Stand C, numbered standing room	„	**3.—**

2. *Ski-jumping (combined event)*

on the Small Olympic Jump,
on the 13th February at 11 a.m.

Stand G, numbered standing room (beside the Small Olympic Jump)	RM.	10.—
Stand D, numbered seats	,,	6.—
Stand A, numbered seats	,,	5.—
Stand C, numbered standing room	,,	5.—
Stand B, numbered standing room	,,	3.—

3. *Ski-jumping (special event)*

on the Great Olympic Jump
on the 16th February at 11 a.m.

Stand D, numbered seats	RM.	20.—
Stand A, numbered seats	,,	15.—
Stand C, numbered standing room	,,	7.—
Stand G, numbered standing room	,,	7.—
Stand B, numbered standing room	,,	4.—
Natural Stand West, unnumbered standing room	,,	4.—

C) Ice Sports (in the Olympia Artificial Ice Stadium)

1. *Ice Hockey*

Opening Games on 6th February at 2.30 p.m. and 9 p.m.
Semi-finals on 15th February at 10 a.m. and 9 p.m.

(The following prices are for each separate event)

East and west blocks, numbered seats	RM.	4.—
Standing room in south stand	,,	3.—
Standing room in east and west stands	,,	2.—

2. *Ice Hockey*

Finals and Closing Ceremony on 16th February at 2.30 p.m.

East and west blocks, numbered seats	RM.	8.—
Standing room in south stand	,,	5.—
Standing room in east and west stands	,,	4.—

(The prices include the Closing Ceremony)

3. *Figure-skating*

Figure-skating for pairs on 13th February at 2.30 p.m.
Voluntary figures for men on 14th February at 2.30 p.m.
Voluntary figures for ladies on 15th Febr. at 2.30 p.m.

(The following prices are for each separate event)

East and west blocks, numbered seats	RM.	5.—
Standing room in south stand	,,	3.—
Standing room in east and west stands	,,	2.—

D) Bobsleighing

All stands at the Olympic Bob-run are reserved for the holders of general or season tickets for seats or standing room. The remaining tickets for standing room will be on sale at the day booking office.

Winter Olympia Badges

The price of the official Winter Olympia Badge is RM. 1.—.

The price of the official Winter Olympia Motor-Car Badge is RM. 6.—.

These two badges are enamelled in five colours and can be obtained from the Organizing Committee, Garmisch-Partenkirchen, by remitting the price plus postage (25 resp. 40 pfennigs). Postal Cheque Account: München 3570.

Conditions of sale for Single Tickets

1. When ordering tickets in advance use must be made of the prescribed forms which can be obtained gratis from any advance sale booking office.

2. Orders for unnumbered seats can be sent at once, remitting the price at the same time. They will be dealt with serially after receipt of the remittance.

3. The number of tickets for numbered seats and numbered standing room available is very limited. They must be ordered on the prescribed order forms from the official advance booking offices. If the seats or standing room ordered are still available the person ordering them will receive a provisional ticket, on receipt of which the amount must be remitted within eight days, failing which the seats or standing room will be disposed of.

4. Confirmation of the receipt of the amount will not be sent. The receipt issued by the bank or the post office is treated as confirmation. The despatch of the original tickets, will be begun by the 1st October 1935 at latest.

5. Any number of single tickets may be ordered, but the Organizing Committee reserve the right to limit orders.

6. The public are warned against purchasing single tickets with a view to reselling them at a higher price. It is forbidden to ask for more than the official price. The Organizing Committee will intervene if excessive demands are made.

7. No reductions will be granted to parties or individuals.

8. Refunds. In the event of the cancellation of an event, the official price of single tickets booked in advance will be refunded, less 10% for administrative expenses.

9. Despatch. The tickets will be sent by registered post to the addresses or advance booking offices named in the order forms, unless the advance ticket office is previously informed in writing (mentioning the number of the order) of a change of address. An advance booking fee of 10% on the price of each ticket (at least 30 pfennigs and at most RM. 1.—) will be charged to cover postage and administrative expenses.

10. Remittance of payments

(A) When tickets are ordered direct from the Organizing Committee, payment should be made

a) to the Bayerische Gemeindebank, Brienner Straße 49, München to the account of the "Organisationskomitee E. V. für die IV. Olympischen Winterspiele 1936, Kartenverkauf, Garmisch-Partenkirchen", or,

b) through Postal Cheque Account No. 3570 München, "Organisationskomitee e. V. für die IV. Olympischen Winterspiele 1936, Kartenverkauf, Garmisch-Partenkirchen".

(B) If the tickets are booked at an official advance booking office, payment should also be made there.

11. Disputes will be settled at Garmisch-Partenkirchen.

Note

There are special prospectuses and special order forms for general or season tickets which will be sent gratis on request by the Organizing Committee or the official travel agencies.

Advance Booking Offices

Orders will be accepted and further information gladly supplied by

The Organizing Committee for the IVth Olympic Winter Games, Garmisch-Partenkirchen, all the tourist offices and agencies of the Mitteleuropäisches Reisebüro (MER), the Hamburg-American Line, the Norddeutscher Lloyd, Wagons-Lits-Cook, the American Express Co., the C. I. T., the Cedok, and the other leading travel agencies in Germany and abroad.

Information can also be obtained from all the foreign agencies of the Reichsbahnzentrale für den Deutschen Reiseverkehr.

IVTH OLYMPIC WINTER GAMES 1936

GARMISCH-PARTENKIRCHEN, 6TH – 16TH FEBRUARY 1936

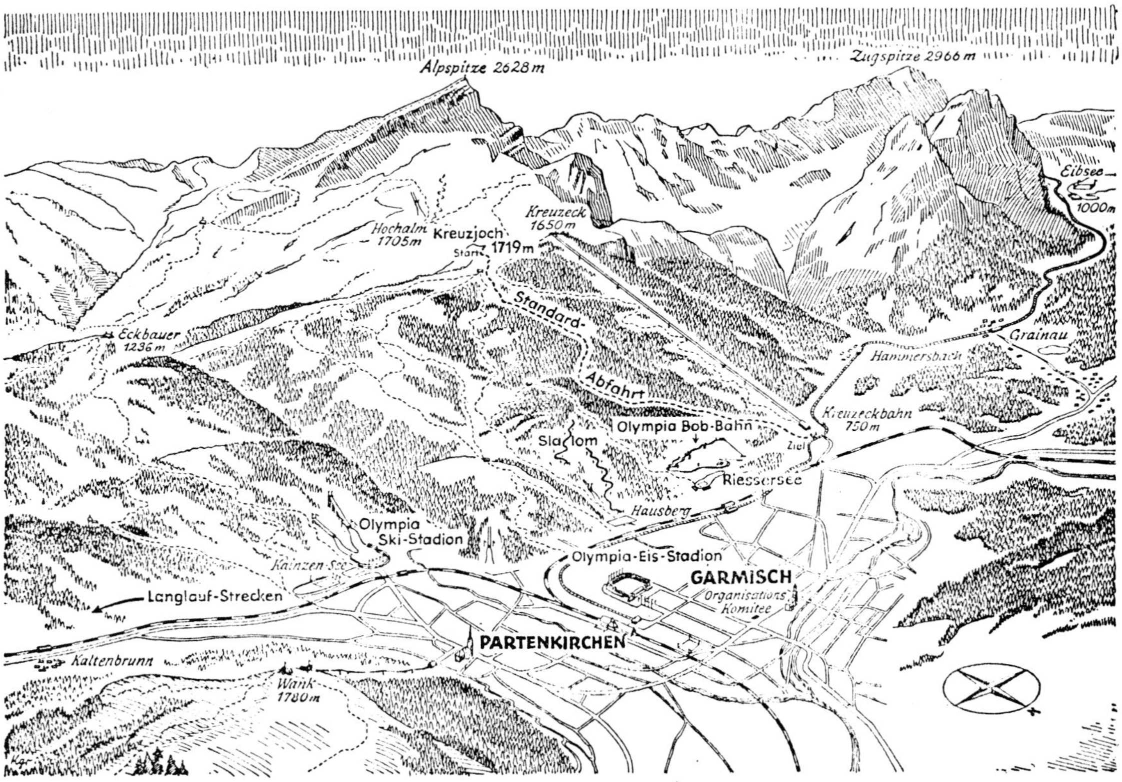

The IVth Olympic Winter Games will be held in the winter of 1936 at Garmisch-Partenkirchen, Germany's most important winter sports centre. The best performers in the whole world will compete there between the 6th and 16th February.

The greatest care has already been devoted to the preparations for these events. The "Great Olympic Jump", specially erected for the special jumping on the Gudiberg, fulfilled all expectations on the occasion of the first time it was used for ski-jumping. The "Old Gudiberg Jump", which is intended for the combination jumping, was reconstructed as a jump with high pressure. A ski-ing stadium was constructed to include both jumps and surrounded by grand stands accommodating almost any number of spectators, and here the opening ceremony of the Olympic Winter Games 1936 will be held. The Olympia Ski Stadium is also the starting and finishing point of the long distance, endurance and relay races.
The downhill and slalom races will be held in the Kreuzeck district and on the Hausberg.
The Olympia Bob-Run on which the four-crew bob sleigh world championships were held in 1934, after the

PROGRAMME 1936

Thursday, 6th February: 11 a.m. Opening Ceremony in the Olympia Ski Stadium / 2.30 p.m. Ice hockey / 9 p.m. Ice hockey.

Friday, 7th February: 9 a.m. Ice hockey / 11 a.m. Ski-ing: downhill race for ladies and gentlemen / 2.30 p.m. Ice hockey / 9 p.m. Ice hockey.

Saturday, 8th February: 9 a.m. Ice hockey / 11 a.m. Ski-ing: slalom for ladies / 2 p.m. Bob-races / 2.30 p.m. Ice hockey / 9 p.m. Ice hockey.

Sunday, 9th February: 10 a.m. Ice hockey / 11 a.m. Ski-ing: slalom for men / 2 p.m. Bob-races / 2 p.m. Figure-skating (compulsory figures) / 9 p.m. Ice hockey / From 9.30 a.m. Eisschiessen display on the Riessersee.

Monday, 10th February: 9 a.m. Ski-ing: 4 × 10 km. relay race and figure-skating (compulsory figures) / From 9 a.m. Eisschiessen display on the Riessersee / Evening: Competitors' Festival.

Tuesday, 11th February: 9 a.m. Figure-skating (compulsory figures) / 11 a.m. Speed skating (500 metres) / 2 p.m. Bob-races / 2.30 p.m. Ice hockey (on the Riessersee) / 9 p.m. Ice hockey.

Wednesday, 12th February: 9 a.m. Figure-skating (compulsory figures) / 10 a.m. Speed skating (5,000 metres) / 10 a.m. Ski-ing: 18 km. long-distance race, special and combined event / 2 p.m. Bob-races / 2.30 p.m. Ice hockey (on the Riessersee) / 9 p.m. Ice hockey.

Thursday, 13th February: 9 a.m. Figure-skating (compulsory figures) / 10 a.m. Speed skating (1,500 metres) / 11 a.m. Ski-jumping, combined event / 2.30 p.m. Pair-skating / 9 p.m. Ice hockey.

Friday, 14th February: 8.30 a.m. Military patrol race (display competition) / 9 a.m. Speed skating (10,000 metres) / 10 a.m. Ice hockey / 2.30 p.m. Free skating for men / 9 p.m. Ice hockey.

Saturday, 15th February: 8 a.m. Ski-ing: 50-km. race / 10 a.m. Ice hockey / 2.30 p.m. Free skating for ladies / 9 p.m. Ice hockey.

Sunday, 16th February: 11 a.m. Ski-jump, special event / 2.30 p.m. Ice hockey / Closing Ceremony in the Olympia Artificial Ice Stadium.

run had been reconstructed, has proved perfectly satisfactory on every occasion.

The Olympic Artificial Ice Stadium close to the Main Railway Station has been completed and taken into use. The actual rink, which can be kept fit for play in any weather, is surrounded by accommodation for 10,000 spectators. The great ice hockey matches and the figure-skating competitions will be held here.

The skating races will be held on the splendidly situated Riessersee, on which, as on the other lakes in the environs of Garmisch-Partenkirchen, there are special rinks available for practice.

Three mountain railways provide an opportunity of reaching altitudes up to 9,370 feet, so that a guarantee is provided that the ski-ing events can be carried out at any time.

The German Railways Company will grant a reduction of fare of 60 per cent on its lines on the occasion of the IVth Olympic Winter Games in 1936 to visitors not domiciled in Germany. Residents in Germany will be granted a reduction of 33⅓ per cent on the return fare to Garmisch-Partenkirchen. The booklets of tickets are valid for three months. The German Luft Hansa and the foreign services associated with it will grant a reduction of 20 per cent to holders of general tickets and active competitors.

The ENTIRE MANAGEMENT of the IVth Olympic Winter Games in 1936 is in the hands of the

Organizing Committee for the
IVth Olympic Winter Games 1936
Garmisch-Partenkirchen. Tel. 2713.

The entire ARRANGEMENTS FOR PROVIDING ACCOMMODATION for competitors and the necessary persons accompanying them will be in the hands of the "Olympisches Verkehrsamt", Garmisch-Partenkirchen (Tel. 3101), and those for spectators in the hands of the "Kurverwaltung" (Tel. 2131).

It is proposed to arrange accommodation in the following groups (with sub-groups for officials and competitors), prices being calculated as follows on the basis of the present economic situation.

Competitors				8	marks
Group	I, from	12	to	18	„
„	II, „	9	to	12	„
„	III, „	7	to	9	„
„	IV, „	5	to	7	„

The prices include full board and lodging. Special requirements are left to private arrangement. Accommodation can be had in good private houses from 2 marks upwards.

The SALE OF TICKETS for the IVth Olympic Winter Games has begun. Forms for ordering tickets and further details can be obtained from travel agencies and other advance booking offices or will be sent on request by the Organisationskomitee, Abteilung Kartenverkauf, Garmisch-Partenkirchen.

L 785400 · e Printed in Germany

Published by the Reichsbahnzentrale für den Deutschen Reisev
in co-operation with the Propaganda Committee for the O

1936 AMERICAN OLYMPIC WINTER SPORTS TEAMS

BOBSLED

Manager
Dietrich Wortmann, New York, N. Y.

Two-Man Bob—Team I
Ivan E. Brown, Keene Valley, N. Y. (Driver.)
Alan M. Washbond, Keene Valley, N. Y.

Two-Man Bob—Team II
Gilbert Colgate, New York, N. Y. (Driver.)
Richard W. Lawrence, Branchville, N. J.

Four-Man Bob—Team I
†John J. Fox, Bronx, N. Y. (Driver.)
Francis W. Tyler, Lake Placid, N. Y. (Substitute Driver.)
James J. Bickford, Lake Placid, N. Y.
*Richard W. Lawrence, Branchville, N. J.
Max T. Bly, Lake George, N. Y.

Four-Man Bob—Team II
J. Hubert Stevens, Lake Placid, N. Y. (Driver.)
Crawford C. Merkel, Lake Placid, N. Y.
Robert P. Martin, Lake Placid, N. Y.
John J. Shene, Lake Placid, N. Y.

Alternates
‡William L. Fiske, No. Hollywood, Cal.
‡Clifford B. Gray, New York, N. Y.
‡E. Hugh Varno, Lake Placid, N. Y.

FIGURE SKATING

Manager
William W. Weigel, Buffalo, N. Y.

Assistant Manager
Mrs. Theresa W. Blanchard, Brookline, Mass.

Chaperons
Mrs. William Weigel, Buffalo, N. Y.
Beatrix Loughran, New York, N. Y.

Judge
Charles M. Rotch, Boston, Mass.

Men—Singles
Robin Lee, St. Paul, Minn.
Erle Reiter, Minneapolis, Minn.
George E. B. Hill, Boston, Mass.
James L. Madden, Newton, Mass.

Women—Singles
Maribel Y. Vinson, New York, N. Y.
Louise E. Weigel, Buffalo, N. Y.
Audrey Peppe, New York, N. Y.
Estelle D. Weigel, Buffalo, N. Y.

Pairs
*Maribel Y. Vinson, New York, N. Y.
*George E. B. Hill, Boston, Mass.
Grace E. Madden, Newton, Mass.
*James L. Madden, Newton, Mass.

*Qualified in more than one event.
†Driver of Team I unable to compete because of injury.
‡Alternate.

ICE HOCKEY

Manager
Walter A. Brown, Boston, Mass.

Committee Representative

TEAM

Albert I. Prettyman, Clinton, N. Y.
Francis F. Baker, Clinton, N. Y. (Hamilton College)
John B. Garrison, W. Newton, Mass. (Boston Olympics)
August F. Kammer, So. Orange, N. J. (St. Nicholas Hockey Club)
Philip W. La Batte, Minneapolis, Minn. (Baltimore Orioles Hockey Club)
John C. Lax, Arlington, Mass. (Boston Olympics)
Malcolm E. McAlpin, New York, N. Y. (St. Nicholas Hockey Club)
Thomas H. Moone, Lexington, Mass. (Boston Olympics)
Elbridge B. Ross, Melrose, Mass. (Boston Olympics)
Paul E. Rowe, Arlington, Mass. (Boston Olympics)
Francis J. Shaughnessy, Montreal, West Canada. (Montreal Victorias)
Gordon Smith, Winchester, Mass. (Boston Olympics)
Francis J. Spain, Waban, Mass. (Boston Olympics)
Frank R. Stubbs, Newton, Mass. (Boston Olympics)

SKI TEAM — MEN

Manager
Dr. Joel H. Hildebrand, Berkeley, Cal.

18 Kilometer Race
Richard E. Parsons, Salisbury, Conn. (Salisbury Outing Club)
Warren H. Chivers, Hanover, N. H. (Dartmouth Outing Club)
Birger Torrissen, Norfolk, Conn. (Norfolk Winter Sports Assn.)
Karl M. Satre, Salisbury, Conn. (Salisbury Outing Club)
†Nils Backstrom, Springfield, Mass. (Norfolk Winter Sports Assn.)
†Alfred D. Lindley, Minneapolis, Minn. (Bush Lake Ski Club)
†Edward J. Blood, Northfield, Vt. (Lake Placid Club)
†Donald W. Fraser, Seattle, Wash. (Washington Ski Club)

50 Kilometer Race

*Birger Torrissen, Norfolk, Conn.
(Norfolk Winter Sports Assn.)
*Karl M. Satre, Salisbury, Conn.
(Salisbury Outing Club)
*Richard E. Parsons, Salisbury, Conn.
(Salisbury Outing Club)
*Nils Backstrom, Springfield, Mass.
(Norfolk Winter Sports Assn.)
†*Warren H. Chivers, Hanover, N. H.
(Dartmouth Outing Club)
†Rolf Monsen, Lake Placid, N. Y.
(Sno Birds of Lake Placid)

Combined 18 Kilometer Race and Jump

*Birger Torrissen, Norfolk, Conn.
(Norfolk Winter Sports Assn.)
*Karl M. Satre, Salisbury, Conn.
(Salisbury Outing Club)
Paul O. Satre, Salisbury, Conn.
(Salisbury Outing Club)
*Edward J. Blood, Northfield, Vt.
(Lake Placid Club)
†*Rolf Monsen, Lake Placid, N. Y.
(Sno Birds of Lake Placid)
†*Warren H. Chivers, Hanover, N. H.
(Dartmouth Outing Club)

Special Jump

Walter I. Bietila, Ishpeming, Mich.
(Ishpeming Ski Club)
Sverre Fredheim, St. Paul, Minn.
(Norwegian American A.C.)
Roy J. Mikkelsen, Auburn, Cal.
(Auburn Ski Club)
Casper Oimon, Anaconda, Mont.
(Anaconda Ski Club)
†Ralph J. Hendrickson, Canton, So. Dakota.
(Sioux Valley Ski Club)
†*Paul O. Satre, Salisbury, Conn.
(Salisbury Outing Club)

Combined Downhill and Slalom

Richard H. Durrance, Hanover, N. H.
(Dartmouth College)
Robert Livermore, Jr., Boston, Mass.
(Ski Club Hochgebirge)
George H. Page, New York, N. Y.
(Amateur Ski Club of N. Y.)
Albert L. Washburn, Hanover, N. H.
(Dartmouth Outing Club)
†Alexander H. Bright, Cambridge, Mass.
(Ski Club Hochgebirge)
†William D. Crookes, Puyallup, Wash.
(University of Washington)
†Edgar H. Hunter, Jr., Hanover, N. H.
(Dartmouth Outing Club)
†*Alfred D. Lindley, Minneapolis, Minn.
(Bush Lake Ski Club)

40 Kilometer Relay Race

*Warren H. Chivers, Hanover, N. H.
(Dartmouth Outing Club)
*Richard E. Parsons, Salisbury, Conn.
(Salisbury Outing Club)
*Karl M. Satre, Salisbury, Conn.
(Salisbury Outing Club)
*Birger Torrissen, Norfolk, Conn.
(Norfolk Winter Sports Assn.)
†*Richard H. Durrance, Hanover, N. H.
(Dartmouth College)
†*Alfred D. Lindley, Minneapolis, Minn.
(Bush Lake Ski Club)
†*Nils Backtsrom, Springfield, Mass.
(Norfolk Winter Sports Assn.)
†*Donald W. Fraser, Seattle, Wash.
Washington Ski Club)

SKI TEAM — WOMEN

Manager

Mrs. Alice D. Wolfe, Tyrol, Austria.

Team

Clarita Heath, Tyrol, Austria.
Mrs. Helen Boughton-Leigh, London, England.
Elizabeth D. Woolsey, New Haven, Conn.
(New York Amateur Ski Club)
Mary E. Bird, Boston, Mass.
(White Mt. Ski Runners)
†Dorothy Brewer, Weston, Mass.
†Hannah H. Locke, Philadelphia, Pa.
(Philadelphia Skating Club)
†Ethylnne Smith, Seattle, Wash.
(Washington Ski Club)
†Kathryn Ward, Boston, Mass.
‡Lillian Swann, New York, N. Y.
‡Grace E. Carter, Seattle, Wash.
(Washington Ski Club)
‡Marian McKean, Beverley Farms, Mass.
(Vincent Club of Boston)
‡Ellis A. Smith, Seattle, Wash.
(Washington Ski Club)
(All competitors defrayed their own expenses.)

SPEED SKATING

Manager

Henry Kemper, St. Louis, Mo.

Coach

O'Neil Farrell, Chicago, Ill.

Judge

Charles J. Gevecker, St. Louis, Mo.

Team

Leo Freisinger, Chicago, Ill.
Delbert T. Lamb, Milwaukee, Wis.
Robert G. Petersen, Milwaukee, Wis.
Allan W. Potts, Brooklyn, N. Y.
Edward J. Schroeder, Chicago, Ill.

* Qualified in more than one event.
† Alternate.
‡ Members of squad—were not entered and did not compete.

The "Wicked" Olympic Rules about Amateurism

The Olympic amateur rules were passed by a majority of the International Olympic Committee against the advice of Baron Pierre de Coubertin, the founder of the modern Games. In 1934 de Coubertin wrote: "The actual rules are wicked. Their terms are indefensible as much from the point of view of logic, which they offered, as of human liberty, which they cheapen."

Nobody today disputes that the Games are entirely due to Coubertin. The International Olympic Committee assembled at Olympia on 26 March 1938 when the Crown Prince of Greece placed a casket containing de Coubertin's heart in the monument commemorating his founding of the modern Games in 1896; I was one of the two Olympic competitors present on that occasion.

The International Olympic Committee showed respect for de Coubertin but continued to insist on rules that he had so trenchantly denounced. One of the rules stated that an Olympic competitor had to be an amateur according to the rules of the relevant international sports federations. The International Ski Federation did not regard ski teachers as professionals. They had not been excluded from the 1924, 1928 and 1936 Olympics. Six months before the 1936 Winter Olympics, the first to include downhill and slalom racing, the International Olympic Committee ruled that ski teachers could not compete because they were professionals.

The French were the first to realize that success in downhill and slalom racing was good publicity for their ski resorts. The German, Italian and French teams were all given lengthy training at public expense but still competed as amateurs. The top Swiss and Austrian racers were all ski teachers and thus excluded from the Games as professionals, even though they were professional ski teachers and not professional racers. The Swiss and Austrians therefore decided to boycott the Games.

There were no ski teachers on the British team. We were amateurs in the strictest sense of the word: however hard we tried we could find no way of making money out of the sports. We nevertheless felt keenly the injustice to our Swiss and Austrian friends. After consulting the captains of the women's and men's teams, who were Jeannette Kessler and me, my father told the International Olympic Committee that the British would join the Swiss and American boycott unless ski teachers were admitted. This was a serious decision. The Olympics, which combine different sports in one overall program, attract far more media attention than do World Championships in the separate sports. They therefore have supreme prestige and are inevitably regarded as the crown of any sporting career. In the end a compromise was reached. Ski teachers would be excluded from the Games but World Championships, in which they were allowed to compete, would also be held in 1936; this reversed an earlier decision that World Championships would not be held in an Olympic year.

The British chances of success in the Games were obviously better if ski teachers were excluded. The British boycott threat is the only occasion—at any rate, the only occasion known to me—when an Olympic team has tried to secure conditions that increased the odds against them. Good sportsmanship was, however, much easier for us than it is for modern competitors, who attract so much media hyperbole and public adulation. Tell young people who are selected for their physical rather than their intellectual qualities that sporting defeat equates with national disaster, then they may be tempted to believe it and to regard bad sportsmanship as a patriotic duty. It was different with us. The press paid scant attention to our activities. *The London Times*, which now covers ski racing so efficiently, gave less space to the 1935 World Championship downhill than they did to a football match won by a police club. Their account was headed "Men's downhill race at Murren." The sub-heading "Best British only tenth," certainly put me in my place.

Our position can be put in four words: we were not famous. We were more interested in journalists than journalists were in us. We were not watched on television screens. We were not bothered by fan mail. Compared with the much-publicized ski heroes of today, we may seem like poor relations. But this attitude overlooks one simple fact: today's newspaper lies in the rubbish bin tomorrow. The cheering fades. The flags vanish. Few things are more evanescent than sporting fame. Races certainly live on in the memory—in one's own memory not that of other people.

by PETER LUNN

While controversy raged in the United States about participation in the games, this sign was displayed at Garmisch. It reads "Admission to Jews Forbidden." AP

DEMONSTRATION EVENTS

MILITARY SKI PATROL RACE

Place—Country	*Time*
1. Italy (Enrico Silvestri, Luigi Perenni, Stefano Sertorelli, Sisto Scilligo)....	2h. 28m. 35.0s.
2. Finland (Eino Kuvaja, Olli Remes, Kalle Arantola, Olli Huttunen)....	2h. 28m. 49.0s.
3. Sweden (Gunnar Wahlberg, Seth Olofsson, Johan Wiksten, John Westberg	2h. 35m. 24.0s.
4. Austria (Albert Bach, Edwin Hartman, Franz Hiermann, Eugen Tschurtschentaler)	2h. 36m. 19.0s.
5. Germany (Herbert Leupold, Johann Hieble, Hermann Lochbuhler, Michael Kirchmann)	2h. 36m. 24.0s.
6. France (Jacques Faure, Marcel Cohendoz, Eugene Sibue, Jean Morand)	2h. 40m. 55.0s.
7. Switzerland (Arnold Kaech, Josef Jauch, Eduard Waser, Josef Lindauer)	2h. 43m. 39.0s.
8. Czechoslovakia (Karel Steiner, Josef Mateasko, Bohuslav Musil, Bohumil Kosour)	2h. 50m. 08.0s.
9. Poland (Wladislaw Zytkowicz, Jean Pydych, Jozef Zubek, Adam Rzepka)	2h. 52m. 27.0s.

INTERNATIONAL EISSCHIESSEN COMPETITION

Team Competition for Men

Won by Austria—1st Team (Tirol)................2053 Points
(Wilhelm Sibermayr, Anton Ritzl, Otto Ritzl, Wilhelm Pichler, Rudolf Rainer)

Individual Distance Competition for Men

Won by Georg Edenhauser, Austria
Distance—154.6 Meters

Individual Tee Competition for Men

Won by Ignaz Reiterer, Austria............................15 Points

NATIONAL COMPETITION

Team Competition for Men

Won by Sport Club Riessersee..........................3553 Points
(Anton Bader, Martin Reiser, Georg Reiser, Anton Jocher, Egon Hartl)

Team Competition for Women

Won by Altonaer Schlittschuhlaufverein........2630 Points
Agnes Knudsen, Martha Knak, Paula Kulper, Lilli Herboldt, Ruth Becker)

Individual Distance Competition for Men

Won by Johann Hacker, Gotteszell..Distance—95.2 Meters

Individual Tee Competition for Men

Won by Josef Kreitmeier, Bad Aibling................17 Points

Individual Tee Competition for Women

Won by Mathilde Seyffarth, Riessersee................**27 Points**

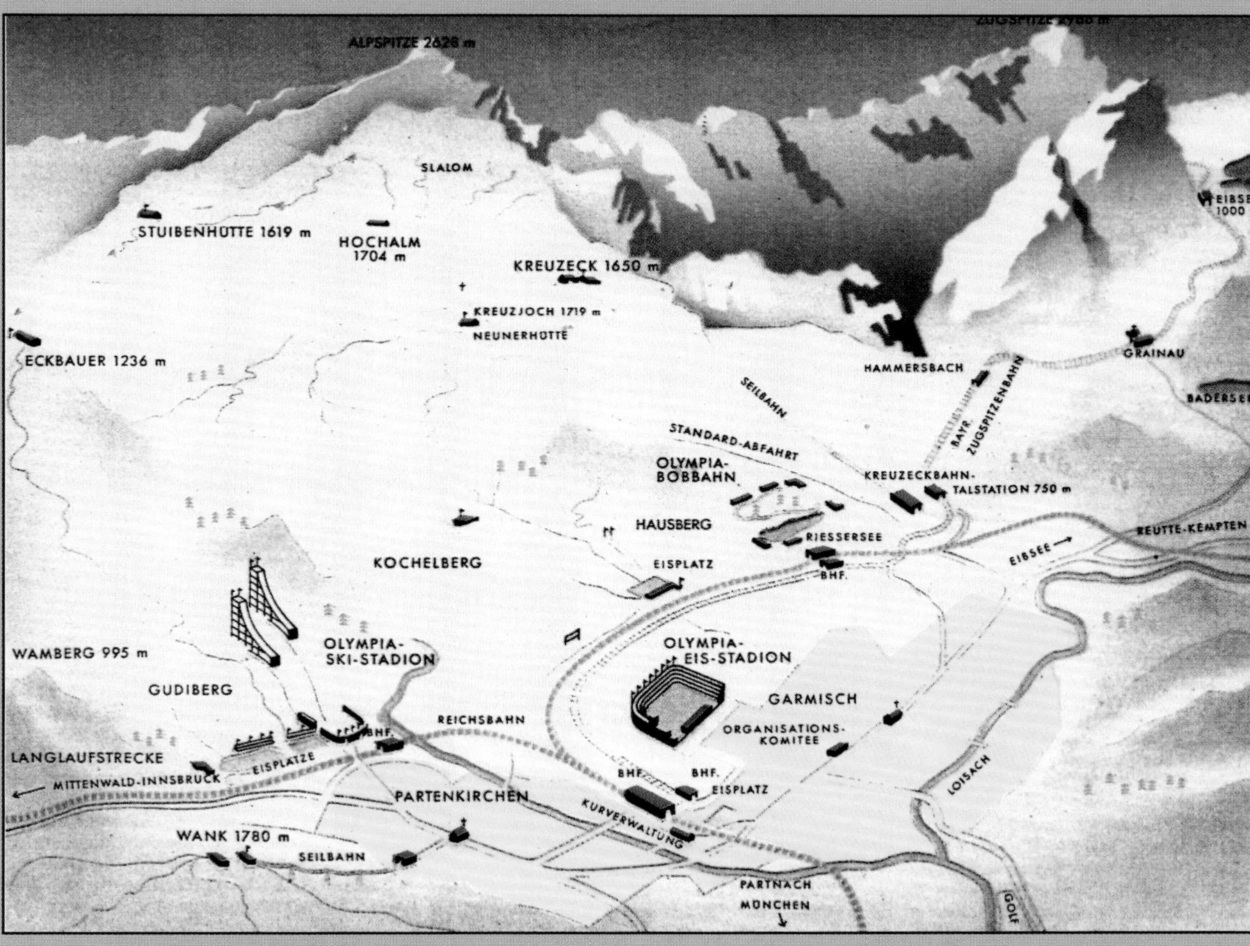

Peter Lunn, the son of Arnold Lunn, the founder of downhill ski racing, was born in London in 1914. Two years later he skied for the first time. Between 1931 and 1937 he skied in seven World Championship races and during the 1936 Olympics he was captain of the British ski team. He was 15th in the downhill and 13th in slalom for a 12th combined place. Lunn is still active in racing (he jumped 66 feet in the Princes Water Ski Club Championship in 1972) and raced in the Inferno Downhill race, recorded as the longest downhill race in the world.

A Nazi swastika was cut into the outrun of the large ski jump, another example of the government involving the games in its morbid ideology. NA, GRIO

Sir Arnold Lunn Speaks Out

Sir Arnold Lunn, regarded as one of the founding fathers of alpine skiing, wrote an article for the February 1949 issue of *Atlantic Monthly* that included this statement about the 1936 Olympics and the Nazis:

"Sport, like other human activities, reflects the dominant philosophy of the age. The dogma 'Sport has nothing to do with politics' is a survival of the age of laissez-fair Liberalism.

"But it is essential for a dictator to prove that the prestige of the country is due to the regime, and sport must therefore contribute to ideological propaganda. The young Nazis were encouraged to believe that a ski race was a competition in which Germans raced to prove, not that they were better skiers than other people, but that Nazism was better than democracy. The thing that mattered, and the only thing that mattered, was victory, and all means which led to this end were justifiable. At the Olympic Games in Garmisch the course was closed to all competitors on the day before the race. The Nazis, we subsequently learned, practiced down the course at dawn.

"Before the Nazis came into power German skiers were decent friendly people who contributed their share to the building of a real freemasonry transcending national frontiers. But the Nazi ski teams were mobilized like ski troops. German competitors were not allowed to accept invitations as individuals. If the team was not invited the individual could not accept. The technique of making protests was developed as a fine art. If the Nazi flag was not displayed with sufficient prominence, a protest was promptly lodged. Any decision which could be challenged was challenged."

Don Fraser and a couple of his teammates napping in their quarters at Garmisch. KSVHS

Program for the final Olympic Alpine tryouts on Mt. Rainier. KSVHS

Don Fraser and three members of the women's ski team traveled to Germany on the *S.S. Oregon Express*. One of the women wrote a series of articles about the trip for a local newspaper. KSVHS

Garmisch-Partenkirchen was a lively, decorated area for the Olympic games.

"We Welcome the Youth of the World" entrance sign in Garmisch-Partenkirchen. NA, GRIO

It took 106 days to build the ice stadium in 1934. The ice sheet measured 30x60 meters and 10,000 spectators could be seated and 6,150 could stand for the skating competitions. The arena was lighted by 28 high-beam floodlights. Space was provided for up to 320 journalists and broadcast personnel. NA, GRIO

The march of the athletes in the ski stadium on Feb. 6, 1936, the opening day of the winter Olympics in Garmisch-Partenkirchen.
TOP: NA, GRIO. BOTTOM: BA

The parking lot was always full at Garmisch for the games. Spectators came from all over Germany and from around the world.
NA, GRIO

The Ski Jumps and Stadium

The Little Ski Jump or Gaudebergschanze, built two decades before the Olympics, was rebuilt for the 1936 games. The Big Ski Jump was built for the 1936 games. A 43-meter high and five-meter-wide tower was constructed with an angle of inclination of 35 degrees. The ski stadium was also the run-off area for the ski jumps, used as the start and finish for the cross-country events and the site for the opening and closing ceremonies. On the last day of the games over 130,000 people were in attendance. The Olympics flame flared day and night during the games from a hill east of the Big Ski Jump.

The American team enters the stadium in a snowstorm for the opening ceremonies. KSVHS and DICK DURRANCE COLLECTION

As in the summer games, the flag of each participating country received a ribbon at the closing ceremony of the winter games.

On February 6 at 10:55 a.m. the special government train arrived at Kainzenbad in a snowstorm.

Heavy snow fell when Hitler, who would open the Olympic games as its patron, is greeted by Dr. Karl Ritter van Halt, president of the Organizing Committee of the IVth Olympic Winter Games.

Hitler in the ski stadium. Next to him is Reichminister Göring and Reichminister Goebbels.

Winter Olympics Results

Two-Man Bobsled
1st – USA, Team 1
2nd – Switzerland
3rd – USA, Team 2
Four-Man Bobsled
1st – Switzerland, Team 2
2nd – Switzerland, Team 1
3rd – Great Britain
4th – USA, Team 1
6th – USA, Team 2
Figure Skating, Men's Singles
1st – Karl Schafer, Austria
2nd – Ernst Baier, Germany
3rd – Felix Kaspar, Austria
12th – Robin Lee, USA
13th – Erle Reiter, USA
22nd – George Hill, USA
Figure Skating, Ladies' Singles
1st – Sonja Henie, Norway
2nd – M. Cecilia Colledge, Great Britain
3rd – Vivi-Anne Hulten, Sweden
5th – Maribel Vinson, USA
12th – Audrey Peppe, USA
21st – Louise Weigel, USA
22nd – Estelle Weigel, USA
Figure Skating, Pairs
1st – Maxie Herber & Ernst Baier, Germany
2nd – Ilse Pausin & Erik Pausin, Austria
3rd – Emilia Rotter & Lazlo Szollas, Hungary
5th – Maribel Vinson & George Hill, USA
11th – Grace Madden & James Madden, USA
Ice Hockey
1st – Great Britain
2nd – Canada
3rd – USA
Nordic Skiing, 18 Kilometer Race
1st – Erik-Aug. Larsson, Sweden
2nd – Oddbjorn Hagen, Norway
3rd – Pekka Niemi, Finland
34th – Karl Satre, USA
46th – Richard Parsons, USA
48th – Warren Chivers, USA
Nordic Skiing, 50 Kilometer Race
1st – Elis Viklund, Sweden
2nd – Axel Wikstrom, Sweden
3rd – Nils-Joel Englund, Sweden
18th – Karl Satre, USA
27th – Birger Torrissen, USA
33rd – Nils Backstrom, USA
Alpine Combined, Men
1st – Franz Pfnur, Germany
2nd – Gustav Lantschner, Germany
3rd – Emile Allais, France
10th – Richard Durrance, USA
13th – George Page, USA
23rd – Robert Livermore, USA
Alpine & Combined, Women
1st – Christel Cranz, Germany
2nd – Kathe Grasegger, Germany
3rd – Laila Schou-Nilsen, Norway
19th – Betty Woolsey, USA
21st – Helen Boughton-Leigh, USA
27th – Clarita Heath, USA
Combined 18 Kilometer Race and Jump
1st – Oddbjorn Hagen, Norway
2nd – Olaf Hoffsbakken, Norway
3rd – Sverre Brodahl, Norway
40 Kilometer Ski Relay Race
1st – Finland
2nd – Norway
3rd – Sweden
11th – USA
Special Ski Jump
1st – Birger Ruud, Norway
2nd – Sven Ericksson, Sweden
3rd – Reidar Andersen, Norway
11th – Sverre Fredheim, USA
13th – Casper Oimon, USA
23rd – Roy Mikkelsen, USA
30th – Walter Bietila, USA
Speed Skating, 500 Meters
1st – Ivar Ballangrud, Norway
2nd – Georg Krog, Norway
3rd – Leo Freisinger, USA
5th – Delbert Lamb, USA
6th – Allan Potts, USA (tie)
11th – Robert Petersen, USA (tie)
Speed Skating, 1,500 Meters
1st – Charles Mathisen, Norway
2nd – Ivar Ballangrud, Norway
3rd – Birger Vasenius, Finland
4th – Leo Freisinger, USA
12th – Edward Schroeder, USA (tie)
17th – Robert Petersen, USA
32rd – Allan Potts, USA
Speed Skating, 5,000 Meters
1st – Ivar Ballangrud, Norway
2nd – Birger Vasenius, Finland
3rd – Antero Ojala, Finland
11th – Robert Petersen, USA
15th – Edward Schroeder, USA
Speed Skating, 10,000 Meters
1st – Ivar Ballangrud, Norway
2nd – Birger Vasenius, Finland
3rd – Max Stiepl, Austria
8th – Edward Schroeder, USA

Nazi Gauleiter (District Leader) of Münich Adolf Wagner, Hitler and his aide, S.S. General Julius Schaub, watch the ice skating events. NA, EVA BRAUN COLLECTION

Luftwaffe commander Hermann Göring is handed an envelope while watching the ice skating events. At left is his wife, German actress Emmy Sonnemann. NA, HERMAN GÖRING COLLECTION

Members of the U.S. men's ski team on board the S.S. *Manhattan*, January 1936.

The American downhill squad. From left: Al Washburn, Al Lindley, Alec Bright, George Page, Bill Crookes, Dick Durrance and Bob Livermore Jr. Lindley, Bright and Crookes were alternates and did not race. NESM

Ski team members stand at attention at Garmisch. NESM

The only alpine ski event held was the Alpine Combined, consisting of one downhill and two slalom runs with the winner having the most number of total points. Twenty-seven year old Franz Pfnür, from Bavaria, was second in the downhill and first in both slalom runs, thus winning the gold medal. Second place went to Gustav Lantschner of Germany, who was considered an ardent Nazi. Third place went to the great French skier Emile Allais and fourth place to the Norwegian ski jumper Birger Ruud.

Alexander (Alec) Bright was one of the most versatile members of the men's team. He was born in 1897 in Cambridge, Massachusetts, and attended Harvard University.

His passion for outdoor sports lasted all his life. Quoting Bright from the Harvard Class of 1919 25th Anniversary Report: "Competition and new games still interest me," he wrote, "and I have a vain joy in winning or getting away with a foolish stunt."

His love of skiing was a shared experience. He was a charter member of the Ski Club Hockebirge, formed in 1930 and the first and greatest exponent of downhill racing in the United States.

He also was an initiator and promoter of the Cannon Mountain Aerial Tramway in New Hampshire, the first in North America. In 1939 he guided a small group of Harvard undergraduates in raising funds and building the Harvard Ski Club House above Pinkham Notch at Mt. Washington. In addition, he persuaded the Harvard athletic community to reorganize competitive skiing as an official minor sport.

At Harvard he was a crack hockey player. He also played with the Boston Athletic Association. The Montreal pro hockey team offered to sign him in 1923. In 1978 Harvard's new hockey facility was named after Bright.

Bright served in World War I and in World War II was with the 8th Air Force in England. Aviation was also a passion of his, learning to fly in 1927.

As a member of the 1936 team he was, at age 39, the first American to finish the downhill event. A year later he captured the Massachusetts downhill championship. Bright raced into his mid-50s. He was a member of the U.S. Olympic Committee in 1948 and vice-president of the National Ski Association in 1950.

His entire adult working life was in the stock brokerage business, first with his father's company and later with a merged firm. In addition, Bright was quite active in many civic affairs.

In 1959 Bright married Clarita Heath, a member of the 1936 women's ski team. He and Clarita had a son and two daughters. Bright died in 1979 at age 82.

Warren Chivers, member of the 1936 men's cross-country ski team, was the eldest member of the famous Chivers family of Hanover, New Hampshire. He was a diversified athlete at Dartmouth College in the ski jump, cross-country, downhill and slalom. He won the national cross-country championship in 1937 and represented the United States in the 1937 Pan-American championships in Chile.

Roy Mikkelsen was one of America's greatest ski jumpers. Norwegian by birth, he came to the United States in 1924. In 1933 he won his first National Ski Jumping Championship and repeated the feat in 1935. Mikkelsen was the Auburn Ski Club's leading jumper and was a member of the 1936 Olympic team. During World War II he was a member of the 10th Mountain Division and the 99th Norwegian American Battalion. He died in 1967. WASM

Dick Durrance was America's best alpine skier in the mid-1930s. At the Olympic tryouts on Mount Rainier in Washington state in 1935 he placed second in the downhill, third in the slalom, and first in the combined for the first Olympic team spot.

Ironically, Durrance would race at Garmisch where he had spent part of his youth attending a German school and becoming one of the best young ski racers in Europe.

He was attending Dartmouth College when he made the Olympic team. He went to Europe earlier than his teammates to get in shape and get the "feel" of his former home again. In the downhill on February 7 Durrance came in eleventh. In the slalom he came in eighth after a questionable penalty cost him a possible third place. His combined place was tenth, tops for the Americans.

After the Olympics he raced in several more European races and then returned to Dartmouth. In the following years he would be the U.S. collegiate ski champion and winner of Sun Valley's prestigious Harriman Cup three times. Before the war he would help develop the Alta Resort and, along with his wife, Miggs, run its ski school.

He worked for Boeing during the war and then moved to Denver to get back into the ski business, this time the manufacturing end. His next move was to the new resort town of Aspen and he was there in the area's early years and helped develop it into one of America's finest ski areas.

Durrance's interest in films went back to his days in Germany and he would make filmmaking his life's avocation and Miggs would become a well-known still photographer.

The Durrances have skied with the early ski pioneers, and with movie stars and have traveled the world making movies. Their two sons, Dick Jr. and Dave, made careers of filming and skiing.

Dick Durrance has been a major influence in American skiing for 60 years. He and Miggs now make their home at Snowmass Village, Colorado.

Durrance at the start of the downhill on the Kreuzeck course – no starting gate, warm-up shelter, wands or electronic devices, as are common today.

Durrance skis in the slalom. DICK DURRANCE COLLECTION

Miggs and Dick Durrance in 1994. MASON BEEKLEY

Don Fraser, right, and Sven Utterstrom in front of the Post Hotel. Utterstrom was a volunteer coach for the American nordic team. KSVHS

Don Fraser is perhaps best known as the husband of Gretchen Fraser, America's first gold medal winner in alpine skiing. She took gold in the slalom and silver in the alpine combined at the 1948 games in St. Moritz.

Don was himself a prominent racer. Growing up in Seattle, he skied on Mount Rainier and won the first Silver Skis Race in 1934 and again in 1938. He raced for the University of Washington ski team.

When he made the '36 ski team he was given a $50 overcoat, cap and sweater and paid $1.00 a day for a 31-day boat trip from Seattle to Europe.

The Olympic alpine team had to be reduced to four skiers for each race and since Fraser had hurt his leg in practice, he withdrew from alpine competition to concentrate on nordic events, especially the 18-kilometer race. He did not make the final four in this race.

In 1939 he married Gretchen and they lived in Sun Valley, where Don worked at the resort. He also was selected for the 1940 Olympic team. During World War II, Don was in the Navy but after the war the couple moved to Washington state so that Don could take over his uncle's heating fuel business.

After retirement in 1968 they moved to Sun Valley, where they were active in resort affairs. Don died in January 1994 at age 80. Gretchen died just 36 days later. They had one son, who lives in the Seattle area.

The American 18 kilometer cross-country team. From left: Paul Satre, Don Fraser, Birger Torrissen, Nils Backstrom, Coach Sven Utterstrom, Warren Chivers, Ed Blood, Karl Satre and Richard Parsons. Backstrom, Blood and Fraser were alternates and did not race. Another alternate, Al Lindley is not shown and Paul Satre is not on the official list for this race. KSVHS

AMERICAN OLYMPIC COMMITTEE

IV OLYMPIC WINTER GAMES-GARMISCH-PARTENKIRCHEN-FEBRUARY 6 to 16, 1936
GAMES OF THE XI OLYMPIAD—BERLIN, GERMANY—AUGUST 1 to 16, 1936

HONORARY PRESIDENT
FRANKLIN D. ROOSEVELT, PRESIDENT OF THE UNITED STATES
HONORARY VICE-PRESIDENTS
CORDELL HULL, SECRETARY OF STATE GEORGE H. DERN, SECRETARY OF WAR CLAUDE A. SWANSON, SECRETARY OF NAVY
PRESIDENT EMERITUS, DR. GRAEME M. HAMMOND

PRESIDENT
AVERY BRUNDAGE
11 S. LA SALLE STREET
CHICAGO, ILL.
VICE PRESIDENT
DR. JOSEPH E. RAYCROFT
PRINCETON UNIVERSITY
PRINCETON, N. J.
SECRETARY
FREDERICK W. RUBIEN
233 BROADWAY
NEW YORK
TREASURER
GUSTAVUS T. KIRBY
36 EAST 57th STREET
NEW YORK
ASSISTANT TREASURER
A. JOCELYN H. MAGRATH

OFFICE OF THE CHAIRMAN
1936 OLYMPIC GAMES SKI COMMITTEE
LEIB DEYO
790, 141 WORTH STREET
NEW YORK N. Y.

September 24, 1935.

Mr. Donald Fraser
Washington Ski Club
Seattle, Washington

Dear Sir:-

I enclose herewith selections for the squad for the 1936 Olympic Games Ski Squad.

As the Committee was unable to raise all the funds required, we can only donate $75.00 towards your expenses and the balance will have to be raised by your club or community.

We estimate the expenses from New York to Germany and return at $400.00, plus any expenses necessary for you to incur between your home and New York City and return.

Please advise me prior to December 1st, 1935 if you will be in a position to finance this trip.

Very truly yours,

Chairman
1936 Olympic Games Ski Committee.

AMERICAN OLYMPIC COMMITTEE

IV OLYMPIC WINTER GAMES-GARMISCH-PARTENKIRCHEN-FEBRUARY 6 to 16, 1936
GAMES OF THE XI OLYMPIAD—BERLIN, GERMANY—AUGUST 1 to 16, 1936

HONORARY PRESIDENT
FRANKLIN D. ROOSEVELT, PRESIDENT OF THE UNITED STATES
HONORARY VICE-PRESIDENTS
CORDELL HULL, SECRETARY OF STATE - GEORGE H. DERN, SECRETARY OF WAR - CLAUDE A. SWANSON, SECRETARY OF NAVY
PRESIDENT EMERITUS, DR. GRAEME M. HAMMOND

OFFICE OF THE SECRETARY
WOOLWORTH BUILDING, 233 BROADWAY
TELEPHONE CORTLANDT 7-0122 - CABLE ADDRESS: "AMOLYMPIC"
NEW YORK CITY

September 23, 1935.

LEIB DEYO, Chairman, 1936 Olympic Games Ski Committee, announces, that, subject to the approval of the American Olympic Executive Committee, the following squad has been selected for the IV Olympic Winter Games to be held at Garmisch-Partenkirchen February 6th to 16th, 1936.

MANAGER

Dr. Joel T. Hildebrand
University of California
Berkeley, California

MEMBERS OF THE SQUAD

Nils Backstrom, Norfolk Winter Sports Association, Norfolk, Conn.
A. H. Bright, Hochgebirge Ski Runners, Boston, Mass.
Warren Chivers, Dartmouth University, Hanover, New Hampshire.
Richard Durrance, Dartmouth University, Hanover, New Hampshire.
Donald Fraser, Washington Ski Club, Seattle, Washington
Sverre Fredheim, Norwegian-American Athletic Club, Minneapolis, Minn.
James Henriksen, Sioux Valley Ski Club, Canton, South Dakota.
E. H. Hunter, Jr., Dartmouth University, Hanover, New Hampshire.
Robert Livermore, Jr., Hochgebirge Ski Runners, Boston, Mass.
Roy Mikkelsen, Auburn Ski Club, Auburn, California.
Casper Oimen, Anaconda Sports Club, Anaconda, Montana.
Richard Parsons, Salisbury Outing Club, Salisbury, Conn.
Magnus Satre, Salisbury Outing Club, Salisbury, Conn.
Ottar Satre, Salisbury Outing Club, Salisbury, Conn.
Birger Torrisen, Norfolk Winter Sports Association, Norfolk, Conn.

It is possible that all the above will be unable to go unless sufficient funds can be raised but the Committee is confident with the small assessment placed on each community that all the above men can be financed.

The U.S. women's ski team at Davos, Switzerland. Left to right: Mary Bird, Marian McKean, Ellis-Ayr Smith, Lily Swann, Betty Woolsey, Grace Carter, Clarita Heath, Helen Boughton-Leigh and Otto Furrer, the coach. McKean, Smith, Swann and Carter did not compete in the Olympics. CLARITA HEATH BRIGHT COLLECTION

The 1936 women's ski team. From left: Lily Swann, Mary Bird, Ellis-Ayr Smith, Grace Carter, Coach Otto Furrer, Hannes Schneider (father of the Arlberg technique), Assistant Coach Herman Tcholl, Helen Boughton-Leigh, Clarita Heath, Betty Woolsey, Marian McKean. KSVHS

The women's team sitting on a fence at the bottom of the ski jumps. From left: Clarita Heath, Ellen Carter, Helen Boughton-Leigh, Betty Woolsey, Alice Wolfe, Marian McKean and Mary Bird. NA 131-6R-222-9

In 1966 members of the 1936 women's ski team met for a reunion. From left: Clarita Heath Bright, Grace Lindley McKnight, Helen Boughton-Leigh McAlpine, Betty Woolsey, Marian McKean Wigglesworth and Mary Bird Young. WASM

Clarita Heath Bright Reminisces

After my high school graduation in 1934, my mother was ordered by her doctor to take a long trip, preferably around the world. I was her youngest child and was deemed the appropriate one to accompany her. Thus was my whole life changed. We were one month on the boat from Los Angeles to France and were naively saddled with 12 pieces of luggage!

Our travels took us to Kitzbuhel, Austria, for Christmas. It was my big chance to learn about skiing to help my college-age brother who was trying to ski with toe straps. I enrolled immediately in the ski school. I loved it from the first moment and have always felt it to be one of the few sports which is enjoyable in all stages. My mother, who seemed quite old to me at near 50, also joined a class and we encouraged each other.

Before the 1935 season was over I entered races in the Tirol and was subsequently invited to join the first Women's American Olympic team for the next year.

Summer activities were mostly travel in Europe, as our World Tour began to take a back seat. There was also some hiking and tennis. Not until fall did Sigi Engl, teacher and friend, suggest I run the woods on uneven terrain with ski poles. That was my conditioning.

On Jan. 1, 1936, the squad of 13 gathered in St. Anton am Arlberg, Austria: three from the Seattle area who had washed cars and organized bake sales to raise money for the long sea voyage through the Panama Canal; two who lived in Europe; the other eight were from the East Coast, with the exception of our Captain Helen Boughton-Leigh, who had raced for Britain the previous year in the World Championships because she was married to an Englishman.

Training began in earnest. I remember clearly that first day. We were so curious and a bit wary of each other as we measured and speculated about our chances of being one of the chosen four. However, I don't recall any disharmony then nor in the succeeding weeks or even years. Training was then relentless. Since our own two feet were the only method of attaining the top of the mountain, we were limited to two downhill runs per day at the most. Usually we climbed in the morning for downhill and practiced slalom in the afternoon. That was also without benefit of uphill transportation.

After a week or so of this regime we started team selection. That meant an elimination race among ourselves every day. We also went to other resorts where we raced against others and finally to Davos, Switzerland, where there were opportunities to *ride* uphill, giving us more downhill time. Such a demanding schedule was more concentrated than anything we had ever undertaken. Thirty-eight days is not long to prepare for the race of your life. We had to go all-out every day.

Clarita Heath in the 1940s. CLARITA HEATH BRIGHT COLLECTION

Our manager, Mrs. Alice Damrosch Wolfe from New York, who on her own gathered us together and provided our trainer, rounded up her American friends who drove us hither and yon when it was needed. They assisted her in many ways such as timing, organizing and comforting. They all did it for fun and we all enjoyed it. Otherwise we paid our own way and were responsible for assembling our own uniforms. It was decided we would wear navy sweaters, white jackets, navy knickers and red stockings. Underwear was not regulated and we all had a good laugh one day when Alice Wolfe asked me if I had a #3 sewn on my undershirt as I was consistently third in our group. So then I knew I was one of the chosen four.

When we finally arrived at Garmisch-Partenkirchen, Germany, we found little snow on the Zugspitze. Some had been trucked in, shovelled and tamped in place on the course by soldiers. On opening day we assembled to march by the reviewing stand built on a meadow. There had been some discussion as to whether we should dip our Stars & Stripes in front of Hitler. We, of course, did not. The ceremony was not the theatrical extravaganza deemed essential today, but a simple salute to winter sport and the games, the oath in tradition taken by a competitor.

During the brief formalities it grew cold and began to snow heavily. As we stood there getting colder and colder in our light windjackets, one member of the men's squad removed his handsome blue overcoat with the enameled buttons and placed it over my shoulders. I was so grateful! The men, of course, had been provided with complete uniforms and equipment. We later contended that it snowed because Hitler had ordered it.

Along with year-round training, equipment has made the most difference between then and now. Our boots and bindings had to accommodate uphill walking so they were comfortable. Tea dancing was popular in all the resorts and tea drinkers most always danced in their boots. Clothing was woolen and light. Quilted jackets filled with down or synthetics were unknown to us.

International rules mandated that skis be stamped with ink at the starting line of the first event in the competition. Any skis without the stamp were forbidden in the next event. Each contestant made her own decisions favoring downhill or slalom or a good compromise. Thus it was possible for less affluent skiers to compete. This was necessary even though some teams were already subsidized by their fatherlands.

I was sick the last days before the downhill so was unable to practice the course. I was, however, given special permission to look it over. On race day I couldn't quite hold the line I had chosen and went off the little bridge into the brook. Because of the newfallen snow it took what seemed ages to me to climb out. I finished about 24th, but it would have been unthinkable not to finish! The next day, walking up the slalom course for the second run I noticed a man walk around me to view my number (marked only on the front). Then he smiled and said admiringly in German, "I watched your first run. Very schneidig." Our German was pretty good by then, but we had to be told that schneidig meant "plucky" or "courageous." My first big race was not a colossal success in the eyes of the outside world, but the whole Olympic experience was just wonderful and continues to make life more interesting for me even to this day!

Life was so innocent in the '30s. We all had crushes on men's team racers. The associations were not complicated nor demanding. My very own future husband, Alec Bright of Cambridge, Massachusetts, was on the U.S. Men's Squad. We met there, but were not romantically involved until 23 years later.

Our coach was Otto Furrer, a famous guide and climber from Zermatt. Since control flags directing the course were sparingly used, we would ask Otto how we should "take" a certain slope. No matter the contour nor

Clarita Heath Bright skiing at Sun Valley, Idaho, in the 1960s.
CLARITA HEATH BRIGHT COLLECTION

Clarita Heath Bright at her home in Brookline, Massachusetts.

the length, Otto's famous last words were "more or less schuss"—straight down. Otto is no longer living, nor is Alice Wolfe, but of the 13 original young ladies, ten are still going strong. We grow older and change, but inside I love to go fast, rise to the challenge. I still ski—but not like that.

Editor's note: Clarita Heath married Alec Bright in 1959 and they lived in Brookline, Massachusetts. Alec Bright died in 1979 leaving his wife, a son and two daughters. Clarita continues to live in Brookline.

Mary Bird Young was another member of the women's team whose life was devoted to the outdoors. She grew up in the Boston area and learned to ski in New England. She was also a mountain climber and traveled to Europe as much as possible in the 1930s to ski and climb. She holds the distinction of being the first woman to ski the headwall at Tuckerman Ravine in New Hampshire.

Although Mary had not raced much, she was selected for the team and traveled once again to Europe to represent the U.S. After the Olympics she participated in a few more races in Europe and then never raced again. She did, however, continue to ski and mountain climb all over the world and assisted her husband, Christopher Young, in his filmmaking business.

The Youngs were friends with Lowell Thomas and accompanied him to exotic places for filming, writing and skiing. Her friends included some of the pioneers of the United States ski industry.

Mary has been a widow since the 1980s and lives in Sharon, Connecticut. She still loves to cross-country ski.

Mary Bird making a turn. MARY BIRD COLLECTION

Otto Furrer and Mary Bird looking over the downhill course at the 1935 FIS at Mürren, Switzerland. MARY BIRD COLLECTION

Alice Damrosch Wolfe Kaier, a New Yorker, was active for many years in international skiing circles. She assembled the National Ski Association's first women's ski team for the 1935 FIS World Championships and the team for the 1936 Olympics. She represented the NSA at the FIS Congress in 1938, 1949, 1951 and 1953 and continued her involvement with skiing through the 1960 Olympics at Squaw Valley. NESM

Betty Woolsey at her ranch near Jackson, Wyoming, 1995.

Betty Woolsey came from an interesting and ambitious family. Her great-grandfather was president of Yale and her father was an early-day forester in the new Bureau of Forestry. She was born in Albuquerque, New Mexico, in 1908. She grew up living in the outdoors and became America's best woman mountain climber. She attended Vassar College and spent much time climbing in Europe and learning to ski in New England.

She won a race at the Suicide Six ski area at Woodstock, Vermont, and was asked to join the 1936 Olympic ski team. She placed ninth in the combined (downhill and slalom), the highest of any American woman.

She raced again in Europe in 1937 and later in the United States and qualified for the 1940 Olympic team and was named team captain.

During the 1940s she worked as a journalist in Sun Valley and as editor of *Ski Illustrated*. In 1943 she bought a ranch at the base of Teton Pass in Wyoming and since 1948 has operated it as a guest ranch. Betty Woolsey is a true competitor—a ski racer, mountain climber, rancher and outdoorsman.

Olympic Romances

Grace Carter of the women's ski team married Al Lindley of the men's ski team. Helen Boughton-Leigh of the women's ski team married Malcolm McAlpin of the ice hockey team. Clarita Heath of the women's ski team married Alec Bright of the men's ski team.

Friedl Pfeifer, left, and Hannes Schneider, right. Pfeifer coached the American women's ski team in 1937 and would have been their coach for the 1940 Olympics. He was on the 1936 Austrian ski team, but the IOC ruled that ski instructors could not compete, so the Austrians boycotted the games. Schneider was the head of the St. Anton Ski School and was imprisoned by the Nazis in 1938. He was released and moved to the United States in 1939. Pfeifer is shown here accepting the winning cup for the Kandahar race. He would move to the United States and help develop the Sun Valley and Aspen ski areas.

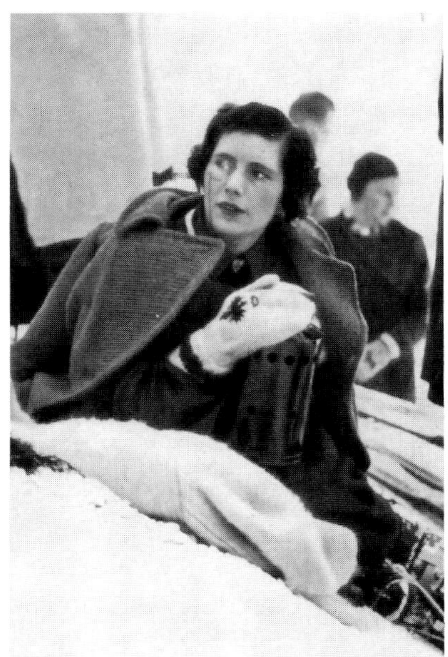

Diana Gordon-Lemmox of Canada finished 29th in the Alpine Combined. She skied with one arm in a cast and a monocle in one eye.

The Greatest Woman Racer of Them All

Germany's Christel Cranz dominated the 1930s like no woman skier has ever dominated a decade of skiing. She was peerless in her own time. Her record is unmatched today.

She was born far from the mountains, in Brussels, in 1914. Her family had earlier emigrated from Hamburg, Germany. The First World War, soon after Christel's birth, forced the family back to Germany to live. Christel spent her childhood in Freiburg, a hundred miles west of Munich, in the Schwabische Alps. She tried on skis for the first time at age four.

The teenage Christel took very confidently to the only form of racing available in the early 1920s, cross-country. But the pure downhill race, the "Alpine events," were slowly coming into their own in the 1920s.

The first big international women's event was at St. Anton, Austria, the Arlberg-Kandahar women's race of 1928. It was the first year that the famous race was held. Three years later, the first woman's World Championship was held at Murren, Switzerland. The very next year 18-year-old Christel took a second, skiing in her first big international race, the Arlberg-Kandahar of 1932.

In 1934, Christel won the slalom and combined women's World Championship at St. Moritz; she won the 1935 women's World Championship downhill and combined in Murren. Her first four gold medals were merely the beginning. Through 1941, Christel Cranz won 17 of 23 Olympic and World Championship gold medals.

Christel Cranz was a better skier than all but a few males in her time. She never lost a race in which she stood up. And her winning margins were incredible.

In the 1936 Olympics, she ran off the course in an icy downhill at Garmisch-Partenkirchen. It took her 50 seconds to get back on course. But she still won the gold medal for the combined (the only gold medal given for Alpine skiing in that Olympics) because of the phenomenal margin she ran up in slalom.

The German women's team of 1936 had been training for two seasons on a cost-is-no-object basis, subsidized by the German state. The German women were the world's best. Alice Wolfe, who had supported the first American women's Olympic team, wrote, "I shall never forget how our hearts sank when those healthy German *frauleins* marched in at mealtime and tucked away their sausage and sauerkraut. Their cheeks were so red and shiny, their figures so strong and solid." (The best U.S. woman's finish was Betty Woolsey's 16th in downhill.)

Christel won the 1937 women's combined world title at Chamonix, France; the next year, 1938, she wiped up the competition by winning the World Championship slalom by a margin of 10 seconds, thus winning the combined. In 1939, her strength was at its peak: she beat teammate Kathe Grasegger in the women's downhill of the Garmisch Winter Sport Week by 10 seconds, and in the World Championship at Zakopane, Poland, she trounced Lisa Resch in the downhill by 14 seconds and Gritti Schaad in the slalom by 20 seconds.

Says Christel today, "The competition in women's ski racing has become much harder. I could not win by the same margins now." Her career began in the era when downhill racers were dressed in fluttering baggies; the courses would run through farmers' fields, with fence gates serving as control gates.

"We were never paid a penny," she says. "We bought our own equipment. There was no pool of ski firms to shower with skis, boots and poles. We were pure amateurs."

In 1941, the shadow of World War II lay on the Alps, but the Italians, who had been awarded the 1941 World Championships, decided to go ahead and hold them despite the fact that the Allied skiers could not compete. Christel's medals were won against a diminished field. Later that year, she met and married Adolph Borcher. She had raced her last big international race.

As the war went on, Christel's husband, Adolph, was shot down over Russia and imprisoned. He remained there after the war ended in Europe in 1945. Christel had been making a living as a sports instructor, a state post. Because she had been granted special status in the official regime, she was imprisoned for nine months after the war. When she was released, she began a children's ski school in the winter resort of Oberstaufen. When Christel's husband was released in 1950, she had a going business, teaching kids to ski and swim.

Had Christel been racing 40 years later, she would undoubtedly—with her extraordinary natural talent—have been phenomenal. Only two or three like Cranz come along every century.

This article was written by Morten Lund and appeared in *Ski* magazine, March 1979.

Christel Cranz. NA GRIO

Laila Schou-Nilsen of Norway won the women's downhill race and placed in the alpine combined.

Christel Cranz, the women's combined alpine champion, is carried on the shoulders of her friends.

A member of the Canadian women's team.

On the downhill course. NESM

IOC president Count de Baillet-Latour, left, talks with the Reichssportführer at the downhill finish.

Memories of the Downhill Race at the 1936 Olympics

Practicing for the downhill I attempted and held a very fast line which caused others on the slope to rate high my chances. I did not take the same line in the race because, overawed by the Olympic name, I felt I must not risk a heavy crash and a discreditable performance. I skied so carefully that this became the only major downhill in which I did not fall. In the 1936 World Championships, held a few days after the Olympics, I fell three times and finished ninth; in that race 17 of the 54 competitors were forced to abandon by injury.

My father had taught me to take the competition seriously but the result light-heartedly, which had been a lesson in good sportsmanship. If only I had applied that lesson to the Olympics, and not been so fussed about where I would finish in the race, my most shameful performance would not have been in the most important race of my career.

—PETER LUNN

The Norwegian Oddbjörn Hagen won two Olympic medals. He won gold in the cross-country combined and silver in the 18 kilometer race.

The finish of the 18-kilometer cross-country race at the ski stadium. It was won by Erik-Aug. Larsson of Sweden. American skiers finished 34th (Karl Magnus Satre), 45th (Birger Torrissen), 46th (Richard Parsons), and 48th (Warren Chivers).

Never before have so many spectators attended a winter sports event. One hundred and thirty thousand people fill the ski stadium to see the special ski jump.

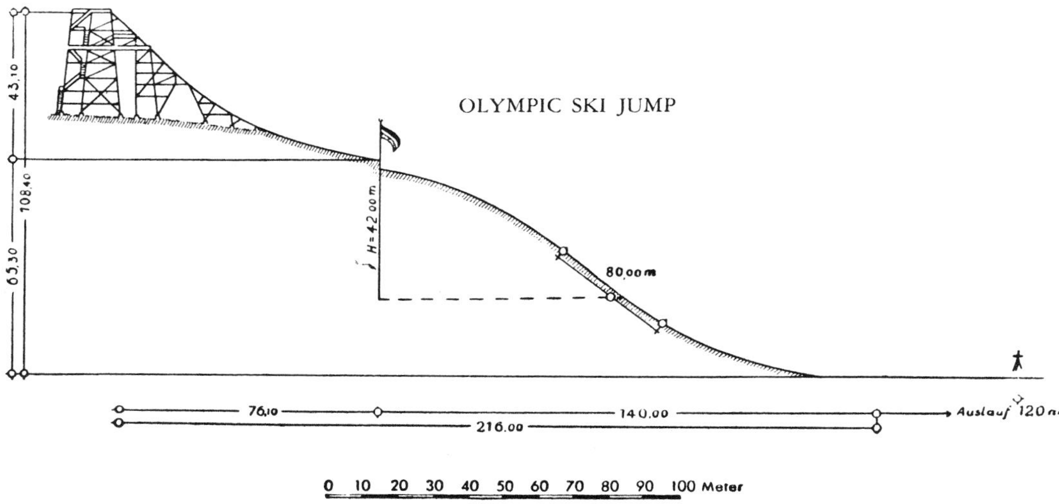

View of Garmisch-Partenkirchen and 60,000 spectators in the ski stadium during a ski jump.

Birger Ruud of Norway won the ski jump in 1932 and 1936. In 1948, at age 36, he was at St. Moritz as a coach. When he saw the poor weather conditions the night before the competition, he decided to take the place of a less-experienced jumper and won a silver medal.

Members of the National Socialist Worker's Service pack the bobsled runs. NA, 131-GR-221-1

The Italien I four-man bobsled team came in tenth. The USA team of Francis W. Tyler, James J. Bickford, Richard W. Lawrence and Max T. Bly came in sixth.

The "Deutschland II" runs off course. The four-man bobsled team weathers the fall but had to drop out of the competition.

Ivan Brown and **Al Washbond** won the two-man bobsled race at Garmisch. Brown was born in 1908 in Keene Valley, New York, and represented the Keene Valley Athletic Club.

Washbond was also born in Keene Valley and started sledding with his brother. The gold medal team at Garmisch also won both the AAU and North American championships in 1935, 1938 and 1939.

Brown lived in Hartford, Connecticut, and died there in 1963. Washbond stayed in Keene Valley and died in 1965.

Getting ready for the two-man bobsled. Twenty-three teams representing 13 nations competed. America's Team 1 was the gold medal winner. NA, GRIO

The first prepared curve in the bobsled run with a marvelous snowy landscape and the Waxenstein in the background.

The American figure skating team. 1) Maribel Y. Vinson, 2) Louise E. Weigel, 3) Estelle D. Weigel, 4) Audrey Peppe, 5) group of skaters, 6) Robin Lee, 7) Erle Reiter, 8) George E. B. Hill.

The American speed skating team on the S.S. *Manhattan*. From left: Manager Henry Kemper, Delbert Lamb, Allan Potts, Coach O'Neil Farrell, Leo Freisinger, Robert Petersen, Edward Schroeder and Judge Charles Gevecker.

Maxie Herber and Ernst Baier, German winners of the pairs figure skating. The American team of Maribel Vinson and George E. B. Hill came in fifth.

Cecilia Colledge was a 15-year-old skater from Great Britain who came close to beating Sonja Henie in 1936. She had placed eighth at the 1932 games. After she skated onto the ice at Garmisch and she gave the Nazi salute, it was discovered that someone had put on the wrong music. After a delay the right music was put on. Colledge almost fell, but then went on to score only one-tenth of a point behind Henie.

Sonja Henie

There are a few names in sports history that are synonymous with a particular sport, Babe Ruth in baseball, Joe Louis in boxing, Bobby Jones in golf. There is one name in ice skating that everyone knows—Sonja Henie.

Henie was the world's greatest woman ice skater from the late 1920s through the mid-1950s. Born in Oslo, Norway, in 1913, she learned to dance at four and at eight she began to ice skate. At 11 she won the Norwegian figure skating championship. Two years later she placed second in the world championships.

Her father paid for the best teachers in skating and ballet including the great Russian ballerina Tamara Karsarina.

In 1924 at age 11, Henie competed in her first Olympics at Chamonix, finishing eighth out of eight places. Starting at age 14 in 1927 she won 10 straight world championships. Her ballet routines on ice, plus her wardrobes, set her apart from the other skaters. She won gold medals in the 1928, 1932 and 1936 Olympics.

Henie's looks and mannerisms enthralled spectators whenever she performed. She was the darling of royalty, especially in her native Norway.

In 1940 she married millionaire New Yorker Dan Topping, but six years later they were divorced. In 1949 she married socialite-sportsman Winthrop Gardiner Jr., but this marriage only lasted seven years.

Hollywood and ice revues beckoned her after the Olympics and at one time she ranked third behind Shirley Temple and Clark Gable as a box office attraction and earned more than $200,000 a year. One of her best-known movies was *Sun Valley Serenade*. Produced in 1941 it did a lot to promote the new resort nationwide.

Henie's ice shows were consistent moneymakers and she was not only the star skater, but eventually manager and then owner of her own ice revue company. She became a multi-millionaire, as well as a shrewd businesswoman.

In 1953 she returned to her native Norway for the first time in 15 years. She renewed an acquaintance with a Norwegian shipowner whom she had known since she was a child. Neils Omstad and Henie were married in 1956 and their passion turned to art collecting.

The couple had homes in Manhattan, Los Angeles, Lausanne, Switzerland, and Oslo, where they spent four months a year at their estate, Grandholet.

The world lost a great athlete and personality too early. Henie died of leukemia in her husband's arms aboard an air ambulance taking her from Paris to Oslo on Oct. 12, 1969. Henie was only 57 years old.

During a snowstorm, Sonja Henie waits in front of the stadium to march with the Norwegian team in the opening ceremonies.

Sonja Henie in her best form. NA, 131-GR-222-6

One of Sonja Henie's best-known movies was the 1941 production *Sun Valley Serenade.* She worked with the great band leader, Glenn Miller. It was a light musical comedy with Henie as a war refugee, John Payne as her foster parent, traveling with the Miller band and its manager, Milton Berle, to Sun Valley. Henie did her skating sequences in Hollywood. Gretchen Fraser doubled for her in the ski sequences, which were shot in Sun Valley. She also starred in *Happy Landing, My Lucky Star, Second Fiddle and Everything Happens at Night* in the late 1930s and early 1940s.

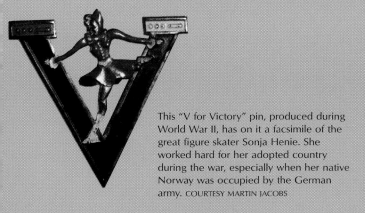

This "V for Victory" pin, produced during World War II, has on it a facsimile of the great figure skater Sonja Henie. She worked hard for her adopted country during the war, especially when her native Norway was occupied by the German army. COURTESY MARTIN JACOBS

Souvenir program of Henie's Hollywood Ice Revue for the 1941-42 tour. Henie and Arthur Wirtz, Executive Vice President of the Chicago Stadium, opened America's first ice theater - the Center Theatre in New York's famous Rockefeller Center in 1939.

One in a Million, 1936, was Sonja Henie's first film set around the Garmisch Winter Olympics.

Seventeen girls from all over the world in the Olympic Ice Stadium. From left: Landbeck (Belgium), Botond (Hungary), Hruba (Czechoslovakia), Sisters Weigel (U.S.A.), Stenuf (Austria), Metznerova (Czechoslovakia), Lindpaintner (Germany), Jepson-Turner (U.K.), Colledge (U.K.), Frey-Dexler (Switzerland), Vinson (U.S.A.), Schenk (Austria), de Ligne (Belgium), Inada (Japan), Anderes (Switzerland).

Leo Freisinger was an American speed skater who came in third in the 500 meters and fourth in the 1,500 meters.

The speed skating races were held on Lake Riessersee. Ivar Ballangrud of Norway won the 500-, 5,000- and 10,000-meter races.

The silver medal winning Canadian hockey team scored 54 goals in eight games and allowed only seven goals. Great Britain won the gold, sparked by the miraculous play of Jimmy Foster, a British-born Canadian who had defected to Great Britain. The United States placed third.

The final ice hockey pool included Great Britain, Canada, the United States and Czechoslovakia. Great Britain went into the finals with a two to one victory over Canada. Great Britain and the United States played to a scoreless tie. The United States dropped a close game to Canada, two to one, which gave Great Britain first place. Had the United States defeated Canada in the final game, it would have been possible to win the gold medal. Great Britain's goal average was seven goals for and one against. The United States entered the game two goals for and none against so that victory over Canada would have resulted in an equality of points in which case the goal average would have decided the title.

Japan's ice hockey goalie Homma.

Wir bringen aus der Olympiastadt

Ein spannendes Moment aus dem olympischen Eishockeykampf Amerika—Deutschland, den die Amerikaner bekanntlich

At the closing ceremonies, each of the flag carriers of the 28 participating countries received a commemorative ribbon and a gun salute.

1936

OLYMPICS

The XII Olympiad in 1940

THE INTERNATIONAL OLYMPIC Committee decided at the 1936 games to award the 1940 Olympics to Japan—Tokyo for the summer games and Sapporo for the winter events. The Japanese government contributed five million yen as did the city of Tokyo. A fund was also established in hopes of providing at least half of the traveling expenses for the athletes and officials from around the world.

The Outer Gardens of the Meiji Shrine were chosen as the location of the main stadium. The regatta course would be in the northeastern part of Tokyo and the yacht course somewhere in Tokyo Bay. A big coliseum was to be erected in memory of the late Dr. S. Kishi, former president of the Japanese Olympic Committee, and a member of the IOC. It would include a gymnasium to seat 10,000 spectators. A nine-story office building was to be built adjacent to the coliseum to house the Japanese Olympic Committee. Another indoor stadium was to be built near the Tokyo Municipal Auditorium.

The Olympic Village was planned for Kinuta Hill, about 10 kilometers from the main stadium, overlooking the Tama River. The area for the village would be about 800 acres and would be built similarly to those in Los Angeles and Berlin—with individual cottages for participating countries. A charge for lodging and food was hoped to not exceed $1.50 per day per person.

However, by 1937 the Japanese had taken over Manchuria (1931) and invaded mainland China. The nation was increasingly being taken over by a militaristic government.

Opposition increased around the world and in the IOC to having the games held in Japan, but it was actually the Japanese government that decided the games were a costly distraction. So in July 1938 the government asked to be let out of its commitment.

The IOC had already decided before this to move the summer games to Helsinki, Finland, and the winter games back to Garmisch-Partenkirchen where all the facilities were still in place.

All this shifting of sites became a moot point, however, when on Sept. 1, 1939, Germany invaded Poland and started World War II. There would of course be no games in 1944. In 1948 a still war-ravaged London was chosen for the summer games and St. Moritz, Switzerland, for the winter games. Tokyo was selected for the 1964 summer games and Sapporo for the 1972 winter games. The summer games returned to Germany for the first time since 1936 in the 1972 Munich games. In 1998 the winter games again return to Japan.

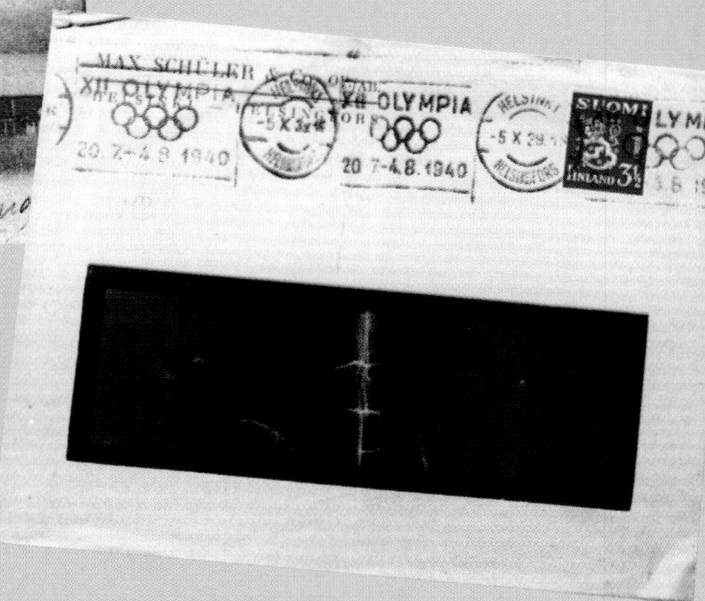

Postal stationery with the stamping of the 1940 summer games in Helsinki.

Stamps were issued by the American Olympic Committee to raise money for the 1940 Olympics, which were to have been held in Helsinki, Finland.

The Jingo (Meiji Shrine) compound where the main stadium and swimming pool were to be constructed.

Kishi Memorial Auditorium where the indoor sports would be held.

1936

OLYMPICS

The Film *Olympia*

Leni Riefenstahl and *Olympia*

Leni Riefenstahl was born in 1902 in Berlin. She grew up in a prosperous environment and started dancing lessons at age eight. She later joined the famous classical Russian Ballet School in Berlin and by 1920 she was dancing in the major cities of Europe.

At about this time she met Dr. Arnold Fanck and began her career in films. Fanck was producing mountain adventure films and picked Riefenstahl in 1924 to appear in the film *Der heilige Berg (The Holy Mountain)*. She went on to star in six of his adventure films and later wrote, produced, directed and starred in *Das blaue Licht (The Blue Light)*. It was released in 1932.

Riefenstahl became a well-known film producer and gained direct access to the newly installed Nazi government of Adolf Hitler. (She always maintained that she was not a member of the Nazi party and was not interested in politics.)

Joseph Goebbels was appointed head of the Reich Film Association and all through the years of the Third Reich Goebbels and Riefenstahl would clash.

The subject of Riefenstahl's first documentary film for the government in 1934 was the 1933 Nazi party rally. Her most famous propaganda film was the 1935 release Triumph des Willens (Triumph of the Will) featuring the 1934 Nuremberg party rally. It has been called one of the greatest achievements, perhaps the most brilliant of all in the history of film propaganda.

Riefenstahl was approved to film the summer Olympics in Berlin, but agreed only reluctantly. Nonetheless she used every trick at her disposal to gain access to the multitude of sports events both in Berlin and at the water sport locations. She was a master of innovation and editing and used her talents in staging some scenes so as to not interfere with the actual performance of the event.

After nearly three years of work with a team that at one point numbered almost 300, after 18 months of post-production, after political arguments and personnel rows, the 250 hours of shot film was edited down to a two-part film of three and three-quarters hours.

The first part of the film was called *Fest der Völker* (Festival of the People) and the second part *Fest der Shönheit* (Festival of Beauty). They were originally intended to be shown as separate films, but the film today is a single epic, with two distinct parts.

An English version of the film was produced called *Olympia* but was not shown in Britain until after the war. Riefenstahl took the film to the United States but was boycotted by all the major Hollywood studios. (Walt Disney was the only studio executive even willing to meet with her, but he was not willing to show the film.) In 1939 the International Olympic Committee awarded Riefenstahl an Olympic Medal. The film itself didn't fare as well. With the start of the war in 1939 the film was put in storage.

During the war Riefenstahl tried to shoot and edit a film based on the opera *Tiefland* but made no more propaganda films. She was arrested after the war on charges relating to her supposed pro-Nazi activities but was released from all legal problems in 1948. She spent several years trying to clear her name and return to making films.

She eventually gained back the master negatives to the film and in the 1950s re-edited a shorter version, taking out the Nazi flags and images of Hitler.

In the fifty years since the end of the war she has fought to regain her respectability and has gained worldwide acclaim for her work photographing the natives of Africa. At this writing (1996) she is almost 94 and lives near Munich.

Her film achievements will live on for their artistic rendering, which overshadows their propaganda role.

Leni Riefenstahl on the Film *Olympia*

The following interview was taken from Andrew Sarris' *Interviews with Film Directors*, published in 1967.

The Beginning

First of all, it took me a long time before I knew whether or not I was going to make this film. My first interest in it was sports. I had done a lot and was always interested in it. In addition, thanks to *Triumph of the Will*, I knew the cinema. I wanted to make a liaison of sports and the cinema.

Once I had this idea, I started to doubt again, persuaded that this would be too hard. Everything hesitated, vacillated for a long time until, finally, I decided. After that everything went very rapidly. I immediately attacked the problem of the camera work, all the while telling myself that it would be nearly impossible to render the plenitude of the event on film. Thus I came, automatically to the solution of doing two films, one reserved for gymnastics and the other for other sports.

After I had made up my mind to that, my interest was principally attracted by two things. The title of my book, *The Beauty of the Olympic Contest*, contains both of them. It implies first of all, from an individual point of view, the complete domination of the body and the will; after that, a great tolerance, introduced by the feeling of camaraderies and loyalty which is at the very heart of the contest. For, in such a confrontation, all men and all races must, for themselves and for others, give the best that they have. From this results an extraordinary atmosphere that is lifted well above ordinary life. This is what I sought to render. In the film, the human point of view and the aesthetic point of view are linked, to the extent that they are themselves already linked in the event, by the nature of the Olympic contest. The problems I started with were not resolved so easily. Among other things, it had become evident to me that the film could only be interesting on one condition. It would doubtless be possible for the camera to capture everything that could interest the spectator, but for that, it would have to take on the weight not so much of the event in itself, as in a newsreel but the form ("Gestaltung") of the event. From that moment on, I began to look at each sport with the eyes of the lens.

Each time, it was necessary that I think about things in order to find the reason behind the camera's position in relation to this or that event. There was no principle at all that demanded that the camera always be one or two meters from the ground, that it always be far from the object or even on the object. Little by little, I discovered that the constraints imposed at times by the event could often serve me as a guide. The whole thing lay in knowing when and how to respect or violate these constraints. Thus, there were some perspectives that had to be respected. There were others that had to be found. At the time of a race, for example, we had installed a hundred meters of track, and the camera ran along it very well, but it seemed to me that the image of the race should be completed with extremely close shots. There was no middle course between extreme proximity and following the movement at a constant distance. As there was no question of getting close to the runner, it called for the use of a telescopic lens. I withdrew to find a vantage point. It was at this moment that we began to employ the gigantic telescopic lenses that were to serve us from then on. It was the fusion of static shots, rhythmic shots and shots animated by technical movement that were to give its life, its rhythm. Thus, in the face of problem, it was necessary to feel one's way, to make tests, and each test resulted in new ideas, some small and some big. For the horses, for example, we tried to attach the camera to the saddle, but in order to keep it from bouncing too much, it was necessary to put it in a rubber bag, full of feathers. While the marathon was in progress, we had a little basket on us, in which was a miniature camera that was set off automatically, by movement—all this was so that the runner wouldn't notice anything. And so it went, from idea to idea, for we always had to find new ones. This also provided us with as much amusement as possible.

I must say that we formed an extraordinary crew. For entertainment, as well as while working, we always stayed together, even on Saturday and Sunday. When we stayed in the tents, we talked, always letting the ideas come, and they always came. That's good practice. There were also nocturnal conversations.

The Means

We had less than people said. Look at the photos and documents of the period: they give rather a feeling of improvisation: . . . For the most part the effects obtained by our crew were improvisatory coups. Much obliged: people didn't know or it wasn't pointed out, how many things we discovered. The noiseless camera, made so as not to bother the athletes, was brought about by one of my cameramen, and the camera for underwater shots, by another. During this time we were looking for other tricks and even the most modest were made use of. Thus we had the idea of digging trenches (and it was very hard to obtain permission for this) from which we might film the jumpers, in order to give a better rendering of their effort.

The swimming pool, above all, inspired us enormously. We had a little rubber boat, the camera was on a little frame attached to the edge of the boat and we pushed this with a pole—oars being out, because of the motion. In this way we were able, during a shot, to start with a face, seen from close, and move off from it. There were also underwater shots, sometimes followed by emergence, shots made at water level, as well as shots made with the lens half-submerged. Naturally, this required a lot of very hard work on the part of the technicians, given the working conditions and the abrupt changes of light. For the ten meter dive, for example, the cameraman, after having set the focus in order to be able to follow the diver, dove with him, filmed him as he fell, filmed him under the water and came to the surface with him. Obviously, the focus was difficult to hold and the brutal variations of light didn't make things easier. In addition, the operation included, at the bottom of the pool, a change of lens. But everything had been carefully rehearsed in such a way that this could be done as rapidly and as mechanically as possible. Obviously, with these methods, for every 100 meters of exposed, 95 were no good.

The Resources

We didn't have gigantic resources for the good reason that we didn't have gigantic sums of money. Quite simply. And we didn't have gigantic sums for the good reason that no one believed that a reportage on the Olympic games could be a success. I had exactly 750,000 marks at my disposal for each part. A million and a half in all. And it was little enough, when you consider the quantity of film used: 400,000 meters—of which 70 percent turned out to be unusable. In addition, the tests, tentative procedures and improvisations that I told you about absorbed a lot of money. Beyond that: we had the problem of lack of experience with certain of the cameramen. We had engaged the best that we could, but for the most part the very best cameramen were out of our reach, as the big companies had a monopoly on them. Afterwards, the film's immense success allowed Tobis [the film's production company] to recoup the money they had (imprudently, according to some) advanced. Several weeks after the opening the film was reimbursed; six months later, Tobis had taken in 4,210,290 marks and the money continued to come in. . . . But in the beginning no one believed in it and we had to arrange things so as not to go over the budget we had been allotted. Then, the cranes . . . we had, above all, ladders. They went from ordinary ladders to firemen's ladders. But we rapidly eliminated the first because they had an inconvenient way of oscillating. Scheil, the cameraman who specialized in this type of work, often had a depth of field of no more than 30 cm (12″ approximately). It is obvious that with the slightest oscillation everything would be ruined.

To off-set that, we had towers. Steel towers, set in the middle of the stadium, from the top of which the cameraman could take in, and follow, the total panorama. This type of tower, used for the first time, afterwards appeared at other Olympiads. As for the balloons, yes, from time to time we had some. A balloon, during that period, was as ordinary as a helicopter is now. Except that directors had forgotten to attach cameras to them. We took care of that oversight.

The balloons in question were furnished with automatic cameras, which led to the necessity of running ads in the papers every day so that when they came down in Berlin, people would know they had cameras inside. With this system, out of a thousand meters of exposed film, perhaps ten were good. But they were very good. We had one just above the finish line of the sculls (which was equally assured by a 120 meter travelling shot). Unfortunately, at the last minute the games committee vetoed the whole operation. Sad end to an experiment . . . I cried.

As for the cameras, there was nearly always one camera for one shot. But I remember that one time we were able to work with two big cameras at the same time: this was the first day of the games, when Hitler gave the opening speech. In the event of mechanical troubles there was no question of retakes for a shot like that. Therefore we had an auxiliary camera.

Here is the way our crew was composed. Six cameramen formed the principal crew—they were the only ones with the right to go into the stadium. Sixteen others (eight cameramen and eight assistants) took care of the trials that took place elsewhere. To which should be added ten non-professionals whom I had asked to mingle with the crowd, with little cameras, to get reaction shots. Thus, there were thirty-three people in all, who had to suffice for the shooting of all the trials, in all the localities in which they took place. Including the sequence in Greece. I can swear to you that my cameramen would have wanted to be a little more numerous! . . .

The Script

I didn't write a single page of text for either *Triumph* or *Olympia*. The moment I had a clear picture of the film in my head, the film was born. The structure of the whole imposed itself. It was purely intuitive.

Starting from that idea, I organized, then sent the technical crew out on different tasks, but the true establishment of the form began with the editing. I edited

Olympia alone, as I had edited *Triumph of the Will* alone. This was necessary for each editor sets his own stamp on a film. Experience shows that if two or three different people edit a film, it is impossible for any sort of harmony to emerge. The nature of my films demands that they be edited by a single person. And that person must be the one who had the idea for the film, who was looking for precisely such a harmony. Harmony would not be born out of another montage.

For *Olympia*, I lived in the editing room for a year and a half, never getting home before five o'clock in the morning. My life was tied to the material and the film. In my editing rooms, I had glass partitions built, on each side of which I hung filmstrips that went down to the floor. I suspended them one next to the other, in order to look at them, compare them, so as to verify their harmony in the scale of frames and tones. Thus, in the long run, as a composer composes, I made everything work together in the rhythm.

But I had to make many tests. I made and I unmade. Sometimes I would change a detail in function of the ensemble, sometimes the whole ensemble in function of a detail, for where one left off, the other began. In this way, I was able to establish that with the same material, edited differently, the film wouldn't have worked at all. If the slightest thing were changed, inverted, the effect would be lost. Therefore, I was engaged in a continuous struggle to arrive at what I wanted. I wanted the film to have, silent, a dramatic efficacity. For the rest, I refer you to what I said concerning the relationship between the editing and the architecture of the film.

However, I am going to try to be precise about certain things, although all that is very hard to explain. It's a little like the foundation of a house. There is, first of all, the plan (which is somehow the abstract, the precis of the construction); the rest is the melody. There are valleys, there are heights. Some things have to be sunk down, some have to soar. And now, I am going to be specific about another thing; this is that as soon as the montage takes form, I think of the sound. I always have a representation inside of me and I always take every precaution so that the sound and the image never total more than a hundred percent. Is the image strong? The sound must stay in the background. Is it the sound that is strong? Then the image must take second place to it. This is one of the fundamental rules I have always observed.

Archie Williams, the gold medal winner in the 400 meters, gets some direction from film maker Leni Riefenstahl for her film *Olympia*. BA

Poster courtesy Bruce Hershenson
White Plains, Missouri.

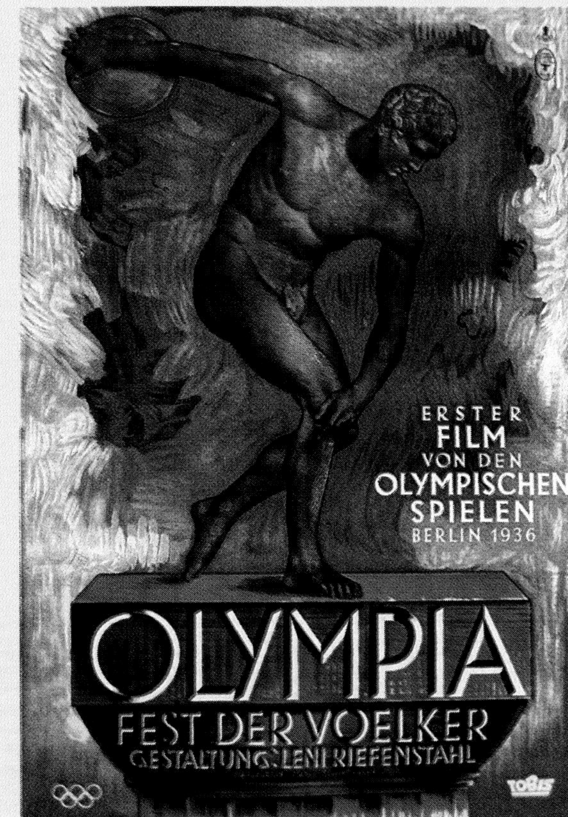

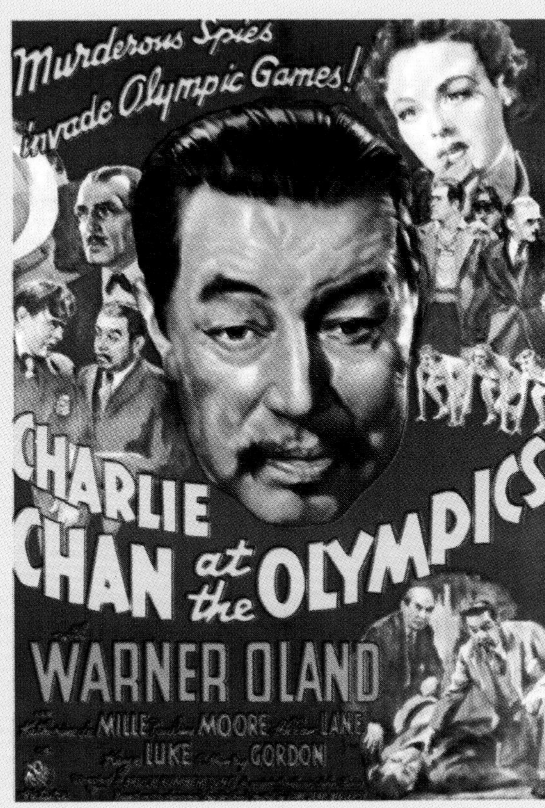

One-sheet movie poster
courtesy Bruce Hershenson
White Plains, Missouri.

The lighting of the Olympic flame had to be staged for the film at Delphi in Greece, a place with no connection to the original Olympic games. TOP LEFT: NA, HH-242-HD-0001, ABOVE: NA, HH-242-HD-20

To film ground-level action of the track and field events a pit was dug for placement of a camera.

Many ingenious means were employed to get action shots. Here a cameraman is riding on a motorcycle ahead of a cyclist.
NA, HH-242-HD-00

Trade, Public Balk At Nazi "Olympia"

NEW YORK—A poll of producers and editors reveals strong opposition to any domestic showings of "Olympia," German film which Leni Riefenstahl presumably is seeking to introduce in this market, according to the Non-Sectarian Anti-Nazi League.

"This visit," League officials declare, "is part of the Nazi campaign to flood the United States with Nazi doctrines and is in accord with recent statements by German consuls here and German officials abroad in which they attacked American principles and ethics and sought to prove the superiority of Nazism."

It is understood Miss Riefenstahl, following a trip to Florida, plans a visit to Hollywood. Vittorio Mussolini, the last representative of the totalitarian form of government to tour the studios, was greeted by an anti-Fascist campaign engendered by the Motion Picture Artists Committee and the Hollywood Anti-Nazi League.

Nov. 2, 1938.

Film Trivia

It is hard to calculate the value of the Nazi reichsmark to the U.S. dollar in 1936 as it was a non-convertible currency at the time. If it is calculated at one dollar to two-and-one-half Reichsmarks, this converts to an approximate budget of $600,000, an extraordinary sum of money for the time.

■

The premiere of the German film version was held on April 20, 1938, at the Ufa-Palast am Zoo in Berlin. It also happened to be Hitler's 49th birthday and he viewed the film with high Nazi officials, film industry personnel, the International Olympic Committee and the entire diplomatic corps.

■

At the Venice Film Festival in September 1938 the film won the "Coppa Mussolina" (first prize). The American and British thought the American entry, Disney's *Snow White and the Seven Dwarfs*, should have won.

■

There were five different language versions produced in 1938, some of which had a more positive view of the Nazis than others. After the war the film was seized and different versions were edited by censors. Perhaps none available today is the same as first shown in Berlin in April 1938.

Upper photo: The largest telephoto lens available in 1936 was used when close-up shots were not practical. Lower photo: Special cameras were used to capture underwater scenes of the swimming and diving competition. LC

"Transcendentally Superb"
"Unbelievably Beautiful"

The greatest Film

—and Sport Spectacle of all Time

may now be seen!

„Olympia"

Festival of the Nations

Leni Riefenstahl's Motion Picture Record of the XI. Olympic Games (I. Part)

dedicated to the Honor and the Glory of the Youth of the World

ENGLISH NARRATION

●

Presented by F. K. FERENZ at the

Criterion Theatre

612 So. Grand Ave., Los Angeles

For One Week

starting SATURDAY, JUNE 8th, 1940

ADMISSION: Lower floor 68c plus 7c tax — 75c
Balcony 40c —— Minors (under 18 years) 25c
Children (under 12 years) 10c

Riefenstahl sent this note to Hitler, Christmas 1936. It reads: "Dedicated to my Führer with indelible loyalty and sincere gratitude as a memento of the Olympic Games in Berlin. Christmas 1936 Leni Riefenstahl"

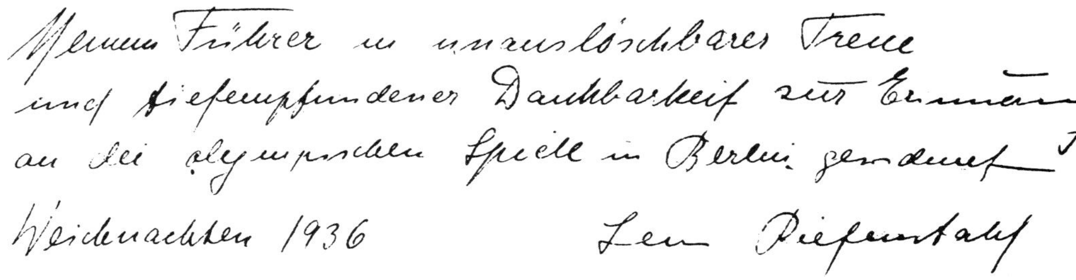
Meinem Führer in unauslöschbarer Treue und tiefempfundener Dankbarkeit zur Erinnerung an die olympischen Spiele in Berlin gewidmet.
Weihnachten 1936 Leni Riefenstahl

The long-range camera on the high platform at the swimming arena.

1936

OLYMPICS

Olympic Trivia

Thomas Wolfe Visits Germany in 1936

Thomas Wolfe was born in Ashville, North Carolina, in 1900. He graduated from the University of North Carolina in 1920 and from Harvard University in 1922. He was teaching at New York University when his most well-known novel, *Look Homeward Angel*, came out in 1929. He published several other novels and short stories and at the time of his death in 1938 he was considered one of America's finest authors.

Wolfe visited Germany in 1936 at the time of the Olympics. His brother Fred related Wolfe's experience to Professor John Griffin, University of South Carolina, Lancaster, who provided this information.

IN 1936 TOM went to Germany. He didn't care much for the English or French, but the Germans were the first Europeans to publish him, plus Papa's people were from Germany and so Tom was eager to go and visit the country of his ancestors.

They were having the Olympic games in Berlin and Tom's German publishers invited him to be their guest in their box for the games. Their box, by the way, flanked Hitler's box. That was the year that Jesse Owens, the great Negro athlete, won four gold medals and every time they'd bring him out there to crown him Tom would jump to his feet and give a rousing western North Carolina war-whoop and yell, "Come on, Jesse, you're doing this for America!" And Tom said that each time he did that Hitler and Goering would turn around and give him a baleful stare. But it didn't bother Tom one bit.

The real reason that Tom went to Germany was because his publishers there owed him 50,000 Reichmarks, but they said he'd have to come to Germany to get it and that he'd have to spend it there. He could only take fifty marks out of the country. So he went to Berlin and they paid him and he stayed there for three months, or until he'd spent all the money.

You see, the Germans would search your baggage at the border and if you were caught with more than fifty marks, why they'd pull you off the train and arrest you.

Tom met a Jewish boy on the train coming out and he wrote an article about him called "I Have A Thing To Tell You," published in *The New Republic*. This young Jew was scared to death. He had a visa and he was leaving the country, but at the checkpoint the Germans caught him. Just before the police came aboard, the Jew handed Tom 500 marks and said, "Take it. You've already been examined." So Tom did. The Germans opened the boy's suitcase and found several thousand marks in it and they pulled him off the train. That was the last Tom ever saw of that boy. He said they unquestionably threw him in a concentration camp and in all probability killed him.

"Charlie Chan at the Olympics"

This is another of those elaborately complex detective yarns in which Charlie Chan, played by Warner Oland, with his customary finesse and Oriental adages, outwits a powerful ring of international spies. This time it is a robot airplane piloting gadget with which the film plays hide-and-seek. Action swings all the way from Honolulu to the Berlin Olympics.

"Charlie Chan at the Olympics"
(20th Century-Fox)

Associate Producer	John Stone
Director	H. Bruce Humberstone
Original Story	Paul Burger
From Stories of Earl Derr Biggers	
Screenplay	Robert Ellis, Helen Logan
Photography	Daniel B. Clark
Art Direction	Albert Hogsett
Associate	Chester Gore
Musical Direction	Samuel Kaylin
Film Editor	Fred Allen

Cast: Warner Oland, Katherine de Mille, Pauline Moore, Allan Lane, Keye Luke, C. Henry Gordon, John Eldredge, Layne Tom Jr., Jonathan Hale, Morgan Wallace, Fredrik Vogeding, Andrew Tombes, Howard Hickman.

Chan, with a party of U.S. Navy officials, tracks the foreign agents by clipper ship, airliner and, finally the *Hindenburg*, to the Olympics. In his sleuthing he is aided by his No. 1 son Lee Chan, a member of the U.S. swim team.

In Berlin the invaluable gadget is recovered only to be temporarily lost again in a series of fairly exciting incidents. It had been hidden in the luggage of a woman member of the swim team on shipboard and Chan has quite a time tracking it down and uncovering the real villain. The actual head culprit is disclosed to be the least suspected member of the film's cast.

Newsreel shots of the Olympic games are effectively blended into the action by director H. Bruce Humberstone. The film, released in 1937 by 20th Century-Fox, was adapted from stories by Earl Derr Biggers. Jesse Owens was supposed to be in the film, but only about 10 seconds of his newsreel made it in the film. This was one of 42 Charlie Chan movies produced from 1929 to 1949 by various studios. Oland died after the Olympics movie was made, but other actors took his place in subsequent films.

This article was released by 20th Century-Fox's publicity director Harry Brand:

"Air conditioning is a pretty well known technique by now, but oxygen conditioning is something else again.

"This new wrinkle of science was necessary on the 'Charlie Chan at the Olympics' set at 20th Century-Fox the other day to prevent the asphyxiation of the entire cast and crew.

"While Director Bruce Humberstone was shooting a spectacular police raid on the European palace where a sequence of the action takes place, the exhaust fumes of so many cars, belching carbon monoxide upon the close sound stage, was so overpowering that oxygen tanks were resorted to in order to keep the air breathable.

"Opening the huge doors between shots was found insufficient, so a battery of the tanks was placed to pump the oxygen continuously into the set.

"All the cars used in this scene had to be imported cars because the action is laid around the locale of the last Olympic games, Berlin, so Katherine de Mille's Isotta, Warner Oland's and producer Sol M. Wurtzel's Minerva all were called out for police duty. The police raid is one of the most exciting ever to be filmed." ■

ACADEMY OF MOTION PICTURE ARTS & SCIENCES

Olympic Trivia

Francis Amyot, the only Canadian to win a gold medal (in the canoeing competition), was a hero in Canada because he had saved three members of the Ottawa Roughriders football team from drowning. Unfortunately he had to pay his own way to Berlin.

■

Martin Gison from the Philippines placed fourth in the rifle event. In 1942 he was captured along with thousands of Filipino scouts and American soldiers at Bataan. He survived the war and participated in the 1948 games for the Philippines.

■

Oliver Halassay from Hungary was a member of the championship water polo team. He won two gold medals and one silver medal in three Olympics (1928, 1932, 1936), swimming with just one leg. He lost a leg at age 11. In 1946 he was murdered in Budapest.

■

Fanny Blankers Koen of the Netherlands is the only woman in Olympic history to win four gold medals in track and field in one Olympics. At Berlin, as an 18 year old, she participated in the high jump and 4×100-meter relay. In the 1948 games she took gold in the 100- and 200-meter dash, the 80-meter hurdles and ran a leg of the winning 4×100-meter relay team. If she had been allowed to compete in five events, she would probably have won the long jump as the winning length was 20 inches short of her own world record.

■

Ko Nakamura, who threw the discus for Japan in 1936, and Toyoko Yashiro, who threw the discus for Japan in 1952, were the same woman. This was only found out in 1980 when Olympic records were examined in Japan.

■

Birger Ruud, gold medal winner at Garmisch, and his two brothers were imprisoned in their native Norway during the war by the German occupiers for refusing to assist the Nazis.

■

Germany and Japan first returned to the Olympic Games at the winter games in Oslo in 1952.

■

During World War II the German Navy allowed the Olympic rings to be printed on the front of a U-Boat's conning tower if the commander of that boat had graduated from submarine school in 1936, the Olympic year. One such U-Boat, *U-537* commanded by Captain Schrewe, was sunk on Nov. 9, 1944, by an American submarine, the *Flounder* (SS-251).

■

Two members of the 1936 track and field team went on to play professional football. **Glenn Morris** played for the Detroit Lions in 1940 and **Jack Torrance** played for the Chicago Bears in 1939–40. **Raymond Clemons,** a light-heavyweight wrestler, played for the Los Angeles Bulldogs in 1937 and the Detroit Lions in 1939.

■

Norman Cudworth Armitage was the standard bearer at the 1952 and 1956 Olympic opening ceremonies for the American team. He started his Olympic career at the 1928 games as a fencer and was a participant in every Olympics through 1956, the longest span of any American athlete. He won a bronze medal for Team Sabre at the 1948 games.

■

Dora Ratjen of Germany was a fourth-place finisher in the women's high jump. In 1938 it was discovered that she was a hermaphrodite, a rare sexual group in which a person has both male and female sexual organs. Thus she was barred from participating because there was no provision for this group in athletic competition.

■

Glenn Morris, the decathlon winner, sold automobiles before the Olympics.

■

Luz Long of Germany, runner-up to Jesse Owens in the long jump, was killed at the Battle of St. Pietro on July 14, 1943.

■

Vera Hruba of Czechoslovakia was on her country's figure skating team. She placed 17th in the competition. In the 1940s and 1950s she starred in numerous B pictures as Vera Ralston. Her specialties were westerns and pioneer films.

■

Canadian **Diana Gordon-Lennox** represented her country in the women's alpine combined. She skied the downhill and slalom with one arm in a cast and a monocle in one eye. She finished 29th.

■

The coxswain for the French bronze medal winner in the Four-Oared Shell with Coxswain was 12-year-old Noel Vandernotte whose father and uncle were also crew members.

■

Seventy-two-year-old **General Arthur von Pongracy** of Austria was the oldest competitor at Berlin. He was a member of the Austrian equestrian team dressage. He first competed at Paris in 1924.

Television cameras were set up trackside to capture the track and field events. NA, HH-242-HD-121-2

Special trucks were built for the new medium of television. NA, HH-242-HD-123

Television at the Olympics

In 1925, American Charles Francis Jenkins experimented with the idea of transmitting a picture by combining photography, optics and radio, and using a scanning disc with vacuum-tube amplifiers and photo-electric cells.

His was one of many experimental broadcasts, so many in fact, that no one person is credited with inventing television. The first TV pictures were poor because only a few impulses could be transmitted in a short time. A more efficient system was found in an earlier work in 1923 of American Vladimir Zworykin, who invented the iconoscope, an electron camera tube. Philo T. Farnsworth also had patents on early television including an image dissector, or camera tube.

On July 30, 1930, NBC began operating an experimental television station, W2XBS in New York City. CBS started a station, W2XAB on July 21, 1931.

In Berlin, this new scientific marvel was used for the first time to project a picture on a television tube. Eighteen receivers were set up in halls around the city and at the Olympic Village. In all 3,000 seats were available. Unfortunately the reception left much to be desired. It would be 10 years before the new-fangled electronic device would become useable and popular.

The first sports event to be televised was a double-header baseball game on May 17, 1939, between Columbia University and Princeton at Baker Field in New York.

Several television stations were on the air in the United States by 1940, but World War II put a stop to TV broadcasts for the duration.

Television first was broadcast in Berlin in March 1935.

Spiridon Loues was a 25-year-old Greek shepherd when he won the marathon at the 1896 Athens Olympics with a seven-minute lead. At the end of the race he was joined in his victory lap around the stadium by the royal princess of Greece. At Berlin he marched with the Greek team in the opening ceremonies and was then introduced to Hitler, whom he presented with a sprig of wild olive from Mount Olympus' sacred grove. Here he signs autographs for admiring fans. NA, HH

America's greatest aviation hero, Charles Lindbergh, and his wife, Anne, visited Germany at the time of the Olympics. He toured German aircraft factories and Luftwaffe facilities and was courted by high government officials, especially Hermann Göring, pictured here with his wife. The Lindberghs visited the Olympic village and mingled with the athletes. Lindbergh was impressed by Germany's military buildup and four years later was a spokesman for the America First Committee that promoted American neutrality in the European war. He was partially ostracized by the government after America's entry into the war, but stayed active in aviation, and even flew some combat missions in the Pacific, later in the war. NA HH

It is possible that this car drove all the way from Nepal to Berlin. Even today this would be a very long and difficult trip. Nepal had no representation at the Berlin games. NA, HH 242-HB-22119

These two photos supplied by Alice Arden Hodge show some of the Olympic participants having a party on board the S.S. *President Roosevelt* on the return trip home. Apparently uniforms were exchanged freely and some members picked up Nazi paraphernalia in Germany.
ALICE HODGE COLLECTION

Jewish Athletes on the American Team

Herman Goldberg—baseball
Sam Stoller—track
Marty Glickman—track
Sam Balter—basketball
Morris Doob—pistol shooter
David Mayor—weight lifter
Max Bly—bobsled

Blacks at Berlin

United States

Jesse Owens—gold in the broad jump, 100- and 200-meter dashes, leg of the 4×100-meter relay
Ralph Metcalfe—gold in the 4×100-meter relay, silver in the 100-meter dash
Matthew Robinson—silver in the 200-meter dash
Archie Williams—gold in the 400-meter run
James LuValle—bronze in the 400-meter run
John Woodruff—gold in the 800-meter run
Cornelius Johnson—gold in the high jump
David Albritton—silver in the high jump
Frederick Polland—bronze in the high hurdles
John Brooks—long jump
John Terry—featherweight weightlifter
Jackie Wilson—boxer
James Clark—boxer
Arthur Wilson—boxer
Louise Stokes—track
Tidye Pickett—track

Canada

Dr. Phil Edwards, bronze in the 800-meter run
Sam Richardson—hop-step-jump

Brazil

Several athletes

Haiti

The country's only entry

A poster for the Japanese team at the Berlin Olympics. BA

A sailor from the German cruiser *Emden* presents a ribbon from the ship to an American athlete. BA

1936 Olympics: Principal Medal Winners
(German points system)

Nation	Gold	Silver	Bronze	Points
Germany	33	26	30	181
United States	24	20	12	124
Italy	8	9	5	47
Finland	7	6	6	39
France	7	6	6	39
Hungary	10	1	5	37
Sweden	6	5	9	37
Japan	6	4	8	34
Netherlands	6	4	7	33
Great Britain	4	7	3	29
Austria	4	6	3	27
Switzerland	1	9	5	26
Czechoslovakia	3	5	0	19
Canada	1	3	5	14
Argentina	2	2	3	13
Estonia	2	2	3	13

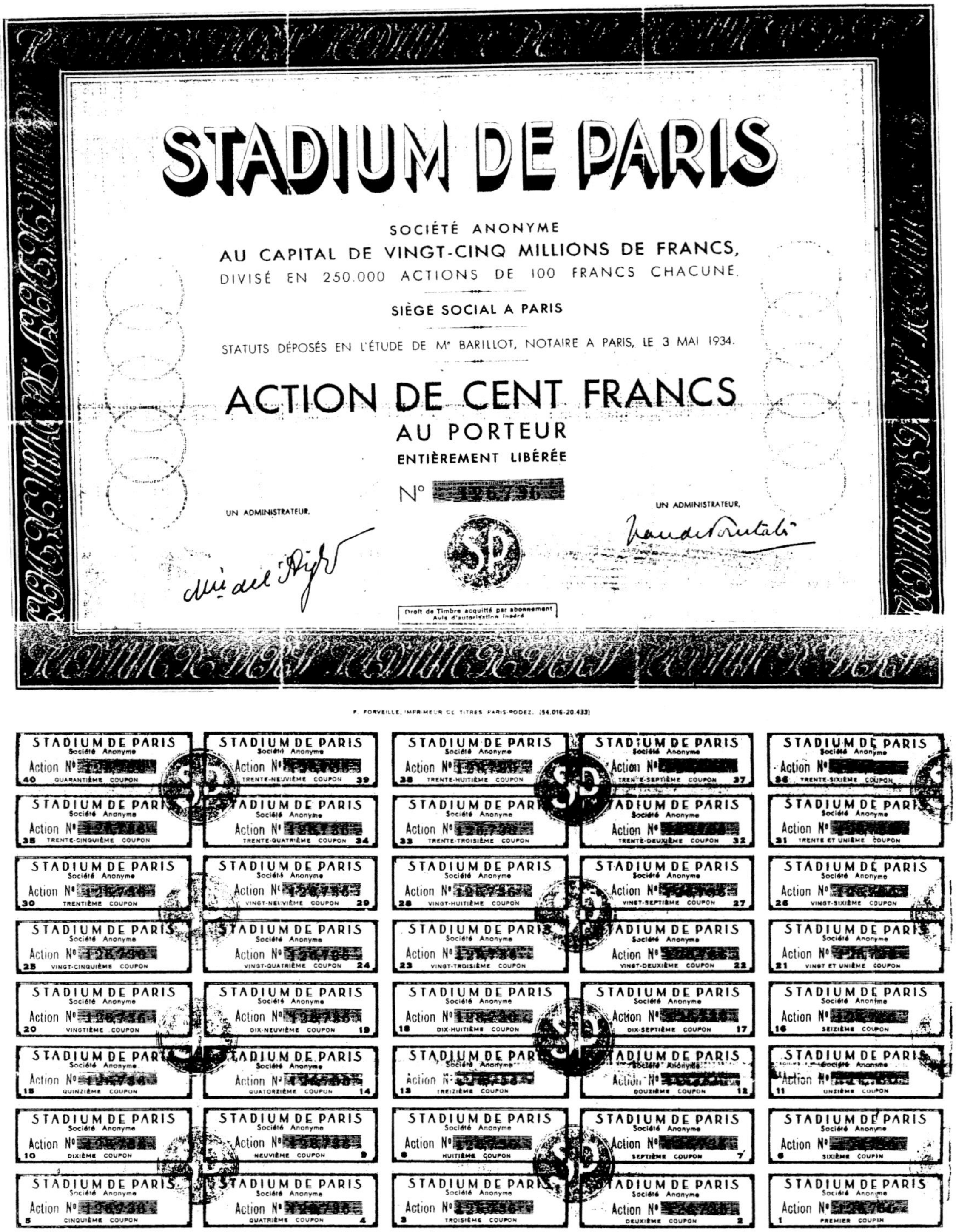

STADIUM DE PARIS

SOCIÉTÉ ANONYME

AU CAPITAL DE VINGT-CINQ MILLIONS DE FRANCS,

DIVISÉ EN 250.000 ACTIONS DE 100 FRANCS CHACUNE.

SIÈGE SOCIAL A PARIS

STATUTS DÉPOSÉS EN L'ÉTUDE DE Mᵉ BARILLOT, NOTAIRE A PARIS, LE 3 MAI 1934.

ACTION DE CENT FRANCS

AU PORTEUR

ENTIÈREMENT LIBÉRÉE

N° [redacted]

UN ADMINISTRATEUR. UN ADMINISTRATEUR.

Droit de Timbre acquitté par abonnement
Avis d'autorisation inséré

F. FORVEILLE, IMPRIMEUR DE TITRES PARIS-RODEZ. (54.016-20.433)

STADIUM DE PARIS Société Anonyme Action N° [redacted] 40 QUARANTIÈME COUPON	STADIUM DE PARIS Société Anonyme Action N° [redacted] TRENTE-NEUVIÈME COUPON 39	STADIUM DE PARIS Société Anonyme Action N° [redacted] 38 TRENTE-HUITIÈME COUPON	STADIUM DE PARIS Société Anonyme Action N° [redacted] TRENTE-SEPTIÈME COUPON 37	STADIUM DE PARIS Société Anonyme Action N° [redacted] 36 TRENTE-SIXIÈME COUPON
STADIUM DE PARIS Société Anonyme Action N° [redacted] 35 TRENTE-CINQUIÈME COUPON	STADIUM DE PARIS Société Anonyme Action N° [redacted] TRENTE-QUATRIÈME COUPON 34	STADIUM DE PARIS Société Anonyme Action N° [redacted] 33 TRENTE-TROISIÈME COUPON	STADIUM DE PARIS Société Anonyme Action N° [redacted] TRENTE-DEUXIÈME COUPON 32	STADIUM DE PARIS Société Anonyme Action N° [redacted] 31 TRENTE ET UNIÈME COUPON
STADIUM DE PARIS Société Anonyme Action N° [redacted] 30 TRENTIÈME COUPON	STADIUM DE PARIS Société Anonyme Action N° [redacted] VINGT-NEUVIÈME COUPON 29	STADIUM DE PARIS Société Anonyme Action N° [redacted] 28 VINGT-HUITIÈME COUPON	STADIUM DE PARIS Société Anonyme Action N° [redacted] VINGT-SEPTIÈME COUPON 27	STADIUM DE PARIS Société Anonyme Action N° [redacted] 26 VINGT-SIXIÈME COUPON
STADIUM DE PARIS Société Anonyme Action N° [redacted] 25 VINGT-CINQUIÈME COUPON	STADIUM DE PARIS Société Anonyme Action N° [redacted] VINGT-QUATRIÈME COUPON 24	STADIUM DE PARIS Société Anonyme Action N° [redacted] 23 VINGT-TROISIÈME COUPON	STADIUM DE PARIS Société Anonyme Action N° [redacted] VINGT-DEUXIÈME COUPON 22	STADIUM DE PARIS Société Anonyme Action N° [redacted] 21 VINGT ET UNIÈME COUPON
STADIUM DE PARIS Société Anonyme Action N° [redacted] 20 VINGTIÈME COUPON	STADIUM DE PARIS Société Anonyme Action N° [redacted] DIX-NEUVIÈME COUPON 19	STADIUM DE PARIS Société Anonyme Action N° [redacted] 18 DIX-HUITIÈME COUPON	STADIUM DE PARIS Société Anonyme Action N° [redacted] DIX-SEPTIÈME COUPON 17	STADIUM DE PARIS Société Anonyme Action N° [redacted] 16 SEIZIÈME COUPON
STADIUM DE PARIS Société Anonyme Action N° [redacted] 15 QUINZIÈME COUPON	STADIUM DE PARIS Société Anonyme Action N° [redacted] QUATORZIÈME COUPON 14	STADIUM DE PARIS Société Anonyme Action N° [redacted] 13 TREIZIÈME COUPON	STADIUM DE PARIS Société Anonyme Action N° [redacted] DOUZIÈME COUPON 12	STADIUM DE PARIS Société Anonyme Action N° [redacted] 11 ONZIÈME COUPON
STADIUM DE PARIS Société Anonyme Action N° [redacted] 10 DIXIÈME COUPON	STADIUM DE PARIS Société Anonyme Action N° [redacted] NEUVIÈME COUPON 9	STADIUM DE PARIS Société Anonyme Action N° [redacted] 8 HUITIÈME COUPON	STADIUM DE PARIS Société Anonyme Action N° [redacted] SEPTIÈME COUPON 7	STADIUM DE PARIS Société Anonyme Action N° [redacted] 6 SIXIÈME COUPON
STADIUM DE PARIS Société Anonyme Action N° [redacted] 5 CINQUIÈME COUPON	STADIUM DE PARIS Société Anonyme Action N° [redacted] QUATRIÈME COUPON 4	STADIUM DE PARIS Société Anonyme Action N° [redacted] 3 TROISIÈME COUPON	STADIUM DE PARIS Société Anonyme Action N° [redacted] DEUXIÈME COUPON 2	STADIUM DE PARIS Société Anonyme Action N° [redacted] 1 PREMIER COUPON

This 1934 bond was issued in France for a projected "Stadium de Paris" for the 1936 Olympic games. This must have been issued when there was some question as to whether the summer games would actually be held in Berlin.

Artifacts and Legacy

AMERICAN OLYMPIC FLASHAD

A small live oak tree was presented to each gold medal winner at the summer games. Perhaps some of these are still in existence somewhere in the United States. NA, GRIO

A special decoration to reward work on the games was instituted on Feb. 4, 1936, in two classes. First class (middle) was worn on a 50mm-wide ribbon at the throat and second class (right) was worn from a 30mm-wide ribbon on the left breast. Seven hundred and seventy-six first awards and 3,364 second awards were made. The model on the left is the Commemorative Medal. JIM OBSORNE COLLECTION

PREIS 1 MARK
Berliner Illustrirte Zeitung
1-49
OLYMPIA - SONDERHEFT

SONDERHEFT
PREIS 1 MARK
Berliner Illustrirte Zeitung
BERICHT
in Wort und Bild
„Die 16 olympischen Ta

ILLUSTRIRTE
ZEITUNG
R. LIPUS
Nr. 108 - 23. April 1936

Deutschland
1. Olympia-Heft
Was bietet Deutschland?

OLYMPIC GAMES 1936
BERLIN JUNE 1935
NUMBER 1

OLYMPIC GAMES 1936
BERLIN JULY 1935
NUMBER 2
PRIEN
SCHULZ

OLYMPIC GAMES
1936
NUMBER 3

OLYMPIC GAMES 1936
NUMBER 6

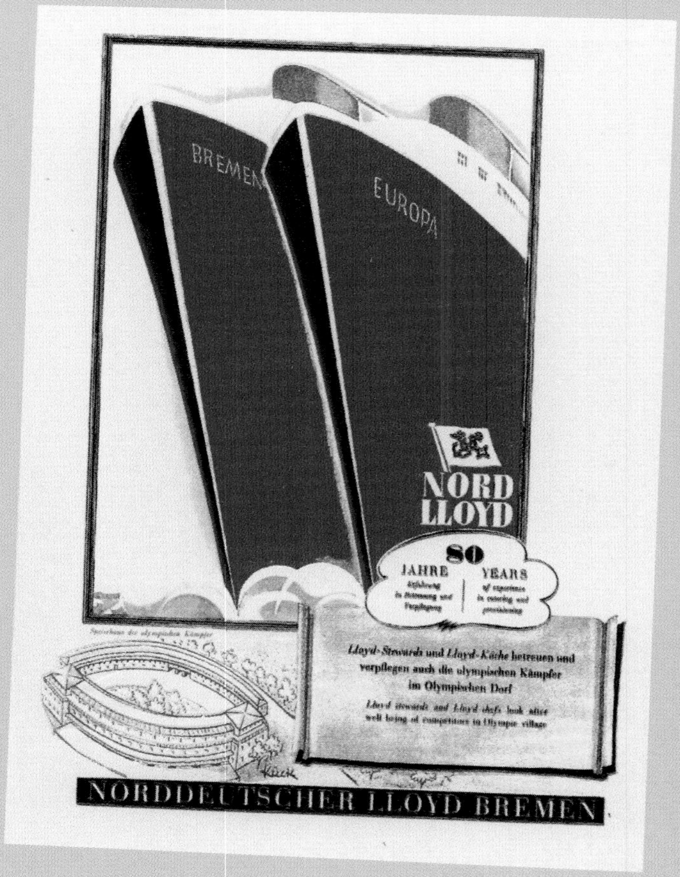

An invitation to a summer festival at the end of the games.
ALICE HODGE COLLECTION

ALICE HODGE COLLECTION

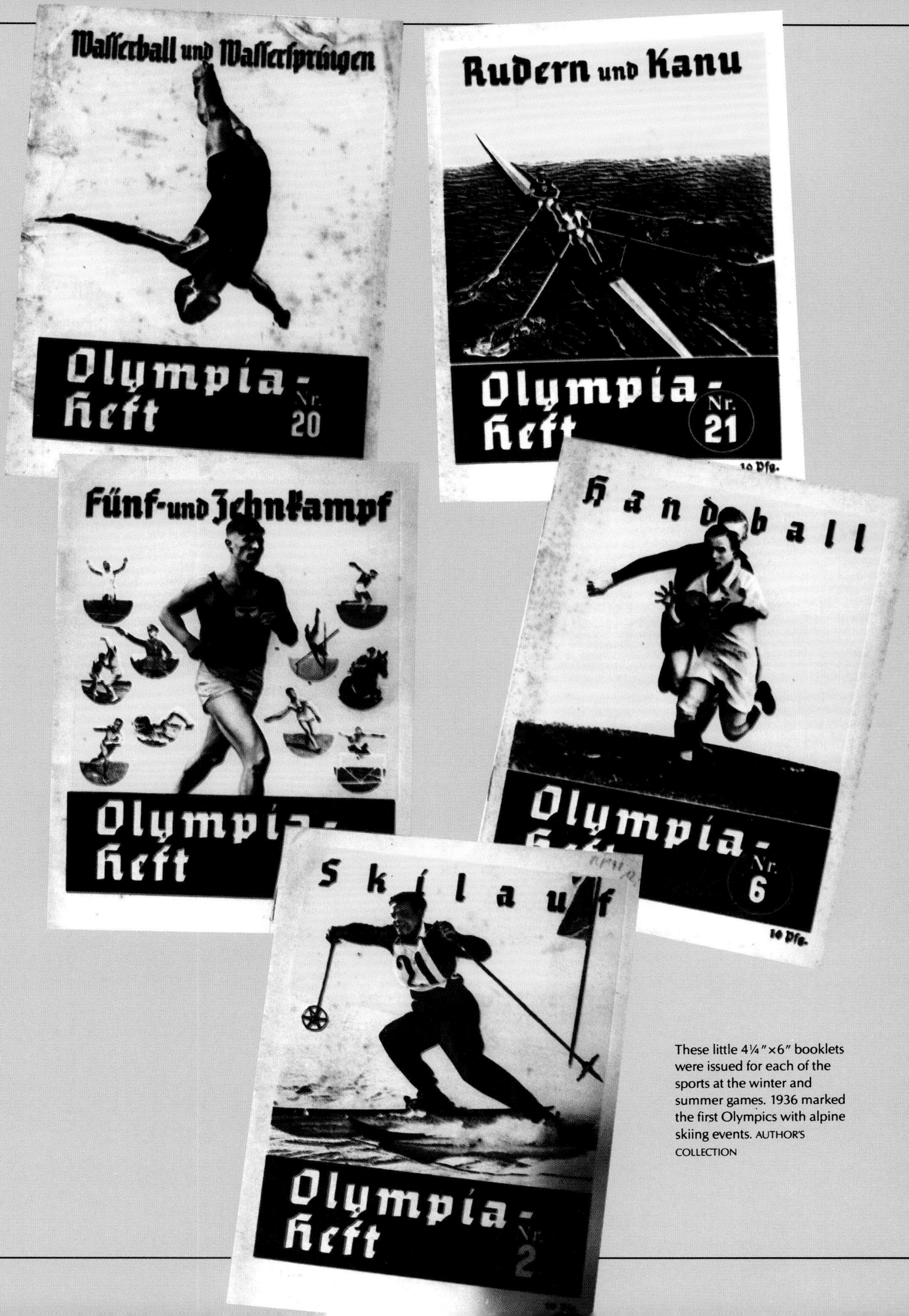

These little 4¼″×6″ booklets were issued for each of the sports at the winter and summer games. 1936 marked the first Olympics with alpine skiing events. AUTHOR'S COLLECTION

Mayor Fiorello H. La Guardia of New York presented one of these medals to each athlete who was honored in the city after the Olympics.
MARTY GLICKMAN COLLECTION

ALICE HODGE COLLECTION

GUIDE BOOK TO THE CELEBRATION OF THE XITH OLYMPIAD BERLIN 1936

PUBLISHED BY THE ORGANISATIONSKOMITEE FÜR DIE XI.OLYMPIADE BERLIN 1936

REICHSSPORTVERLAG. BERLIN SW 68

ALICE HODGE COLLECTION

Deutsche Reichspost

Telegramm

aus

HAMPSTEADNY

Nr. OLX , 30 W. vom 7 / 8 1936 , Uhr

ALICE ARDEN
WOMENS DORMITORY
CARE AMERICAN OLYMPIC
COM REICHSSPORTFIELD
BERLIN

HERES TO WIN WHEN YOU GO
UP AND OVER WITH A BIG
BOOST LUCK AND LOVE

RUTH AND ADA

A telegram and its folder were used for propaganda purposes.

Menu from the Norddeutscher Lloyd Bremen Company, which catered the food for athletes at both summer and winter games.
ALICE HODGE COLLECTION

A film guide put out by the German film company Agfa.

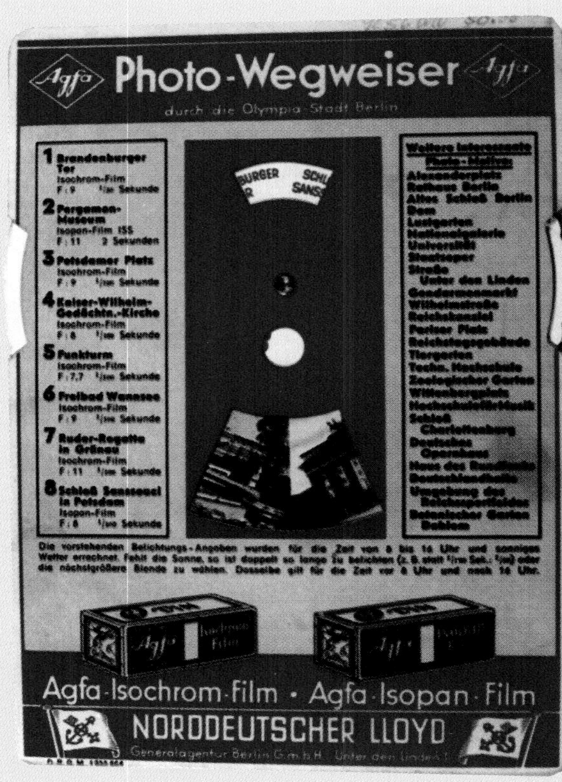

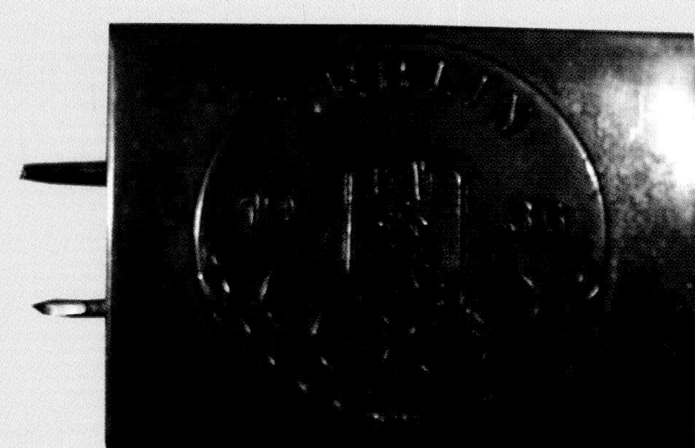

Belt buckle from the Berlin games.

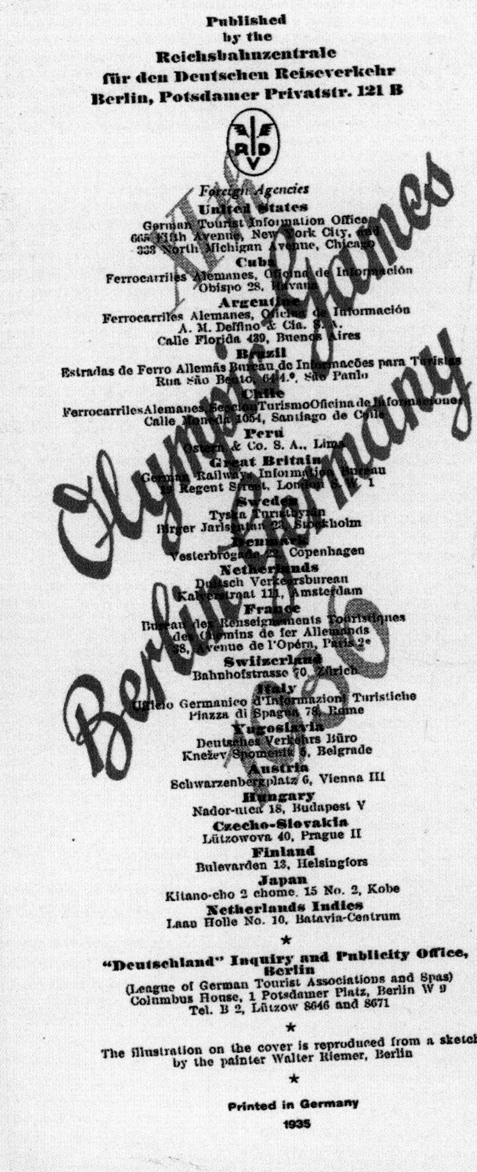

Published
by the
Reichsbahnzentrale
für den Deutschen Reiseverkehr
Berlin, Potsdamer Privatstr. 121 B

Foreign Agencies

United States
German Tourist Information Office
665 Fifth Avenue, New York City, and
333 North Michigan Avenue, Chicago

Cuba
Ferrocarriles Alemanes, Oficina de Información
Obispo 28, Havana

Argentine
Ferrocarriles Alemanes, Oficina de Información
A. M. Delfino & Cia. S. A.
Calle Florida 489, Buenos Aires

Brazil
Estradas de Ferro Allemãs Bureau de Informacões para Turistas
Rua São Bento, 64 4.°, São Paulo

Chile
FerrocarrilesAlemanes,SeccionTurismoOficina de Informaciones
Calle Moneda 1054, Santiago de Chile

Peru
Ostern & Co. S. A., Lima

Great Britain
German Railways Information Bureau
19 Regent Street, London S. W. 1

Sweden
Tyska Turistbyrån
Birger Jarlsgatan 22, Stockholm

Denmark
Vesterbrogade 22, Copenhagen

Netherlands
Duitsch Verkeersbureau
Kalverstraat 111, Amsterdam

France
Bureau des Renseignements Touristiques
des Chemins de fer Allemands
38, Avenue de l'Opéra, Paris 2°

Switzerland
Bahnhofstrasse 70, Zürich

Italy
Ufficio Germanico d'Informazioni Turistiche
Piazza di Spagna 78, Rome

Yugoslavia
Deutsches Verkehrs Büro
Knežev Spomenik 5, Belgrade

Austria
Schwarzenbergplatz 6, Vienna III

Hungary
Nador-utca 18, Budapest V

Czecho-Slovakia
Lützowova 40, Prague II

Finland
Bulevarden 13, Helsingfors

Japan
Kitano-cho 2 chome. 15 No. 2, Kobe

Netherlands Indies
Laan Holle No. 10, Batavia-Centrum

★

"Deutschland" Inquiry and Publicity Office, Berlin
(League of German Tourist Associations and Spas)
Columbus House, 1 Potsdamer Platz, Berlin W 9
Tel. B 2, Lützow 8646 and 8671

★

The illustration on the cover is reproduced from a sketch by the painter Walter Riemer, Berlin

★

Printed in Germany
1935

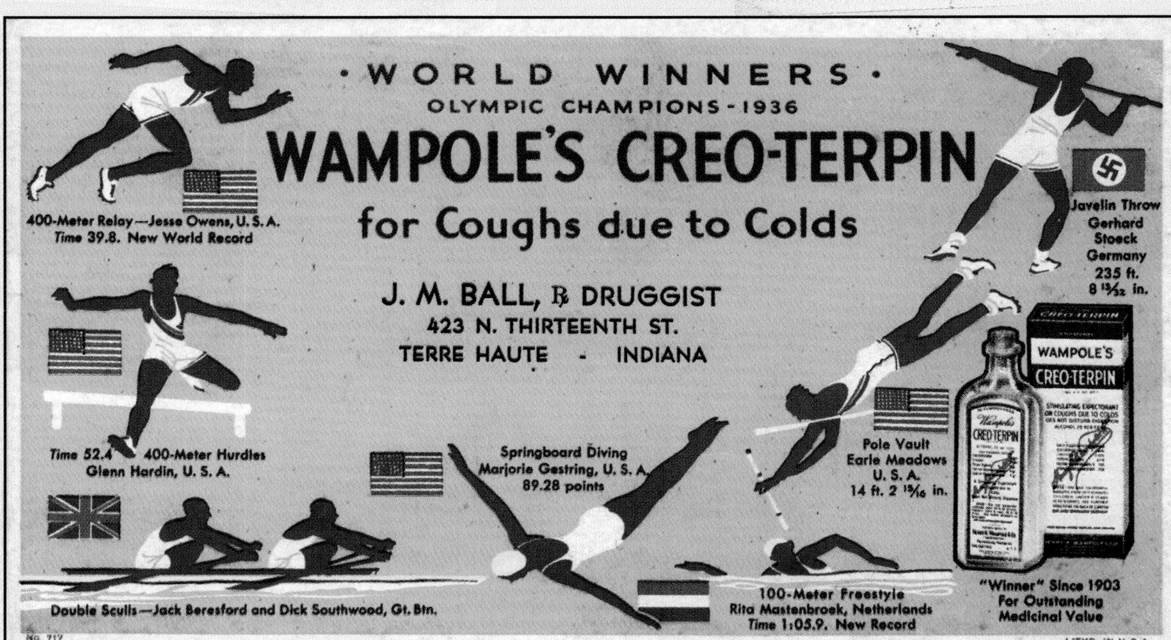

JIM OSBORNE COLLECTION

The Commemorative Medal, front and rear, awarded for work on the games. 54,915 were produced.
COURTESY JOHN REYNOLDS.

The Memorial Medal, designed by Otto Placzek, was awarded to each participant. The medal is made of bronze.

Visitor's souvenir pin.

German pin produced for fundraising for the equestrian events.

An enamel plaque about three inches in diameter, probably used on automobiles.

Winter games souvenir pin.

A
Badge with ribbon (one-piece)

B
Badge (two-piece) with bar and ring for looping ribbon through

*) Olympic ribbon:
Blue, yellow, black, green and red

OFFICIAL BADGES Design: Professor Raemisch

A BADGE WITH RIBBON (one-piece)

	Lettering and Description	Colour of Ribbon (Insignia)
1. International Olympic Committee (I. O. C.)	I. O. K. gold-plated	White, with short Olympic ribbon*)
2. I. O. C. Jury of Honour, Executive Commission	I. O. K. gold-plated	White, with short Olympic ribbon (Honorary Judges)
3. National Olympic Committee President	N. O. K. gold-plated	Dark blue, with Olympic ribbon (National Committee)
4. N. O. C. General Secretaries and Members	N. O. K. silver-plated	Ribbon as No. 3 (National Committee)
5. Chefs de Mission	N. O. K. silver-plated	Ribbon as No. 3 (Chef de Mission)
6. International Federations President	I. V. gold-plated	According to sport (International Federation)
7. International Federations General Secretaries	I. V. silver-plated	According to sport (International Federation)
8. O. C. Members	O. K. gold-plated	Light grey, with Olympic ribbon (Organizing Committee)
9. O. C. Active Members, Commissions	O. K. silver-plated	Ribbon as No. 8 (Organizing Committee)
10. Attachés	Attaché silver-plated	Dark blue, with Olympic ribbon (Attaché)
11. Referees	Referee silver-plated	According to sport (Sport)
12. Team Leaders	See appendix bronze	According to sport (Team Leader)
13. Active Participants	See below bronze	According to sport (Sport)
14. Press	Press, bronze	Red-yellow
15. Film	Film, bronze	Red-green
16. Photographers	Photo, bronze	Red-blue
17. Radio	Radio, bronze	Red-white

B BADGE (two-piece)

1. Organizing Committee Executive Officials	Name, O. K. silver-plated	Olympic ribbon
2. Organizing Committee Officials	Official, Sport silver-plated	According to sport
3. Organizing Committee Bureau	Staff, O. K. silver-plated	Light grey
4. Olympic Village	Staff, Olympic Village silver-plated	Light grey
5. Physicians	Staff, Physician silver-plated	White with red cross

RIBBON COLOURS

1. Athletics . orange
2. Fencing . . deep lavender
3. Wrestling . canary yellow
4. Weight-Lifting . . sand colour
5. Football . tomato red
6. Hockey . . dark green
7. Modern Pentathlon light lavender
8. Polo . . . . light brown
9. Yachting . medium green
10. Handball . pink
11. Cycling . . rust brown
12. Shooting . olive
13. Rowing . . light blue
14. Swimming cornflower blue
15. Basketball light green
16. Gymnastics raspberry red
17. Boxing . . bordeaux red
18. Canoeing . light grey
19. Equestrian Events . . . dark lavender
20. Gliding . . ochre
21. Baseball . stone gray

For other badges, see page 65

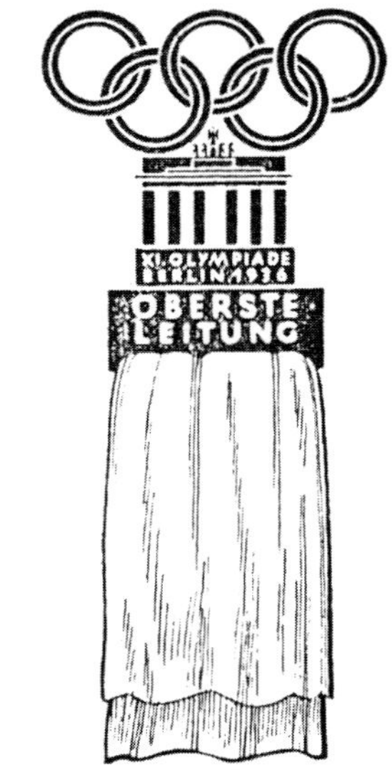

OFFICIAL OLYMPIC BADGE

Automobile pennant of the Organizing Committee

Olympic track uniform worn by Marty Glickman.

JIM OSBORNE COLLECTION

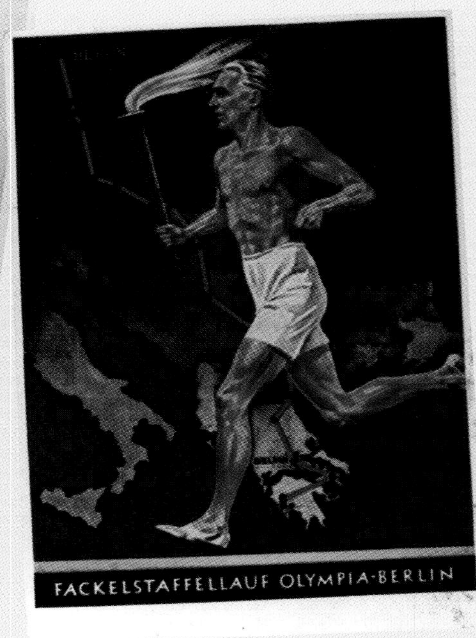

This poster was designed by Berliner Frantz Wurbel. Two hundred and forty-three thousand copies were printed in 19 languages and distributed in 34 countries.

Official Olympic Posters

Stamps issued by the German postal service for the winter and summer games.

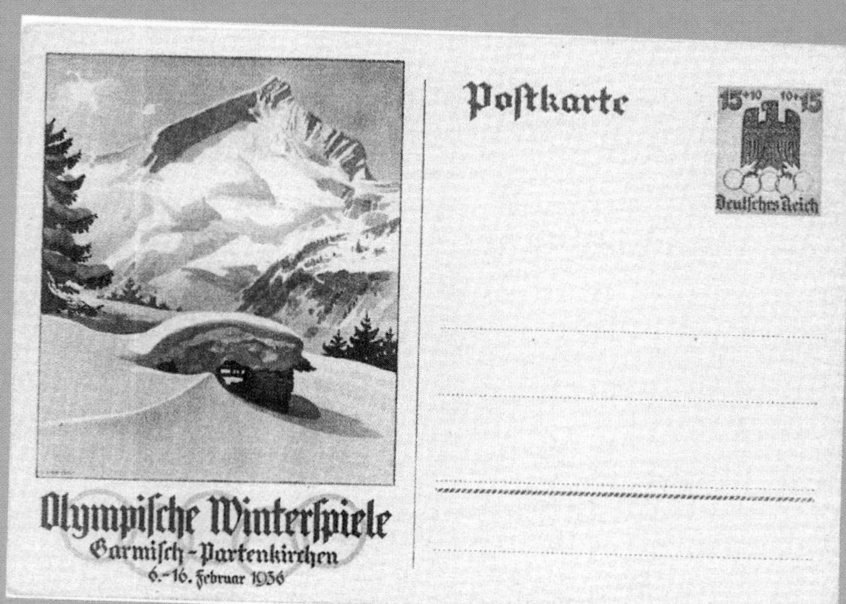

Postcards and Postal Stationery for the Winter and Summer Games

This postal card was sent from Germany on Oct. 4, 1936 via the *Hindenburg* to Lakehurst, New Jersey and then to Los Angeles. Note the 75RM air mail stamp attached.

The use of postcards and postal stationery for both winter and summer Olympics provided the German government with a convenient mode for propaganda. Special stamps were issued for both Olympics, along with dozens of cards that were sent out worldwide. Over 100,000,000 pieces of mail were posted during the summer games, a figure that practically overwhelmed the government postal system. Special post offices were set up at all Olympic sites and even some mobile postal vans were used. Olympic cards and letters from the German Olympics, as with all Olympics, are highly collectible today.

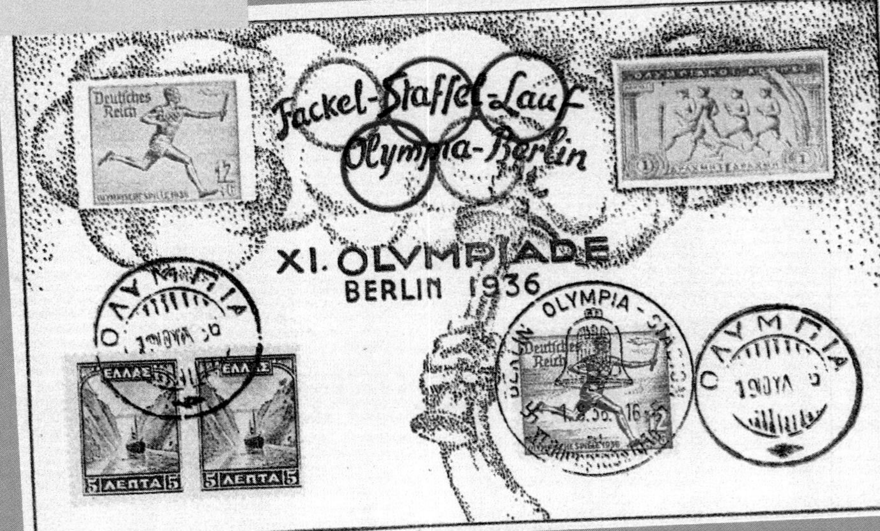

This postal card states Fackel-Staffel Lauf (Torch Relay Run) was cancelled in Olympia, Greece on July 21, 1936, the day after the Olympic Flame Ceremony. On Aug. 1, 1936 it was cancelled in Berlin, the opening day of the Olympic Games.

Postal card carried by the *Hindenburg* and cancelled on August 1 at Frankfurt and Berlin.

During the winter games from February 6 to 16 the German Postal system handled over 50,000 long distance calls, 14,000 telegrams, 400 photo telegrams, 3.5 million letters and postcards were sent and 1.8 million received.

THE OLYMPIC STADIUM TODAY

Parts of the Olympic rings suffered damage during the war but have been restored to the 1936 appearance.

A side view of the stadium. The cinder track was replaced with a synthetic track in 1969.

The stadium was entirely renovated in 1974. Two acrylic roofs were added, along with floodlights and an electronic scoreboard.

The bell tower was completely destroyed but has been rebuilt and rises 77 meters above the Maifeld.

The Olympic Flame Bowl still stands above the Marathon Tunnel.

The large stone tablets on either side of the gap near the Maifeld bear the names of the 1936 Olympic Medallists.

The swimming station was renovated for the 1978 Third World Swimming Championships. A fountain was built on the north where a spectators stand stood in 1936.

Statuary in the stadium area from the 1936 games.

Plaque on the stadium wall.

Plaque on the stadium wall.

GARMISH - PARTENKIRCHEN TODAY

The ski stadium at the foot of the two jumps.

The picturesque villages of Garmisch-Partenkirchen in Bavaria.

Inscription in the ski stadium for the 1936 Olympic Winter Games and the cancelled 1940 games.

The little and big ski jumps are still in use along with the other facilities built for the 1936 games. GARMISCH-PARTENKIRCHEN CHAMBER OF COMMERCE

Index

This index covers the text only, not the captions.

Bibliography

American Olympic Committee Report, 1936, Games of the XIth Olympiad, Berlin, Germany, IVth Olympic Winter Games, Garmish-Partenkirchen, Germany.

Baker, William J., *Jesse Owens, An American Life*. The Free Press, New York, 1986.

Downing, Taylor, *Olympia*, BFI Publishing, London, England, 1992.

Durrance, Dick, *The Man on the Medal, The Life & Times of America's First Great Ski Racer*, Durrance Enterprises Inc., Snowmass Village, Colorado, 1995.

Guttmann, Allen, *The Games Must Go On, Avery Brundage And The Olympic Movement*, Columbia University Press, New York, 1984.

Hart-Davis, Duff, *Hitler's Games, The 1936 Olympics*, Harper & Row Publishers, New York, 1986.

LeTissier, Tony, *Berlin Then and Now*, After the Battle, London, England, 1992.

Mallon, Bill, Ian Buchanan, *Quest For Gold, The Encyclopedia of American Olympians*, Leisure Press, New York, 1984.

Mandell, Richard D., *The Nazi Olympics*, The MacMillan Company, New York, 1971.

Riefenstahl, Leni, *Olympia*, BFI Publishing, London, England, 1992.

Wallechinsky, David, *The Complete Book of the Olympics,*, Penguin Books, New York, 1984.

Woolsey, Elizabeth, *Off the Beaten Track*, Paragon Press, Salt Lake City, Utah, 1984.

Plus a number of German books and magazines published in 1936.

The author with his 1936 Olympic collection.

About the Author

Stan Cohen is a native of West Virginia and was born two years after the Berlin Olympics. He was on the track team in high school but never won a race. After graduating from West Virginia University with a degree in geology he headed west to Montana to work for the government. After many years as a consulting geologist, owner of a ski and sporting goods company and director of a historical museum, he founded Pictorial Histories Publishing Company in 1976. Since then he has written or co-authored 55 books and published more than 180. He lives in Missoula, Montana, with his wife, Anne, and spends considerable time traveling around the United States and Europe selling and researching books.

About the Cover Artist

In 1975 Robert Gunn was catapulted to national prominence when he won the Third Annual Norman Rockwell Cover Award for *The Saturday Evening Post*. The painting, published in January of 1976, was the Bicentennial painting for that year. He did other cover paintings for the *Post* and was soon acclaimed by the publishers to be the artist most likely to carry on the tradition of Americana established by Norman Rockwell. His rapidly soaring fame was soon enhanced by a commission from Sears to do several paintings commemorating great events in the Olympic Games. These paintings were displayed on a national tour organized to raise funds for the American participation in the 1976 Winter Olympics. From 1976 to 1980 Gunn produced more than fifty cover paintings for a prominent trade journal of the oil and gas industry. In addition he has done many special commissions for various national corporations and presently his work is eagerly sought by investors throughout the U.S. and Canada. To contact Mr. Gunn write 715 Windsor Road, Olathe, Kansas 66061.